Edith Wharton: Sex, Satire and the Older Woman

Also by AVRIL HORNER:

BODY MATTERS: Feminism, Textuality, Corporeality (*ed. with Angela Keane*)

DAPHNE DU MAURIER: Writing, Identity and the Gothic Imagination (*with Sue Zlosnik*)

EUROPEAN GOTHIC: A Spirited Exchange, 1760–1960 (*ed.*)

GOTHIC AND THE COMIC TURN (*with Sue Zlosnik*)

IRIS MURDOCH AND MORALITY (*ed. with Anne Rowe*)

LANDSCAPES OF DESIRE: Metaphors in Modern Women's Fiction (*with Sue Zlosnik*)

LE GOTHIC: Influences and Appropriations in America and Europe (*ed. with Sue Zlosnik*)

Also by JANET BEER:

AMERICAN FEMINISM: Key Source Documents, 1848–1920 (*4 volumes; series ed. & volume ed.*)

THE AWAKENING: A Sourcebook (*ed. with Elizabeth Nolan*)

THE CAMBRIDGE COMPANION TO KATE CHOPIN

EDITH WHARTON: Traveller in the Land of Letters

EDITH WHARTON

THE HOUSE OF MIRTH (*ed. with Elizabeth Nolan*)

KATE CHOPIN, EDITH WHARTON AND CHARLOTTE PERKINS GILMAN: Studies in Short Fiction

LIVES OF VICTORIAN LITERARY FIGURES IV: EDITH WHARTON

ROUTLEDGE GUIDES TO LITERATURE: Edith Wharton's *The House of Mirth*

SPECIAL RELATIONSHIPS: Anglo-American Antagonisms and Affinities, 1854–1936

Edith Wharton: Sex, Satire and the Older Woman

Avril Horner
Emeritus Professor of English, Kingston University

and

Janet Beer
Vice Chancellor, Oxford Brookes University

palgrave
macmillan

First published 2011 by
PALGRAVE MACMILLAN

Palgrave Macmillan in the UK is an imprint of Macmillan Publishers Limited, registered in England, company number 785998, of Houndmills, Basingstoke, Hampshire RG21 6XS.

Palgrave Macmillan in the US is a division of St Martin's Press LLC, 175 Fifth Avenue, New York, NY 10010.

Palgrave Macmillan is the global academic imprint of the above companies and has companies and representatives throughout the world.

Palgrave® and Macmillan® are registered trademarks in the United States, the United Kingdom, Europe and other countries.

ISBN 978–1–403–94126–8

This book is printed on paper suitable for recycling and made from fully managed and sustained forest sources. Logging, pulping and manufacturing processes are expected to conform to the environmental regulations of the country of origin.

A catalogue record for this book is available from the British Library.

Library of Congress Cataloging-in-Publication Data
Horner, Avril, 1947–
Edith Wharton : sex, satire, and the older woman / Avril Horner, Janet Beer.
   p. cm.
Includes bibliographical references and index.
ISBN 978–1–4039–4126–8 (hardback)
1. Wharton, Edith, 1862–1937—Criticism and interpretation.   2. Women and literature—United States—History—20th century.   3. Older women in literature.   4. Sex in literature.   5. Satire, American—History and criticism.   6. Wharton, Edith, 1862–1937—Political and social views.   7. Modernism (Literature)—United States.   I. Beer, Janet, 1956– II. Title.   III. Title: Sex, satire, and the older woman.
PS3545.H16Z669 2011
813'.52—dc22   2011016932

10   9   8   7   6   5   4   3   2   1
20   19   18   17   16   15   14   13   12   11

Transferred to Digital Printing in 2012

Contents

Acknowledgements

An earlier version of Chapter 1 first appeared in *American Modernism: Cultural Transactions* edited by Catherine Morley and Alex Goody, Newcastle upon Tyne: Cambridge Scholars Press, 2009; Chapter 2 draws on an essay published in *The Yearbook of English Studies, From Decadent to Modernist and Other Essays*, edited by John Batchelor, Volume 37, No. 1, 2007.

The authors and publisher would like to thank the following for permission to quote from the work of Edith Wharton: The Collection of American Literature, Beinecke Rare Book and Manuscript Library, Yale University; and the estate of Edith Wharton and the Watkins/Loomis Agency. They also thank Scribner, a Division of Simon & Schuster, Inc., for permission to quote from *The Mother's Recompense, The Children and Twilight Sleep*.

Avril Horner thanks the British Academy for funding which enabled a month's research in the Beinecke Library, Yale University and the librarians at London City University for facilitating access to *The Nation and Athenaeum*.

We also wish to thank Pamela Knights for her lively interest in our project, Paula Kennedy of Palgrave Macmillan for her patience and Dale Bauer for suggestions made during the final stage of writing. Janet Beer would like to thank Bev Watson for her magical diary skills and for her endless good humour. We are both very grateful for the unfailing support given by our husbands, Howard Horner and David Woodman.

Avril Horner and Janet Beer
London and Oxford, 2011

Introduction

There still exists a critical consensus that Edith Wharton's final works, from the late 1920s onwards, represent a falling-off from her greatest novels, *The House of Mirth* (1905), *The Custom of the Country* (1913) and *The Age of Innocence* (1920). This consensus had its genesis in Edmund Wilson's description, following Wharton's death, of her novels from *The Age of Innocence* onwards as a 'feebler second boiling from the tea-leaves', gained momentum with R.W.B. Lewis's query as to why Wharton 'permitted herself such relatively slack work in the 1920s' and continues in more recent dismissals of her writing after 1920.[1] Conversely, contemporary reception of Wharton's last six novels was mixed, much of it very positive. More recently, the consensus that these works are not Wharton's best has been reflected in the relatively small output of academic studies that focus on the novels published after 1925. While critics continue to publish frequently on the earlier novels, the short stories and Wharton's war and travel writing, the output on her late fiction is comparatively meagre. Dale M. Bauer's *Edith Wharton's Brave New Politics* (1994) remains, to date, the only book-length study of the fiction Wharton published after 1925.[2] The Edith Wharton Society's 'Current Bibliography, 1999–present', while not comprehensive or fully up to date, confirms this trend.[3] At the time of writing, the bibliography lists 282 works on Wharton. Excluding review articles and new editions of Wharton's novels, only eight of these focus exclusively on her post-1925 fiction.[4]

Even Wharton herself lost faith occasionally in her talents in the last two decades of her life, despairing at the critics' misunderstanding of her later work and realising that she was being unfavourably compared with younger novelists and the rising stars of Joyce and Woolf. By 1924 she was already being described as a 'distinguished representative of the old school'[5] whereas, looking back from the 1930s, she perceived the work she had done in the 1920s as 'revolutionary', particularly in her '"audacious treatment of unpleasant themes"'.[6] Writing to Scott Fitzgerald in 1925, to thank him for sending her a copy of *The Great Gatsby*, Wharton declared: 'I feel that to your generation, which has taken such a flying leap into the future, I must represent the literary equivalent of tufted furniture and gas chandeliers'.[7] Critics have perhaps too easily acquiesced with this humorous self-deprecation, not appreciating its ironic undertow. In *Edith Wharton: Sex, Satire and the Older Woman*, we argue that Wharton's last six novels – *The Mother's Recompense* (1925), *Twilight Sleep* (1927), *The Children* (1928), *Hudson River Bracketed* (1929), *The Gods Arrive* (1932) and *The Buccaneers* (1938) – are hybrid and experimental works, intellectually ambitious in both form and content. As Pamela Knights has noted, 'the oblique and fragmented vision of these later fictions' do indeed 'suggest some experimentation', all six novels offering 'meditations on the depredations of a commodity culture, new versions of the self in a "make-over" society and the nature of writing itself'.[8] Although flawed in certain respects, they are hardly the second-rate productions of a mind in decline. Rather, like the late work of many writers, from Shakespeare to Joyce, their problems and puzzles are best understood as the results of a deliberate attempt to break away from generic formulae and to present new challenges to the reader.

By 1925, the publication date of *The Mother's Recompense*, Wharton was 63 years old and had lived in France for half of her adult life. Not surprisingly, her late work is even more marked by European culture and values than her early writing. This did not please everyone: several American critics, as Kristin Olson Lauer has documented, castigated Wharton during the 1920s for writing fiction that no longer accurately reflected the American experience, claiming that her residence in France had resulted in her losing touch with the country of her birth.[9] However, although Wharton continues her earlier portrayal of America and its values with a mixture of satire and melancholy in *The Mother's Recompense, Twilight Sleep* and *The Children*, her last three novels – *Hudson River Bracketed, The Gods Arrive* and *The Buccaneers* – show a distinct desire to complicate the dialogue between Europe and America. This is most evident at the level of plot: characters journey frequently between America and France, Spain and England and the idea of a transatlantic alliance is literalised in the various marriages of *The Buccaneers*. Her desire to present a more sophisticated dialogue is also evident at the level of language. The last three novels, in particular, are marked by a rich intertextuality with the literary legacy of

Europe, represented by authors such as St Augustine, Dante, Goethe, Jane Austen, Wordsworth, Shelley, Keats, Trollope, Thackeray, George Eliot, Meredith, Tennyson, Dante Gabriel Rossetti and with more recent writings, both American and European, including popular novels such as Frances Hodgson Burnett's *The Shuttle* and Margaret Kennedy's *The Constant Nymph*. Wharton was nothing if not an eclectic reader. Given this, it is surprising, as Richard A. Kaye has noted, that 'Almost all of the major critics of Wharton's fiction have emphasized the novelist's allegiance to the American literary tradition.'[10] The rich legacy of European history is also stressed through place and the evocation of times past through certain buildings: the mezquita at Cordova in *The Gods Arrive*, and Honourslove in Gloucestershire in *The Buccaneers*, for example. The Willows in *Hudson River Bracketed* and *The Gods Arrive* represents her desire that America should pay attention to and learn from European culture while celebrating its own legacy, signified by the architecture of the house. Significantly, it is to the Willows that Halo Spear and Vance Weston return, after their long sojourn in Europe.

We have suggested that Wharton's late novels are best understood as experimental works. However, they are not experimental in the 'high' modernist sense. Indeed, Wharton famously dissociated herself from writers such as Gertrude Stein, Djuna Barnes, Virginia Woolf and James Joyce, dismissing their claims to innovation and articulating her own misgivings about modernism through the character of Vance Weston. Yet, during this phase of her life, she constantly laid claim to writing innovatively herself, both in terms of form and content. Her dismissal of modernist writing did not impede her interest in and ability to learn from writers and artists associated with modernism. As Hermione Lee has noted, 'She had well-attested passions not only for Yeats and Stravinsky, but for Isadora Duncan, Cézanne, Gauguin (though not Matisse), Gide, Huxley and Rilke'.[11] Her refusal to give easy answers or to deliver conventional endings in these late novels necessitates an actively interpretative reader, something we associate more with modernism than with realist writing. Her subject matter was also far from the 'tufted furniture and gas chandeliers' of Victorian fiction. As Robert A. Martin and Linda Wagner-Martin have pointed out:

> who among the American writers in Paris was more 'contemporary' than Wharton? *The Gods Arrive* features Halo Tarrant's out-of-wedlock pregnancy, *A Mother's Recompense* has a run-away mother looking for complete sexual satisfaction, and *The Children* deals, discretely, with the theme that Nabokov was to make a fortune from years later in *Lolita*.

Another of the conundrums of literary history is that the so-called repressed and proper 'Mrs. Wharton' was writing fiction that was as 'advanced' as anything Modernism produced...[12]

Hermione Lee has also commented on the very contemporary nature of Wharton's late work, noting that during the 1920s:

Wharton [was] extremely preoccupied, at this time – in 'Beatrice Palmato' and other works – with how to write about the truths of female sexuality, the cruelty that is in marriage, and taboo subjects like incest, homosexuality, prostitution, adultery, the horrors of repression, and the baleful effects of silencing.[13]

Our focus in *Edith Wharton: Sex, Satire and the Older Woman* is on both the shocking subject matter – which Wharton employed in order to continue her searching critique of social constraints and hypocrisies – and on the formal nature of her experimentation. As we have noted, her emphasis on the particular moral dilemmas facing her female characters marks her as a very modern, if not a modernist, writer. In particular, her subtle exploration of sexual desire in the older woman – still a taboo subject in the 1920s and 1930s – is striking. Kate Clephane, Pauline Manford, Rose Sellars and Laura Testvalley, whose ages range from nearly forty to fifty or thereabouts, are all portrayed in the melancholy light of societies that allow no expression of such desire. Even Halo Spear in her late twenties suffers the experience of being discarded for a younger woman and feels consequently prematurely aged. Wharton frequently departs from realism in these late novels, using (for example) gothic effects to convey these women's subsequent crises of identity: they experience themselves at this stage as 'ghosts' and their environments as unreal or suffocating. As Kathy A. Fedorko has remarked, 'Wharton's Gothic allows her to press the limits of rationality, to utter the unutterable about sexuality, rage, death and fear, and, especially, the nature of men and women'.[14]

We suggest that Wharton's interest in hybridity becomes more evident in the late novels and that it is the key to understanding her ambivalent engagement with modernism. As Amy Kaplan has noted, Wharton was 'an author who wrote at the intersection of the mass market of popular fiction, the tradition of women's literature, and a realistic movement which developed in an uneasy dialogue with twentieth-century modernism'.[15] There has been much critical debate over the last 20 years as to how far Edith Wharton's fiction can be described as modernist.

Wharton herself, of course, recorded in *The Writing of Fiction* (1925) her impatience with the modernist claim that the stream of consciousness technique represented, for the first time, 'a slice of life':

> The stream of consciousness method differs from the slice of life in noting mental as well as visual reactions, but resembles it in setting them down just as they come, with a deliberate disregard of their relevance in the particular case, or rather with the assumption that their very unsorted abundance constitutes in itself the author's subject.[16]

In her view, authors such as Flaubert, Zola and Maupassant had all done the 'slice of life' before in a less pretentious and more skilful manner, thereby preserving the aesthetic coherence of their work. For Wharton, continuity with the past was vital if Europe and America were to resist barbarism and disintegration, particularly in the period that followed the First World War. Her loyalty to realism, and its rougher offspring, naturalism, was rooted in her admiration of many nineteenth-century writers, particularly Austen, George Eliot, Thackeray, Hawthorne and Meredith, who managed to combine a respect for tradition with an irony that offered a searching critique of contemporary manners. Hence her praise for one of the few modernists whose work she did admire – Proust – whom she described as a 'renovator' rather than an 'unintelligible innovator'.[17] Like many writers of the 1920s and 1930s, then, Wharton was insistent that the novel should provide a lens through which to examine social behaviour *and* the morality of the individual and the group. This was, of course, partly a reaction to what she perceived as the solipsism of much modernist writing. Indeed, her attitude to modernism resonates interestingly with Patrick Hamilton's statement made in 1939 – that modernists 'are for the most part hopelessly and morbidly turned in upon themselves, and sterile in consequence...'.[18]

In retrospect, however, recent critics have suggested that many authors of the 1930s – just like Wharton – drew on modernism even while they repudiated it:

> The history of the novel in this period is at once a move away from modernism and a continuation of it. In the 1930s, for example, there was a rejection of the modernist preoccupation with aesthetics and formal experimentation in favour of a sustained focus on social reality. But it is also the case that the novel of the 1930s, with its awareness of psychoanalysis and elements of fantasy, was as much concerned with the nature of consciousness, as was Virginia Woolf or James Joyce.[19]

This description of British fiction in the 1930s aptly captures the nature of Wharton's writing from the mid-1920s onwards. As Stephanie Lewis Thompson has noted, after the First World War Wharton's main project 'was an attempt to find a literary aesthetic that suited her ideals about form and order'.[20] And as Sharon Kim has argued, she adapted the modernist epiphany for her own ends, always situating it in relation to history as well as to the ephemeral experience of an individual character.[21] In this, she certainly revealed an interest in the 'nature of consciousness' while refusing to accept the modernist representation of consciousness as technically groundbreaking. Indeed, Wharton's own attempt to 'make it new' included a regard for how past writers had plotted and expressed dilemmas similar to those faced by her own characters.

Those excluding Wharton from modernism include Frederick Wegener and Robin Peel, who are adamant that Wharton's dislike of formal experimentation and her affinity with the values of a particular social world (whether that is Old New York or the cultivated class of old Europe) preclude her from being considered as a modernist.[22] On the other hand, there are those who, while acknowledging that Wharton distanced herself from modernism, nevertheless see her novels as either modernist or as presaging modernism. Candace Waid and Clare Colquitt, for example, portray Wharton as 'a radical experimentalist *malgré lui*' and argue that 'she anticipated many of the defining elements of literary modernism'.[23] In the same spirit, several feminist critics during the 1980s described her as a 'transitional' figure within a linear development model of fiction that led to modernism.[24] Katherine Joslin, Stephanie Lewis Thompson and Jennifer Haytock have more recently claimed that Wharton's focus on issues of gender, desire and creativity, and on the fracturing of identity, distinguish her as a modernist writer.[25] In defining 'transatlantic modernism' as a 'realm of experiential morality' in which writers 'attempted to discover a passage between personal value and social action', Martin Halliwell widens the net to embrace decadent and naturalist writers, including Wharton.[26] He points, for example, to her use of ellipsis in *Ethan Frome* as a device which moves writing and reading away from the narrative certainties and 'moralism' of much nineteenth-century fiction into a mode of unreliable narration we associate with the dawn of modernism.[27] Well-practised in the use of ellipsis through her interest in the gothic – she comments in the Preface to her collection of ghost stories that she expects her readers to meet her 'halfway among the primeval shadows' to fill in 'the gaps in my narrative with sensations and divinations akin to my own'[28] – Wharton develops its use to communicate uncertainty, ambiguity and vacuum in the late fiction. Jean-Michel Rabaté argues that 'Wharton's and Proust's novels of 1913 belong to an early modernist moment of discovery, as both probe the links between form and technique'. Noting 'many modernist elements' in *The Custom of the Country*, including an 'abundance of cuts and jumps in the narrative', he suggests that its 'main modernist feature is the novel's ethical ambivalence...we are not to judge Undine', a character he sees as 'a Nietzschean heroine'.[29] While not arguing specifically for Wharton as a modernist, Nancy Bentley nevertheless claims her as a very modern writer:

> the very energies of modernity that fuelled the new emergent order – technologies of speed and mobility, the pleasures and hazards of trading the familiar for the novel and the transitory – are also absorbed into Wharton's literary practice, transforming both the texture and the critical vision of the novel of manners she inherits from Austen and Eliot.[30]

The debate about whether or not Wharton can be admitted to the modernist canon is exacerbated by the difficulty of defining modernism itself – not a monolithic or coherent movement, by any means, but a series of experimentations, avant-garde groups, small magazines and individuals whose only common aim was the desire to 'make it new', in Pound's words. It is thus not surprising that it has, so far, been easy to make the case for or against Wharton's inclusion within the modernist canon since this depends on how modernism itself is defined. In *Edith Wharton: Sex, Satire and the Older Woman*, we wish to offer a rather different proposition: that Wharton's fiction after 1925 can be fruitfully read in the context of novels published in the late 1920s and 1930s that are often described as 'late modernist'. Such work, according to Tyrus Miller, 'reopens the modernist enclosure of form onto the work's social and political environs, facilitating its more direct, polemical engagement with topical and popular discourses'.[31] Given this agenda, late modernist texts are, not surprisingly, frequently characterised by hybridity and generic experimentation. In the six novels we analyse here, Wharton mixes gothic effects with parodic gothic, realism with mysticism and satire with melancholy, creating hybrid fictions quite unlike her earlier work.

It is worthwhile exploring further the contiguities between Wharton and certain writers of the 1930s, particularly in relation to her tendency to combine satire and melancholy in her later work. It is not surprising to find that she identified far more closely with Evelyn Waugh and Aldous Huxley than with 'high' modernists such as Virginia Woolf and James Joyce. Like Huxley and Waugh, she lamented what she saw as the junking of history and of tradition; feared the worst effects of consumerism and state control; used satire to expose contemporary folly and the dangers of progress unharnessed by moral sensibility. Indeed, Wharton's *Twilight Sleep* has much in common with Huxley's *Brave New World*, published in 1932, which she greatly admired. Writing to Laurence ('Larry') Grant White on 19 March, 1932, Wharton declared:

> I suppose you've ready [*sic*] Huxley's book, by the way? It seems to me by far the biggest English satire since Gulliver, great fun, every line of it, & chaps XVI and XVII really great...[32]

In the same month she wrote to John Hugh Smith, commenting on *Brave New World* that 'Up to Chap. VXI...I thought it an amazingly brilliant performance – now I think it is a great one' and she assured Gaillard Lapsley that *Brave New World* is 'really great' and (in part) 'incredibly brilliant'.[33] Huxley's dystopia, in which suffering has been eliminated and morality sidelined in the pursuit of pleasure and state control, strongly echoes the thematic concerns of *Twilight Sleep* in which hedonism is advanced by consumerism, cult beliefs and the betrayal of family loyalties, all in the name of 'progress' in a Taylorized world. Indeed, in a letter to Margaret 'Daisy' Chanler, Wharton expressed delight that Huxley saw similarities in their work:

> I suppose you have read his 'Brave New World', which is a masterpiece of tragic indictment of our ghastly age of Fordian culture. Get it at once, if you haven't. He wrote to me that I had 'put the case' already in 'Twilight Sleep', & I own I was much set up by his recognition of the fact![34]

Her correspondence also suggests great admiration of Evelyn Waugh's work; *à propos* of Gerhardi's *Pending Heaven*, she comments 'I don't know when I've laughed more of late – though "Vile Bodies" gave me some good guffaws'.[35] She had also much admired Gerhardi's earlier novel, *Futility* (1922), especially its combination of humour and melancholy. Like Waugh, whose *A Handful of Dust* resonates particularly with Wharton's late work, she was quick to see the potential for comedy in depicting barbaric behaviour in modern society and lamented what she saw as a cultural decline into mediocrity. In this, she shared his socially conservative views – including his casual racial and religious stereotyping – but they are the views of a radical conservative who, in Waugh's own words, enjoys 'all the fun of detecting hypocrisies and inconsistencies' through the use of satire.[36] Indeed, as early as 1921 Wharton was expressing delight that an eminent critic had recognised her as a satirist: 'Mr. Ed. Wilson Jr. speaks words that are as balm to me, for it has dawned upon him that perhaps satire *is* my weapon!'[37] Her later fiction, while continuing the satirical vein evident in her earlier writing, is much more hybrid and allusive than earlier works, such as *The House of Mirth* (1908), which had established her as an important writer. That generic hybridity, laced with social satire, puzzled many contemporary readers while the subject matter of novels from *The Mother's Recompense* onwards alienated many former American admirers.

As a female novelist, Wharton was particularly interested in the roles of women in the social world and, despite the similarities between her late work and novels by Waugh and Huxley, this is what finally differentiates them. Always concerned to create complex female characters, in her last novels the perspective shifts and her focus on the situation of women becomes even sharper. Comparing *The Mother's Recompense* with the original version of the story, entitled 'Disintegration', drafted in 1902, Katherine Joslin remarks:

> What is finally enlightening about reading the two works together is that they suggest a progression in Wharton's thinking. She moves from daughter to mother or from the concerns of youth to those of middle age, and from husband to wife or from the paternal to the maternal point of view.[38]

This is an astute observation. In these late works we share Demeter's perspective as well as Persephone's.[39] Wharton's late work is notable for its inclusion of older women as main, rather than ancillary, characters. In this respect, it illustrates what Margaret Morganroth Gullette has described as a new tendency in the literature of the first few decades of the twentieth century: main characters are frequently mature or ageing.[40] Novels of this period by women about middle-aged or older women include Rebecca West's *The Judge* (1922), Willa Cather's *A Lost Lady* (1923), Grace Atherton's *Black Oxen* (1923), Virginia Woolf's *Mrs Dalloway* (1925) and Wharton's *The Mother's Recompense* (1925) and *Twilight Sleep* (1927). In the last two, Wharton also explores the tension between mothers and daughters. This tension ultimately evolves into a desire for 'good' mothering and reconciliation between the generations, represented by Laura Testvalley's decision to sacrifice her own happiness in order to secure that of Nan St George in *The Buccaneers*. The culturally induced neglect of children, as portrayed in *Twilight Sleep* and *The Children*, is replaced by Halo Spear's ability to nurture and to love unconditionally – maternal aspects that will be more appropriately bestowed on her child than on her immature male partner. The older woman in these novels moves from being completely self-obsessed (Pauline Manford) to wryly observing the younger generation with wisdom and sadness (Rose Sellars, Laura Testvalley). In mid-life and endowed still with sexual energy and desire, these women characters are nevertheless haunted by the prospect of old age. In Wharton's late works, as Pamela Knights has noted, 'the narrative eye dwells on signs of aging – dropped mouths, freckled hands, stiffening forms; on modes of growing old, and painful efforts to stay young...'.[41] Mature woman, such as Kate Clephane, Rose Sellars and Laura Testvalley, are often also rootless and homeless. All are willing exiles of course, but that sense of homelessness as the 'modern condition' – combined with a fear of ageing – make them very twentieth-century women despite the fact that *The Buccaneers* is set in the 1870s. In short, Wharton's older women characters in her late novels are allowed an unusual complexity for the time. Indeed, the portrayal of the older woman's anguish is one of the features that lends Wharton's late work a particular poignancy.

In conclusion, then, we suggest that, like several women authors of the 1930s (Ivy Compton-Burnett, for example), Wharton combined generic forms in order to challenge contemporary attitudes. Many of her female protagonists (Nona in *Twilight Sleep*, Kate Clephane in *The Mother's Recompense*, Halo Spear in the Vance Weston novels, for example) are often melancholy, unhappy and out of joint with the conventional morality of the time. Anticipating the work of authors such as Sylvia Townsend Warner and Rosamond Lehmann in the 1930s, Wharton eschewed obvious modernist experimentation in favour of re-working and fragmenting traditional narratives, imbuing them with a twentieth-century consciousness. With the exception of *The Buccaneers*, Wharton – like many women writers of the 1920s and 1930s – abandons the traditional 'death or marriage' plot in her late work. At the same time, however, all her late novels draw on a long tradition of literary representations of female suffering in one way or another. This is not surprising, given Wharton's insistence in her essays and elsewhere that the literary tradition, from the Greeks onwards, still has much to teach us. Refusing to subscribe to conventional or sentimental narratives about love, sexual desire, marriage, mother-daughter relationships and ageing, in the last 12 years of her life Wharton sought to offer witty and satirical critiques of society and moving portraits of individuals in novels that are hybrid and experimental. It is our hope that *Edith Wharton: Sex, Satire and the Older Woman* will contribute usefully to a reassessment of six novels that have been relatively neglected but that we have found funny, fierce and often very moving.

1

The Mother's Recompense

'something vanishing and sweet'[1]

Edith Wharton's interest in the older woman is evident throughout her writing career. Her first published short story, 'Mrs Manstey's View', which appeared in Scribner's Magazine in 1891, has as its main character a lonely widow living quietly in a New York boarding-house who has become estranged from her only daughter and who suffers from gout. The potential loss of the view from her window, which will follow inevitably from a neighbour's plan to extend her house, results dramatically in an act of arson and in Mrs Manstey's death. Wharton's last short story, 'All Souls'', which was published in *Ghosts* in 1937, centres on an experience of the uncanny for an older woman living alone with her servants in a large house in Connecticut. The events of one night render Sara Clayton's home uninhabitable for her; in spite of all the trappings of civilised living that surround her and that have made her existence well ordered and comfortable, she is suddenly dispossessed by stories which attach to Halloween, stories of sexual abandon and the breaking down of barriers, including those of class. The many gaps and evasions in this tale, combined with the skilful use of an unreliable narrator, show Wharton at her most sophisticated as a story-teller. Other stories and novellas which feature older women include 'The Lamp of Psyche' (1895), 'The Pelican' (1898), 'The Lady Maid's Bell' (1902), 'Autre Temps' (1911), 'Xingu' (1911), 'Bunner Sisters' (1916), 'Bewitched' (1925), 'Miss Mary Pask' (1925), 'Mr. Jones' (1928), 'Pomegranate Seed' (1931), and 'Roman Fever' (1934).

However, from the early 1920s, by which time she was in her sixties, Wharton's interest in the older woman seemed to intensify. In each of the four tales comprising *Old New York*, published in 1924, 'we see life defying the bounds prescribed for it by the complacent conventionality of Old New York...[a]...self-sufficing little society of inter-marrying families, smugly Philistine and Pharisaical', as Gilbert Thomas put it in his review of the volume on its publication.[2] Two of the tales, 'The Old Maid' and 'New Year's Day', feature older women whose secrets are those of sexual transgression. These transgressions, concerning illegitimacy and prostitution, challenge not only the respectable surface of Old New York as Wharton presents it in both tales, but also various stereotypes of female identity, such as the angel in the house, the old maid and the whore. Interestingly, in 1921, when Wharton was awarded the Pulitzer Prize for *The Age of Innocence*, she was having great difficulty placing 'The Old Maid' for publication because of its subject matter. Several magazines turned it down on the grounds of its 'immorality', a decision which drew from Wharton the astonished response: 'Have the readers of the Metropolitan never read "The Scarlet Letter" or "Adam Bede" to mention only the two first classics that come to my mind? And how about my own "Summer"?'[3] Like the short story 'All Souls", both 'The Old Maid' and 'New Year's Day' turn on gaps, evasions and invisible scenarios; both are structured through secrets, silences and encryptment.

In *The Mother's Recompense* Wharton continues to hone these techniques while developing the theme of the older woman and sexuality. The novel is more ambiguous and puzzling, however, than the stories and novellas that preceded it, as if Wharton came to a turning point in the mid-1920s. It is, as Hermione Lee notes, 'a disconcerting and troubling book'.[4] The short story, 'Miss Mary Pask', published in the same year as *The Mother's Recompense*, uses the comedic potential of parodic gothic to present an older woman deliberately passing as a vampire in order to claim sexual attention.[5] In her more usual role as a respectable older woman living alone in northern France, Mary Pask – like Kate Clephane – politely observes the social taboos which prevent the older woman from appearing sexually active and demanding. She is able only to express the needs that 'the living woman had always had to keep dumb and hidden' once she realises that her visitor thinks she is a member of the living dead (a performance that perhaps contributes to the young man's subsequent nervous breakdown).[6] While the short story uses parodic gothic to undermine conventional beliefs and stereotypes, *The Mother's Recompense*, a work that is sustained by hybridity, uses irony, satire and a reworking of various tragic, gothic and sentimental narratives to achieve the same end. Both fictions, then, offer critiques of conventional attitudes to female desire, albeit in different moods and modes. Taken together, 'The Old Maid', 'New Year's Day', 'Miss Mary Pask' and *The Mother's Recompense* present a considerable challenge to contemporary values and beliefs concerning the older woman and sexuality. Additionally, in order to sharpen and spice her treatment of this topic, Wharton added the theme of incest to her 1925 novel, further complicating the predicament of the sexually active older woman.

The Mother's Recompense opens with Kate Clephane, aged 45, settled in the south of France where she has made a life for herself in the American and British expatriate community. We learn that between the ages of 39 and 42 she had a passionate affair with Chris Fenno, an American 14 years her junior, a slightly bohemian and emotionally unreliable character who had settled in France to paint. The affair finished when Chris drifted away from her, volunteering to fight in the First World War, leaving her with still poignant memories of happiness and sexual fulfilment. Shortly after the novel opens, Kate is recalled to New York by her daughter, Anne, now 21, who warmly welcomes her back into the family home. She tries to readjust to the very society that had formerly stifled her and is courted afresh by an old admirer, Fred Landers, a retired lawyer. In a coincidence which is more reminiscent of non-realist genres such as melodrama, the gothic and the sentimental novel than of realism, Kate discovers that her ex-lover is the man with whom her daughter has fallen in love and wishes to marry. In anguish, she confesses the situation to the Parish Rector, Dr Arklow, who advises silence in order to avoid 'sterile pain' (p. 266). Finding the situation intolerable, she finally returns to France, abandoning her daughter for a second time and rejecting the offer of marriage made by the amiable but dull Fred Landers who, by now, knows her secret. There is no actual incest in Wharton's text: the dimension of incestuous desire – or near incestuous desire – is deferred. The sexual relationship between Chris and Kate remains innocent until she is about to be replaced in her lover's bed by her daughter, at which point the intensity of Kate's emotions forces her to make important decisions about her life. The sense of disappointed desire and lost love lends the novel a great deal of poignancy, although the ambiguity of the ending tempers any tendency towards nostalgia or melancholy. Love, it seems, for Kate Clephane, can only ever be 'something vanishing and sweet' (p. 276). The reasons for this are partly to do with Kate's own intense and romantic temperament but they derive also from cultural perceptions of motherhood and the older women.

Wharton thus places the older woman at the very heart of *The Mother's Recompense*, combining her increasing interest in ageing and sexuality with observations on postwar displacement and modern America, which she saw as materialistic and compromised by moral inertia and hypocrisy. The narrative is governed by the relationship between Kate Clephane, Chris Fenno and Anne Clephane. Wharton's development of the erotic dynamic between these characters is yet another variation of the Demeter–Persephone relationship to which she so often returned.[7] Here she uses it to explore not only the mother-daughter relationship but also displacement as well as the taboo topics of the older woman as sexually engaged and the nature of incestuous desire. Indeed, Wharton suggested 'Demeter' as well as 'Le Retour' and 'Vendages' – wine-harvests – for the title of the French translation of the novel.[8] At this stage of her career, Demeter, rather than Persephone, becomes her focaliser and her subject matter. Demeter's agony at losing her child to Hades and to sexual knowledge is reflected in Kate Clephane's pain at having finally to renounce her rediscovered daughter to her own lover. Significantly the novel opens in early spring and ends in the autumn with winter advancing and Demeter's adult female sexuality, indicated by her role as the goddess of fertility and harvests in Greek mythology, is reflected in Kate Clephane's mature sensuality. Indeed, Kate's highly erotic nature, never addressed directly, is nevertheless conveyed by Wharton obliquely but effectively. In her frequent descriptions of Kate's hair, for example, as rich, wild, abundant and still luxurious, and of Anne's as always tightly braided, she manages to suggest that the mother's sexual knowledge and capacity for erotic enjoyment and abandon is far greater than that of her daughter. The invisible scenario that the novel constantly invokes is Kate in bed with Chris Fenno, who, unlike her husband and previous lovers, was able to awake his 39-year-old lover to the pleasure of orgasm for the first time.[9] Kate is finally unable to reconcile this sense of herself as erotic and alive with her new identity of mother to Anne and of mother-in-law to Chris, roles which would redefine her as a passive, asexual, marginal figure in American society. Drawing on Josephine Donovan's argument, Sarah Whitehead points out that:

> Persephone's descent into the Underworld becomes an allegory of the New Woman's rejection of the essentially domestic women's sphere of their mothers for what had previously been the exclusively male realm of education and employment. Central to this transition is the problematic relationship between daughter and mother, in which the maternal realm 'represents a horrifying stasis'.[10]

Kate Clephane abandoned 'the essentially domestic women's sphere' in 1900, at the age of 26. Returning to New York as an older woman in

1919, she finds herself expected to adjust to a maternal role that indeed 'represents a horrifying stasis' for her. Thus in Wharton's revision of the myth in *The Mother's Recompense*, it is Kate, the Demeter figure, not Persephone, who finally feels trapped and in limbo. Her solution to this crisis of morality and identity, like Ellen Olenska before her, is to return to Europe and the anonymity of a society less 'bathed in the bright publicity of the American air' as Henry James put it when describing the milieu in Wharton's 1913 novel, *The Custom of the Country*.[11]

The societies of New York and the French Riviera, the novel's settings, are portrayed as respectable because of the accommodation of the necessary hypocrisies and inconsistencies which maintain this hard-won determination. New York comprises an older generation that has become stultified by the conventions of the social round and a younger generation that is 'curiously undifferentiated and immature' (p. 79), their youthful faces uniform and 'as inexpressive as a football' (p. 83). The French Riviera, which has become Kate Clephane's home and to which she returns at the end of the novel, is shown as a retreat for English and American expatriates, ranging from the sickly seeking a warm climate to the socially disgraced or displaced, all of whom confound the threat of loneliness abroad by organising endless rounds of bridge and numerous events that replicate the social life they left behind many years ago. With occasional exceptions – Fred Landers, for example – members of both societies seem to embody superficiality, inertia and moral compromise. One of the many paradoxes of this novel is that, in such contexts, Kate Clephane – a woman who left her husband and abandoned her three-year-old daughter at the age of 26 in order to pursue her freedom in Europe – emerges as an individual of some integrity. As Wharton pointed out in a letter to John Hugh Smith, when writing *A Mother's Recompense* she deliberately dissociated herself from the extreme techniques of modernism and her heroine from the morals of the post-First World War 'jazz age': 'I was not trying to follow the new methods, as May Sinclair so pantingly & anxiously does; & my heroine belongs to the day when scruples existed'.[12] However, many readers, from early reviewers to more recent critics, have found it hard to locate these 'scruples' and have been harsh in their condemnation of Kate Clephane as heroine.[13]

Published in 1925, the same year as *Mrs. Dalloway*, *The Mother's Recompense* was seen as old-fashioned, in technique if not in content, compared with Woolf's experimental modernist novel. Although Wharton's novel sold very well, competing with *The Great Gatsby* as a best-seller,[14] she was disappointed by the mixed reviews it received. Nowhere is this disappointment more evident than in a letter to her lifelong friend Daisy Chanler written on 9 June 1925:

> No one else has noticed 'desolation is a delicate thing' or understood that the key is there. The title causes great perplexity, but several reviewers think it means that the mother was 'recompensed' by the 'love of an honest man'. One enthusiast thinks it has lifted me to the same height as Galsworthy & another that I am now equal to Scott Fitzgerald. And the Saturday Review (American) critic says I have missed my chance, because the book 'ought to have ended tragically' – *ought to*! – You will wonder that the priestess of the Life of Reason shd take such things to heart; & I wonder too. I never have minded before; but as my work reaches its close, I feel so sure that it is either nothing, or far more than they know.... And I wonder, a little desolately, which?[15]

It is no wonder that Wharton felt discouraged. The reviewers, in the main, misread the novel, and avoided engagement with the substance of the narrative: the sexuality of the older woman and taboo desire. Surprisingly, outside the rather mealy-mouthed reviews in the literary magazines, those writing on the novel in the mass media were rather less oblique in their comments. For example, *The Boston Herald* reviewer noted: 'Throughout the novel, there is a horrible thing impending – the marriage of a girl to a man who has been the lover of her mother years before – and the menace of the thing, like the fear of something following one in the dark, fills the pages... There seem[s] something revoltingly incestuous in the thought of marriage between her daughter and her former lover'. Writing in *The New York Herald Tribune* on 17 May 1925, Stuart P. Sherman goes further, raising the question of 'whether the mother's impassioned opposition is actually due to incestuous horror or to normal, though acute, sexual jealousy.'[16] The words 'incest', 'sexual jealousy', 'impassioned', 'a horrible thing', 'menace' and 'fear' used by reviewers accurately reflect the visceral subject matter of Wharton's novel in which the word 'horror' and its variations recur frequently. What the critics missed, however, was Wharton's exposure of the taboos surrounding mature female sexuality and desire. She noted in her diary for 1925:

> Reading most reviews of my books – the kindest as well as the most disappointing – is like watching somebody in boxing-gloves trying to dissect a flower. I don't mean to suggest that my novels are comparable

to flowers – real ones – but they are certainly more nearly like these than they are like the conception of my work in the mind of the average reviewer.[17]

The petal-like layering of the text, produced by a rich density of allusion, locates the plot in an ancient tragic tradition while giving it new melancholic expression – and a satiric dimension - through the modern setting. Thus the bleakness of Kate's life is expressed by desolation rather than death, and 'desolation is a delicate thing', as the novel's epigraph, taken from Shelley's *Prometheus Unbound*, intimates. The spirit who utters these words in Shelley's dramatic poem is answering the question 'Has thou beheld the form of Love?', and responds that 'desolation' is the inevitable outcome for those who 'Dream visions of aëreal joy, and call the monster, Love,/ And wake, and find the shadow Pain'.[18] The anguish of the novel is rooted in the tension between Kate Clephane's dreams of love and her experience that love can only ever be temporary, 'something vanishing and sweet' (p. 276). Harbouring such an intensely romantic, in the Shelleyan sense, attitude toward love, Kate is likewise doomed to 'desolation'.[19] Having found her 'real self' (p. 18) relatively late in life, she loses the love of the man who sexually awakened her, only later to lose the love of a daughter, having briefly experienced a return to motherhood as 'so sweet' (p. 323). Desolation, the 'shadow Pain', in Shelley's words, carries its own consolation or recompense, for it is the aftermath of love; it is the state that results from having both found love and lost it. The word 'desolation' thus tolls through the novel like a bell, reflecting both Kate Clephane's individual situation and that of a postwar modern world in which everything, even love itself, has become transient. Accordingly, homes and relationships can only ever be temporary for Kate:

> Every gesture, every act, denoting intimacy with that house, or the air of permanence in her relationship to it, would also have been impossible. Again she had the feeling of sitting in a railway station, waiting for a train to come in. (p. 218)

The desolation and pain resulting from such transience become a feature of Wharton's late fiction and the image of the railway station is used later in *Twilight Sleep* to suggest instability and impermanence. In that novel, Lita and Jim's state-of-the-art drawing-room is described as 'more like the waiting room of a glorified railway station than the setting of an established way of life', suggesting the temporary quality of their marriage.[20]

Notwithstanding its portrait of an intractably modern world, *The Mother's Recompense*, as several critics have noticed, draws on numerous previous tales and texts. Like all her late novels, it is a richly intertextual work. We have already noted that it reworks the Demeter and Persephone myth and draws something of its mood from 'Prometheus Unbound'. Hermione Lee likens its plot to that of *Anna Karenina* (1873–7) and indeed Kate does liken herself fleetingly to Tolstoy's heroine in the early pages of the novel. Adeline Tinter sees the novel as owing a debt to Henry James's short story 'The Chaperon' (1891) and Hildegard Hoeller argues convincingly that it is in close dialogue with Grace Aguilar's *The Mother's Recompense* (1851), from which Wharton took her novel's title.[21] However, the differences between Wharton's novel and these works are significant, particularly with regard to their endings. Tolstoy chooses death to resolve his heroine's plight; Henry James chooses marriage as closure, albeit a marriage hedged round with ambiguity.[22] Grace Aguilar's *The Mother's Recompense*, as Hoeller argues, embraces melodrama and sentimentality in its portrayal of the mother-daughter relationship and resolves all tensions through marriage as closure. However, with the exception of the Demeter and Persephone myth which, in some versions, has Hades as Demeter's brother, making him the uncle as well as the husband of Persephone, none of these works has as its central focus incestuous desire and the sexuality of the older woman. For example, despite featuring an attractive and disgraced older woman, James's story is focalised entirely through the eyes of her young daughter.

Wharton, in her Notebook of 1924–1928 – contemporary with the writing of *The Mother's Recompense* – experimented with depicting the effects of a stepmother/stepson physical relationship in a story outline called 'Cold Greenhouse'. We were to learn of the liaison through the memories of the two unmarried sisters of Charles Legree – who died in the Civil War – as they deal with the thoughts and memories that arise at the much later death of the stepmother. One of them reports to the other that she witnessed a kiss between stepmother and stepson that was 'the sort of a kiss you and I have never had...She had it'.[23] Insofar as it is possible to speculate, 'Cold Greenhouse' was to focus on the daughters rather than the stepmother, thereby eliding the complexities of portraying the older, sexually assertive woman. In *The Mother's Recompense*, however, the older woman – who still desires the ex-lover who is about to marry her daughter – plays a part in an erotic triangle which is powerfully reminiscent of the plots of ancient Greek playwrights, as well as classical European dramatists. One thing that contemporary reviewers did agree on was that Greek tragedy was a powerful influence in Wharton's novel. Wharton must have felt particularly frustrated by their inadequate responses to her work because they were right in spotting her indebtedness to Greek tragedy and specifically to the story of Phèdre and her stepson Hippolytus.[24] Wharton's library contained Euripides' play *Hippolytus*, in translation by Gilbert Murray, as well as the work of Sophocles in a number of editions, including a German translation, *König Ödipus*. She also possessed a 1677 edition of Racine's *Phèdre et Hippolyte* as well as his complete works in two different editions.[25] Notes and letters in the Wharton archive at the Beinecke Library of Yale University show that she both read and responded creatively to the Greek classics throughout her writing career.[26] Indeed, Wharton's poetic response to Aeschylus's work in the final sestet of an early undated sonnet, entitled 'Orestes', clearly reveals how drawn she was to the classical portrayal of violence at the heart of the family:

> Is this the roof that sheltered me? There swell
> The figs against the wall…such little things!
> How strange it is the palaces of Kings
> Should look like homes where harmless people dwell…
> Far down the wind I hear the hum of hell,
> And in my brain the clang of iron wings.[27]

Wharton was to describe her next novel, *Twilight Sleep* (1927) as 'an Aeschylean tragedy with no Aeschylean moral ideals'[28] and Adeline Tintner has commented that 'it does not seem to me to be forcing the issue if we see the three novels, 'The Old Maid', *The Mother's Recompense* and *Twilight Sleep*, as Wharton's Sophoclean tragedy'.[29] Although contemporary readers failed to interrogate the way in which *The Mother's Recompense* engages with the Greek classical dramatic tradition, one critic dismissing it as 'a Greek play minus the fifth act',[30] Wharton clearly drew on it in order to establish a framework within which she could focus on an older woman's desire for a younger man.

The trope of incest, the foundation of the dramatic tragedies referred to here, became a common feature of Gothic writing in both Britain and America from the eighteenth century onwards.[31] Horace Walpole's play, *The Mysterious Mother*, written in 1768 but considered even by its author as too shocking to stage publicly, is in direct line of descent from Greek through Jacobean Revenge and Racinian tragedy. Given that *Twilight Sleep*, Wharton's next novel, was to draw on Walpole's *The Castle of Otranto*, which was published alongside *The Mysterious Mother* in editions of Walpole's collected works from 1770 onwards, it is quite likely that Wharton had *The Mysterious Mother*, as well as the previously mentioned works, in her mind when writing *The Mother's Recompense*. If so, she would undoubtedly have been attracted, at this stage in her writing career, to Walpole's defence of generic hybridity in literature, set out in his preface to *The Castle of Otranto*, published in 1764 and regarded as the first Gothic novel in English. His agenda for such hybridity, which clearly informs both his novel and his play, includes a blending of ancient romance – tales of chivalry and myth – with modern romance, that is, the eighteenth-century novel. Described by Paul Baines as 'an extreme version of incest narrative' which interfuses 'Greek and French material in a new Gothic form', Walpole's *The Mysterious Mother*, like Wharton's novel, takes as its main focus the sexual desires of the older woman.[32] While the plot of Walpole's play goes beyond anything Wharton would have deemed publishable – his mysterious mother knowingly sleeps with her own son, bears his daughter and ends her own life when she discovers years later that her two children have married – there are nevertheless interesting resonances between the two authors' work, not least in the portrayal of the mature woman's sexuality. In Walpole's drama the mother is an exceptionally sensual and erotically aware woman, having been initiated into 'the sting of pleasure' by her deceased husband who had 'taught her passion'.[33] As we have seen, Kate Clephane has been taught passion not by her husband, nor even the lover with whom she made her escape from New York, but by a man 14 years her junior, 'who had loved and waked her' (*MR*, p. 19). A source of intense pleasure, the affair fills both her memory and her sense of self with a sexual confidence that is displaced only when she is recalled to duty as a mother.

Once back in New York she comes face to face with her past in the shape of Chris, now transformed from a reminder of past happiness into a potentially 'incestuous horror' (*MR*, p. 279) as she learns that her daughter is in love with him. Thus the most shocking revelation for Kate is that she feels an overwhelming sexual jealousy which inevitably disrupts the revived mother–daughter relationship. It is at this point in the novel that the threat to the very fabric of society and family life is made manifest by the older woman's sexual desires. In a letter to John Hugh Smith, dated 25 May 1925, Wharton wrote:

I'm glad you liked 'The Mother.' I felt, in writing it, all the force of what you say about the incest-element, & its importance in justifying her anguish – but I felt it wd be hardly visible in its exact sense to *her*, & wanted to try to represent the business as it seemed to her, culminating in the incest-vision when she sees the man holding Anne in his arms.[34]

This moment occurs when Kate, asked to view the wedding dress which is lying across 'Anne's narrow bed', startles the young couple who, while supposedly looking at the dress, are actually erotically absorbed in each other, 'the curves of their lips, hardly detached...like those of a fruit that has burst apart of its own ripeness' (p. 278). Seeing her daughter and Chris Fenno in a close embrace which suggests their strong sexual passion for each other, Kate feels 'a furious flame of life [rush] through her; in every cell of her body she felt that same embrace, felt the very texture of her lover's cheek against her own, burned with the heat of his palm as it clasped Anne's chin to press her closer' (*MR*, p. 278). This wave of sexual arousal is followed by a moment of anguish in which Kate realises both the intensity of her own jealousy and the impossibility of continuing to live in New York near her daughter. The autumnal tints with which Wharton imbues the scene – 'One of the tall vases was full of branching chrysanthemums and autumn berries' (p. 277) – intimate obliquely the incongruity, in society's eyes if not of that of Wharton or the reader, of a mother in her mid-forties feeling such intense sexual desire and jealousy. In the early pages of the novel Kate defined herself by her sexual relationship in the past with Chris Fenno and she can only envisage happiness in the future if that affair is revived. The removal to New York has been insufficient to effect the transformation to 'mother' rather than 'lover' as her means of self-definition and the emotional complexity of this moment provokes the moral dilemma.

But what exactly is the nature of Kate's dilemma? Before the wedding-dress scene, Kate had determined to put her daughter's happiness before her own: 'Renunciation, renunciation. If she could attain to that, what real obstacle was there to her daughter's happiness?' (p. 276). Moreover, Anne Clephane's marriage to Chris Fenno would certainly not be incestuous, as Kate herself has already realised: 'Legally, technically, there was nothing wrong, nothing socially punishable, in the case' (p. 275). She continues to associate the word 'horror', however, with her daughter's impending marriage: reflecting on her wave of jealousy, she thinks 'Was that why she had felt from the first as if some incestuous horror hung between them?' (p. 279). The dilemma Kate faces results in part from the sense that she cannot tell the truth about her past because this would mean giving voice to herself as a passionate and sexually desirous older woman – an identity which American society construes as incompatible with the role of mother and one which Kate has already partially internalised: 'Anything rather than to be the old woman clutching at an impossible prolongation of bliss' (p. 275). Wharton spells out the cost of such silence but also draws a clear moral line in the novel at the idea of a mother and a daughter sharing a lover. It is plain that, despite the lack of consanguinity, such a relationship would constitute a sort of *emotional* incest, both in Kate's eyes and in Wharton's.[35] The two references to Guido's portrait of Beatrice Cenci – a famous victim of paternal incest[36] – which hangs above the double bed in the best spare room of the Clephane house in New York (*MR*, pp. 45 and 80), obliquely suggest Kate's horror at the thought of her lover being as intimate with her daughter's body as he had been with her own. Her dilemma is understandable. Remaining silent about her relationship with Chris would place Kate almost in the position of a mother who colludes with her husband's seduction of her daughter. It would also mean stifling her sexual identity. On the other hand, if she tells all, she will lose her daughter, having only just found her. In exploring the complexities of Kate's situation, Wharton channels the powerful emotions that can distort family life and aligns her work with a gothic exposure of their potential for destruction rather than with the sanitisation more typical of the sentimental novel.[37]

Because she has nowhere to go and no one to turn to, Kate Clephane, in her desperation to find a way through her torment, seeks advice from the rector who will officiate at the marriage of Anne and Chris. While his original reaction when Kate explains the situation – albeit pretending that the story belongs to another – is one of shock and revulsion, he comes around to the conclusion that if the mother 'has the courage to keep silence – always' then 'sterile pain', as he calls it, will be avoided (*MR*, pp. 265 and 266). Walpole, in his 'Postscript' to *The Mysterious Mother*, reveals one of the sources for his drama. It is a source which resonates strikingly with this episode in Wharton's novel for it concerns a 'gentlewoman' who tricked her own son into making love to her. Many years later the son marries a beautiful young woman who (unbeknown to him) is the fruit of the union with his mother. On discovering this, the horrified mother seeks counsel from an archbishop, who advises her 'never to let her son and daughter know what had passed, as they were innocent of any criminal intention. For herself, he bade her almost despair.'[38] In Walpole's source, then, although not in his play, a senior cleric advises the mother to keep silent, just as Dr Arklow advises Kate Clephane to keep quiet. Church authority which, in terms of spiritual values, plays no part in the narrative of *The Mother's Recompense*, still acts as a form of social control where female desire is concerned. The Rector advises Kate to keep her potentially explosive knowledge to herself, in order to contain the 'secret' of the sexually active mother, thereby preserving the roles conventionally prescribed for her. This echoes the part played by the archbishop in Walpole's source who seeks to punish maternal transgression for, as Elizabeth Ammons notes, 'the free expression of female sexuality represents a profound threat to patriarchal power, and is therefore assiduously guarded against'.[39] Commenting specifically on Walpole's *The Mysterious Mother*, E.J. Clery observes that, 'female desire has its own, autonomous and selfish volition, [such] that it might be impervious to the social desiderata of reproduction and the patriarchal family; that it might even be at war with them'.[40] The law, as well as the Church, constrains the independence of the mature woman in such a world and so it is not surprising to find Kate thinking of 'Lawyers, judges, trustees, guardians' as 'all the natural enemies of woman' (*MR*, p. 10). Many of Wharton's male characters are lawyers, including even the benign Fred Landers: 'She remembered that his profession had been legal – most of one's men friends, in those remote days, were lawyers' (*MR*, p. 46). Wharton was well aware how religious and legal discourses functioned to inflect the social contract with roles and expectations that did not allow women the same freedoms as men.[41] *The Mother's Recompense* shows us that 'the inexorable laws which had governed family affliction' (*MR*, p. 62) in Old New York still pertain in the twentieth century and that their government of female desire is buttressed by the language of the Law and the Church.[42]

Like Walpole, Wharton makes the older woman's active sexuality catalytic to the action; the incestuous desire of the mysterious mother and Kate Clephane's affair with a younger man precipitate chains of events that impact upon innocent members of the younger generation. However, in both texts the authors stand back from judging their heroines: their individual situations are presented sympathetically and the readers are drawn into an understanding of their predicaments. As *The Mother's Recompense* opens, we see a lonely woman thrown too much upon her own scant emotional and financial resources, dwelling on the memory of the one experience in her life that seemed to lift her above the mundane – her affair with a younger man that awakened her sexually. At the opening of *The Mysterious Mother* we are introduced to a 'pious Countess',[43] dispensing alms to the poor, still apparently grieving for her handsome husband and absent son. The women have both worked hard to maintain a public image of respectability; indeed, Kate Clephane's two years of war work and the award of a 'Reconnaissance

France' have made her feel that 'she could carry her head fairly high' (p. 14), at least in Europe. From the outset we know the worst about Kate Clephane's life and her expiation – a somewhat lonely and rather shabby existence abroad – seems sufficient unto the sin; the 'incestuous horror', precipitated by a curious coincidence, has yet to rear its head. In Walpole's play the worst is saved for last; it is only at the end of the drama that we learn the Countess's secret – that she knowingly seduced her own son and hid the disastrous results. Walpole understood that his refusal to damn the Countess made his play even more shocking.[44] Standing back from judgment, he even provided her with mitigating circumstances in so far as her son looks very much like his handsome father, whose premature death the Countess is still grieving and whose physical presence she sorely misses. Wharton similarly refuses to condemn her heroine, focalising the story entirely through Kate so that the reader's sympathy for her is maintained throughout.

This textual strategy is further strengthened by the presentation of Anne as a rather cold, repressed and yet wilful individual so that the reader's sympathy is not deflected to the daughter. Anne is associated throughout with whiteness which, in the context of the novel, connotes not only virginity but also barely contained anger and unnatural restraint. Her face is always pale – 'her pale face hung over her mother's like a young moon seen through mist' (p. 36) – her features usually 'opaque and guarded' (p. 174) and she is linked with 'aloofness' more than once (pp. 68 and 274). Before the conversation about Anne's money, Kate's daughter appears to her 'tall and ghostly in her white linen riding-habit' (*MR*, p. 189), facing her mother 'in a white glare of passion' (p. 192). When she accuses Kate of being 'the other woman' in Chris Fenno's life, she stands before her 'like a blanched Fury' (*MR*, p. 199), in a 'white-heat of ire' which turns her mother cold (p. 200). Indeed, Kate sees something of her mother-in-law, who was a very rigid and domineering woman, in her daughter. Noticing how Anne's eyes are like those of her grandmother, Kate glances away 'frightened at the riddle' (*MR*, p. 68); Anne's tendency to repress her emotions, together with 'a certain asperity of speech, a sharp intolerance of trifles' (*MR*, p. 186) remind her further of old Mrs Clephane. The conservative tendencies of the previous generation, it seems, are being replicated in her daughter and have no doubt been encouraged by Anne's aunt, Mrs Enid Drover, who has acted as a surrogate mother in Kate's absence. As already noted, whereas Kate still has 'unmanageable abundant hair' (p. 6), 'radiant irrepressible hair' (p. 12) – suggesting her passion and desire – Anne's hair is always tightly braided, even in sleep (p. 119). Anne's combination of repressed passion and strong will is reminiscent of Charlotte Brontë's portrait of St John Rivers in *Jane Eyre* and, like that character, Anne is associated with the coldness of marble: 'In the passing flashes of the arc-lights the head at her side, bound about with dark braids, looked as firm and young as a Greek marble' (p. 155).[45] Again like St John Rivers, she invariably maintains a certain 'rigid reserve' about emotional matters so that after her engagement with Chris Fenno is broken off, 'her soul seemed to freeze about its secret' (p. 186). Like her father, she is constrained by 'a certain heaviness of pen, an inability to convey on paper shades of meaning or feeling' (p. 152). Her exemplary behaviour and her conformity to social expectations conceal from most of her friends and relations a self which only Kate and Fred Landers glimpse. Her mother comes to understand 'what reserves of violence still underlay her daughter's calm exterior' (p. 190) and Fred Landers recognises in her 'a young woman of considerable violence of feeling' (p. 250).

Wharton also presents Chris unsympathetically, despite Kate's positive memories of their affair which, at the time, seemed to fill 'her soul's lungs' (p. 18) with air after two stifling relationships: her five-year marriage to John Clephane and a two-year relationship with Hylton Davies who had 'the soul of a club steward' (p. 305). Although intelligent, Chris as a 25-year-old was drawn to 'gambling, casinos, rowdy crowds' and was 'never happy without what he regarded as excitement' (p. 19). Bumping into him unexpectedly six years later in New York, Kate is reminded of his 'bad taste' (p. 112) and tactlessness. Reflecting on the relationship soon afterwards, she realises how selfish he has always been: 'it all came to the question of what he wanted; it always had' (p. 117). Rationalising his dilettante nature as characteristic of 'a sort of intellectual rolling stone' (p. 149), he redeems himself in the First World War by showing courage on the battlefield and is awarded the Legion of Honour and the Distinguished Service Medal for bravery. Although he is now Major Fenno, the war has not transformed him as much as he claims. Still rather lazy and opportunist, he prefers life to come easy: 'He liked money...wanted to have it, but he hated to earn it' (p. 123). Believing that he has broken off their engagement because of her wealth, Anne decides to transfer most of it to her mother. However, Wharton leaves his motives for marrying Anne rather unclear so that there is room to suspect that her money is, indeed, part of her attraction for him. Nollie Tressleton regrets that 'he feels obliged to give up his present job' (p. 149) as Horace Maclew's private secretary once he becomes engaged to Anne but for the reader alert to Wharton's irony, her comment only provides further evidence of his opportunism and indolence. His tactic of distancing himself from his relationship with Kate by referring to himself at that time as a 'boy' who looked up to her (p. 149) and as a 'silly conceited boy' (p. 182) is both inaccurate, because he was 28 at the time they parted, and emotionally cruel, for he must know that such comments, made to Nollie and Anne, will get back to Kate, as indeed they do. Indeed, increasingly, Kate recollects that he has the capacity to be cruel: 'Fear uppermost – yes; was she not always afraid of him?' (*MR*, p. 218); 'When his blue eyes turned to that harsh slate-gray, and the two perpendicular lines deepened between his brows, she had always trembled' (*MR*, p. 219); by the end of the novel she recognises that 'his ways of being cruel were innumerable' (p. 257). It is significant that Fred Landers, a dull man but full of goodness and integrity down to 'his honest boot-tips' (p. 301), 'had never liked Chris', as Kate knows (p. 207). Indeed, she is not blind to 'the weakness of his fallen features' (p. 172) and his 'sullen obstinacy' (p. 222), refusing any longer 'to draw the old tattered glamour over him' (p. 117). However, she still remembers with pleasure the old charismatic Chris: 'the real Chris; always on the spot, easy-going and gay' (p. 122). Above all, she still remembers the powerful sexual current between them and it is this memory that haunts her present and that viscerally undermines her newly acquired identity. Kate is clear, however, that she does not now love Chris Fenno: 'No; she didn't love him any longer; she was sure of that' (p. 117). Nor is she haunted by the memory of him: 'It was as if his actual presence had exorcised his ghost' (p. 116). Rather, she is haunted by the desire that he awakened in her.

In her book *Edith Wharton* Katherine Joslin opens her discussion of *The Mother's Recompense* by describing the novel as one which 'while not strictly speaking a ghost tale, does rely on ghosts for its meaning'. Her terms of reference draw on the gothic in setting up a reading of the novel as one which revolves around the 'spectral nature of [Kate's] desires'.[46] And they are, indeed, 'spectral', insofar as society's refusal to recognise or accept them increasingly renders Kate 'unreal' to herself. Haunted at each turn by both her American and European past, her sense of alienation grows stronger with every New York encounter and is frequently expressed in gothic images of claustrophobia and disorientation: 'At the moment when her very life depended on her knowing their passwords, holding the clue to their labyrinth, she stood outside the mysterious circle and vainly groped for a way in' (*MR*, pp. 135–6); 'for Anne's sake she must try to make the most of it, to grope her own way and the girl's through this ghastly labyrinth...' (*MR*, p. 194). Plunged into a Drover family weekend she feels 'so tenuous and spectral that she almost wondered how she could be visible to their hearty senses' (*MR*, p. 229). The older woman is indeed invisible in a society which prizes only young and beautiful women and Kate's sense of self evaporates within it. All eyes are on Anne. No longer able to identify fully with her younger self – 'was it her own figure she saw fading down those far-off perspectives? Well – if it were, let it go! She owned no kinship with that unhappy ghost!' (*MR*, p. 106) – and unable to slip easily into the role of the middle-aged mother, Kate feels trapped and suffocated: 'there was an obstruction in her throat, as if her voice were a ghost vainly struggling to raise its own grave-stone' (*MR*, p. 132). Images of incarceration permeate the novel from here on: 'There they all were, the faces that had walled in her youth' (*MR*, p. 154); 'how often Kate had driven up to that door inertly huddled in her corner, with her husband's profile like a wall between her and the world beyond the windows' (*MR*, p. 155). Her sure-footedness and confidence slipping away from her, Kate experiences a gothicised sense of dislocation from the real world, indicative of both depression and alienation: 'under the surface-rattle of her thoughts a watchful spirit brooded haggardly on the strangeness and unreality of the scene' (*MR*, p. 231); 'Kate stood behind them like a ghost. It made her feel like a ghost to be so invisible and inaudible' (*MR*, p. 278).

The gothic dimension of the text is discernible in other elements of the novel too. The Clephanes and Drovers, like any clan in a gothic novel, are fading as once ruling elites. The younger generation is represented by two women: the laconic and bovine Lilla Gates and the cold and pale Anne Clephane. The Drover family scheme to wed the recently divorced Lilla to Horace Maclew, a wealthy collector, philanthropist and much older man, both comically inverts the usual gothic plot in which the younger woman is pursued by a predatory older man and offers an ironic critique of society's sexual double standards. A shadowy figure who conveniently provides employment for Chris Fenno, Maclew haunts the text only as a creature to be stalked and captured by a family ambitious for material wealth and anxious to secure a son-in-law who might be able to subdue their wild daughter. Despite the couple's incompatibility – Lilla sparks to life for bridge, dancing and cocktails whereas Maclew is interested mainly in money and his museum – the union is shown to be a matter for celebration in New York society. This marriage plot provides a constant note of satiric counterpoint to the taboo relationship between Kate and Chris. While the union of Horace and Lilla is deemed to be a social triumph rather than a perversion of the natural order, the fact of the liaison between the older woman and the younger man is too abhorrent even to be spoken aloud.

Lilla also has another function in the novel. Representing an extreme version of the moral laxity of 'new' New York society, she embodies everything that Kate Clephane finds abhorrent about modern America, including its casual attitude towards relationships between men and women. New York is, it seems, fast becoming a city of transient coup-lings and quick divorces – a theme to be developed in *Twilight Sleep*; Nollie Shriner's almost immediate marriage to Joe Tresselton after her divorce from Frank Haverford is merely one example. Lilla, a heavy smoker – a 'defining feature of feminine modernity', according to Penny Tinkler[47] – with her 'dyed hair, dyed lashes, drugged eyes and unintelligible dialect' (p. 64),[48] is a much less sympathetic character than Nollie, who at least cares for other people. Indeed, we learn from Anne that it was Nollie who 'arranged' things when 'Lilla came to grief' and 'behaved really badly' (p. 60). Lilla, with her 'sluggish stare' (p. 93) is the most selfish of her set, who are all 'careless self-engrossed young people' (p. 90) in Kate's eyes. Her transgression – probably an affair with another man – clearly prompted a quick divorce and much alarm in her family. Despite her own unconventional history, Kate has no sympathy for Lilla, seeing her as 'smirched and deadened' by her past (p. 64). Later, Lilla is foolish enough to jeopardise her relationship with the wealthy Maclew by abandoning him at a New York party in favour of another man, with whom she leaves in the small hours of the morn-ing (p. 148). As Nollie reveals, it took the combined efforts of all family and friends – including those of Chris Fenno who doubtless has his own motive for championing Lilla – to re-establish the relationship. Yet:

> as a matter of curiosity, and as a possible light on the new America, Kate would have liked to know why her husband's niece – surprising offshoot of the prudent Clephanes and stolid Drovers – had been singled out, in this new easy-going society, to be at once reproved and countenanced. Lilla in herself was too uninteresting to stimulate curiosity; but as a symptom she might prove enlightening. (p. 93)

From this point on, Lilla becomes a touchstone for what Kate finds unacceptable behaviour: casually undertaken and promiscuous sex. Whereas Henrik Drover is shocked by what he imagines to be the 'kind of thing they did in Europe' (p. 67), Kate is repulsed by the conduct so easily embraced by modern America: 'Much as Kate Clephane had suffered under the old dispensation, she felt a slight recoil from the indifference that had succeeded it' (p. 62). Indeed, it is the thought of

Lilla's easy acceptance of her situation, should she reveal it, which helps Kate to decide that she can no longer live with it:

> it suddenly became clear to Mrs. Clephane that no recoil of horror, and no Pharisaical disapproval, would be as intolerable to her as Lilla's careless stare and Lilla's lazy: 'Why, what on earth's all the fuss about? Don't that sort of thing happen all the time?'...She would have felt herself befouled to the depths by Lilla's tolerance. (p. 241)

Kate's strong reaction to Lilla reveals in part the nature of her scruples: able to defend her decision to leave an unhappy marriage and to seek her independence in Europe, and previously eager to resume a sexual relationship with Chris, she nevertheless does not approve of sexual promiscuity. Although she recognises that 'reality and durability were attributes of the humdrum, the prosaic and the dreary' (p. 5), Kate is deeply concerned by the changed nature of relationships in New York despite the fact that her own marriage represented an intolerable confinement. For Kate, such behaviour threatens degeneration and the collapse of tradition and social codes. As Dale M. Bauer has noted, 'The novel is at once both sympathetic to the new spirit of tolerance and its loosening hold on the social scene and, at the same time, deeply split, especially with respect to the threat of unchecked sexual desires, in which Wharton sees social anarchy'.[49] It is thus not surprising to discover that the plot of *The Mother's Recompense* began life as an unfinished novel entitled 'Disintegration', which Wharton started in 1902 and which featured a young New York girl, Valeria Clephane, whose mother ran off with another man.[50] By the 1920s, however, Wharton had switched the focus from the daughter to the mother. In Kate Clephane, Wharton presents an unconventional woman who has shocked society in the past by her behaviour but who has her own standards of morality that derive more from old Europe or America than the present day. An affair may well be secretly celebrated as something 'vanishing and sweet' but promiscuity promises social anarchy. In this respect, the novel echoes Wharton's own concern that sexual activity during the 1920s 'seemed too much like recreation or, worse, addiction, that sex was becoming not a means to pain or pleasure...but an avoidance of intimacy'.[51]

Kate is aware, however, that her own past 'bad behaviour' precludes an open dialogue with her rather conservative daughter, a dialogue that would speak the truth and thereby bring into the daylight the taboo topic of the double awakening to sexual pleasure of the mother and daughter. Indeed, there is much emphasis on silence and secrecy in the last third of the novel, indicating that there is a great deal that must remain hidden: 'Silence fell – always the same silence' (*MR*, p. 214); 'she remained silent' (*MR*, p. 289); 'The silence continued' (*MR*, p. 320). This is the silence surrounding the 'hypocrisies and inconsistencies' which Evelyn Waugh thought it the novelist's duty to expose. Instead of open dialogue between her characters, Wharton uses bedroom scenes to intimate sexual desire and the emotional complexities which result from it. Incidents in or beside beds dominate *The Mother's Recompense*. The novel opens with Kate awakening to a Riviera light which brings back memories of the young man who once shared her bed. On arrival in New York she is given a new bedroom, to avoid the association with her previous married life in the same house; she spends most of her time in that room, eating and receiving old friends in it, but making few appearances in public. The state of the relationship between Anne and Kate is documented by whether or not the daughter brings breakfast in bed to the mother, in so doing endorsing Kate's presence in her life and in the life of her social circle and giving permission, with the delivery of the food, for Kate to believe that she has a part to play in family life. Returning to the Riviera, Kate wakes alone, without the erotic aspirations that once gave her hope for the future. The breakfast is delivered by the paid help and intimacy – with either lover or daughter – is now confined to memory. Violets invariably accompany the breakfast tray, wherever Kate is. Always hoping they have been sent by Chris, Kate is always disappointed. In the novel's opening scene, they have been sent by a lame boy to whom Kate has been kind; in New York they come from Anne; on her return to France they are sent by a new beau, Lord Charles, as a token of his admiration. She even finds a bunch of violets, 'compact and massive' (p. 204) by her dinner plate when she dines with Fred Landers at his home. The many symbolic meanings of this flower accord well with the emotionally complex nature of Wharton's novel. Outside Christian mythology, in which the flower is associated with the Virgin Mary and humility because it grows near the ground, the violet usually signifies faithfulness in love. In a novel in which relationships are portrayed as insubstantial, its traditional meaning becomes imbued with irony. The flower is also connected with Demeter, since Hades carries off Persephone while she is walking through a field of violets. Even more significantly, perhaps, it is part of another famous erotic triangle. In Greek mythology, Io – the Greek word for violet – the beautiful daughter of King Argus, was much loved by Zeus. To prevent Hera's jealousy and rage, Zeus turned Io into a heifer and then created the sweet-scented plants, now known as violets, for her to eat. Refusing to 'internalize decline as [her] dominant private age identity',[52] Kate still feels she is Io in her heart: 'If it had not been for her looking-glass she would never have known she was more than twenty' (p. 299). Fate and time, however, have cast her in the role of Hera.

In order to preserve her freedom and retrieve an authentic sense of her own identity, Kate Clephane chooses exile from her country of origin and sacrifices the chance to establish a bond with her daughter. The cost of integrity is therefore high. Kate has always intuitively been aware that this would be the case: 'At thirty-nine her real self had been born; without him she would never have had a self...And yet, at what a cost she had bought it!' (*MR*, p. 18). The events that follow this early realisation only confirm it for her. The 'cost' of her decision that 'Thy gods shall *not* be my gods' (*MR*, p. 135) eventually includes the loss of her daughter – 'the one perfect companionship she had ever known, the only close tie unmarred by dissimulation and distrust' (p. 87); reversion to a rather rootless and superficial way of living; the sacrifice of a very materially comfortable life in New York for return to life in a hotel room on the French Riviera; and the threat of loneliness and emotional isolation in old age. We have suggested that the recompense for the pain Kate experiences is her memory of sexual fulfilment with Chris Fenno, although this is now contaminated by his new relationship to her of son-in-law. However, this is not how contemporary readers saw it, some even choosing to interpret Fred Landers' devotion as the recompense that would assuage Kate's despair. Wharton, however, briskly dismissed this idea in a letter to John Hugh Smith written in May 1925.[53] Nor is it the 'recompense', celebrated by Grace Aguilar at the end of her novel *The Mother's Recompense*, published posthumously in 1850. Mrs Hamilton, the idealised and sentimentalised mother in that novel, expresses her idea of 'recompense' very clearly: it is seeing 'my children, as I do now around me, walking in that path which alone can lead to eternal life, and leading their offspring with them...and yet lavishing on me, as on their father, the love and duty of former years...Is not this a precious recompense for all which for them I may have done or borne?'[54]

The 'apology' to Grace Aguilar that prefaces Wharton's novel, for 'deliberately appropriating, and applying to uses so different' the former author's title is thus heavily ironic. Aguilar's *The Mother's Recompense* explored the topic of mother–daughter alienation and resolved it in the tradition of the sentimental novel. The acceptance of prescribed roles is offered as the recipe for domestic happiness: passion is confined to the daughter and self-sacrifice to the mother.[55] It also sanitises the spectre of incestuous desire by allowing characters who have regarded each other as 'brothers' and 'sisters' – even though there is no consanguineous link between them – to marry as young adults. Reprinted throughout the nineteenth century, the book became a classic of domestic and sentimental fiction. Wharton appropriated this popular sentimental work in order to offer a critique of the way in which the modern novel, unlike classical Greek, Racinian or gothic drama, confined the 'stories' of women's inner lives to a few limited narratives. As Wharton notes when discussing Proust's work and reputation in *The Writing of Fiction*, 'Original vision is never much afraid of using accepted forms'.[56] In this respect, Hildegard Hoeller is right to claim that 'As much as *The Mother's Recompense* is a story about her heroine…it is a story about literary genres'. Wharton's renovation of sentimental fiction does indeed, as Hoeller suggests, allow her to take issue with the way in which it is informed by a 'domestic ideology' that is blind 'to female desire and the threat of incest'.[57] In renovating sentimental fiction through an engagement with both classical and Racinian tragedy, as well as gothic plots, Wharton sought to explore the nature of female desire and its constraint by a patriarchal culture buttressed by the law and the Church. The use of gothic tropes, in particular, allows her – in Kate Ferguson Ellis's words – to 'speak of what in the polite world of middle-class culture cannot be spoken'.[58] In creating Kate Clephane, she presents a woman who is, according to Dale M. Bauer: 'confronting the demands of modernity to motherhood, erotic companionship, and "the new narcissism" of flapperhood'.[59] In so doing she challenged the platitudes constantly recycled by popular sentimental fiction and presented her readers with a novel that asked them to assess how far the move towards female suffrage and the change of status resulting from women's involvement in the First World War had changed conventional perceptions of 'the mother' and of female desire.

Completely rejecting the sentimentalism of Aiguilar's novel, Wharton shows Kate Clephane deliberately ignoring Anne's comment that 'Mothers oughtn't ever to leave their daughters' (*MR*, p. 235). Kate Clephane's sense of recompense has nothing to do with maternal duty or with self-sacrifice. Instead, it derives from both an authenticity of self that allows the older woman to see herself as sexually desiring and desired and the sad sweetness of having known love and lost it. It is a rejection of the unspoken judgement pronounced on the older woman, a social view Mrs Lidcote acknowledges in the short story 'Autre Temps', which treats in miniature the same subject matter as *The Mother's Recompense*: 'Finis was scrawled all over her'.[60] Anticipating Vita Sackville-West's *All Passion Spent* (1931), it marks a refusal to allow her family to dictate what she should do. It is also a refusal to return to the conformity offered by the companionship of marriage in middle-age to a good man she does not sexually desire; indeed Kate describes her rejection of Fred Landers' proposal as 'the one thing that keeps me from being too hopeless, too unhappy' (*MR*, p. 341) and as 'the most precious thing she could give him in return' for his pity (*MR*, p. 342). This is because in choosing to return to her life abroad she is able to hold on to that time when she felt most alive, most herself; she is able to shut away 'in a little space of peace and light the best thing that had ever happened to her' (*MR*, p. 342). Hildegard Hoeller claims that: 'the best thing that ever happened to Kate is still her sexual fulfilment and her passionate desire for Chris Fenno, and it is precisely this experience which she can guard by refusing to marry'.[61] The ending is not susceptible to such a definitive reading, however. The novel's ambiguous closure celebrates integrity and solitude, however painfully preserved, above duty, family ties and sexual as well as maternal love. This is radical content, even if the form of the novel is hybrid rather than experimental in a more obvious modernist manner. The novel's plot and daring subject matter have challenged readers over the years although at least one contemporary critic resolved the matter by describing *The Mother's Recompense* as a 'problem' novel.[62] In particular, its ambiguous closure has resulted in many different, often conflicting, readings.[63] Wharton creates in Kate Clephane a modern woman who, in Adeline Tintner's words, 'has a new identity, the woman without a traditional role. She is faced with the task of finding one'.[64] In this, as in other ways, Wharton's novel sits more comfortably with fiction of the 1930s than with modernist works of the 1920s. As Janet Montefiore has observed, in many novels by women writers of the 1930s – including those by Naomi Mitchison, Winifred Holtby and Sylvian Townsend Warner – the main female character is freed from the old 'marriage-or-death' plot and her 'quest for consciousness is tied not...to new forms of writing, but to the more familiar goals of autonomy and identity'.[65]

However, it is clear that Kate's 'quest for consciousness' is a difficult and painful one. Throughout *The Mother's Recompense* there are many references to her loneliness and sense of isolation. Even when apparently settled in New York with Anne:

> she was secretly aware of feeling a little lonely; there were hours when the sense of being only a visitor in the house where her life ought to have been lived gave her the same drifting uprooted feeling which had been the curse of her other existence. (p. 103)

To Fred Landers she confesses that she is 'homeless...I've been a wanderer for so many years' (p. 204), later reassuring him that she is 'used to being lonely. It's not as bad as people think' (p. 290). Using the image of a railway station again, Wharton makes clear that Kate Clephane's quest for consciousness will never allow her to settle for a life which constrains her 'real self':

> it was as if this house which people called her own were itself no more than the waiting-room of a railway station where she was listening for the coming of another train that was to carry her – whither? (p. 178)

And, indeed, although Kate returns to rooms in a slightly more upmarket French hotel than those of the Minorque et l'Univers, she 'had the feeling of having simply turned back a chapter' and begins 'to be aware that she was slipping back without too much discomfort into the old groove' (pp. 328 and 329). The novel closes with her having rejoined the community of 'uprooted drifting women' (p. 30) she had left a year ago, making conversation with the Dr Arklow (by a curious coincidence just appointed as the bishop of the American Episcopal churches in Europe) and being romantically pursued by an English noble. Realising she has to remake her life yet again, she takes comfort in 'all the narcotic tricks of evasion and ignoring' (p. 335) which have helped her in the past.

The story of Kate Clephane is not, then, a tragedy nor does it have a happy ending. Indeed, the final conversation with Dr Arklow, who presses Fred Landers' case, moves her to tears: 'Her eyes filled; for a moment her loneliness came down on her like a pall' (p. 341). We leave Kate Clephane trying 'to blot out the old horrors and the new loneliness', recompensed only by the knowledge that 'at least she had stood fast, shutting away in a little space of peace and light the best thing that had ever happened to her' (p. 342). The idea of being nourished by a secret memory might evoke Ronsard's lines: 'Une tristesse dans l'âme close/Me nourrit, et non autre chose', and, as we know, these lines provided Wharton with the title for the journal documenting her affair with Morton Fullerton – 'The Life Apart: L'Âme Close'. Kate Clephane has rejected traditional roles but feels unable to embrace the laxity and carelessness of the modern world. The result is a sense of dislocation, desolation and alienation: a self in limbo, a self that is always between worlds – past and present, Europe and America, youth and age. Although endowed with a romantic sensibility – even at one point feeling 'her real self...blown about on a lonely wind of anguish, outside in the night' while sitting comfortably by Fred Landers' hearth (p. 209) – in some ways Kate Clephane is a very modern woman, particularly in her sense of exile and homelessness. A curious mixture of the old and the new, Kate Clephane typifies the women of Wharton's late fictions, 'characters who are bewildered about and struggling to find niches in modernity'.[66] Rejecting the constraints of realism in an attempt to delineate the complexity and force of emotions that are often irrational, Wharton's hybrid fiction engages with the sentimental novel, the classical dramatic tradition and gothic fiction – genres that enabled her to make use of both coincidence and excess. Wharton's next novel continues this experiment in hybridity and, as we shall see, the dislocation and desolation Kate Clephane embodies will be developed further in the characters of Nona Manford, Rose Sellars and Halo Spear in the late and also 'problematic' novels that follow *The Mother's Recompense*.

2
Twilight Sleep

'What was the sense of it all?'[1]

Reviewing Edith Wharton's 1927 novel, *Twilight Sleep*, Edmund Wilson recognised its experimental nature, acknowledging that there was a freshness in the text: 'It is a striking proof of Mrs. Wharton's insight that *Twilight Sleep* should be something other than...a mere paler repetition of the author's earlier characters and situations. She has really, to a surprising extent, renewed herself with the new age'. However, while praising *Twilight Sleep* as 'a most entertaining novel and a distinguished piece of social criticism', it remained for him, quite reductively, 'a comedy', compared to *The House of Mirth*, which he thought a tragedy and *The Custom of the Country* which he described as 'ferocious satire'.[2] In fact, *Twilight Sleep* is a delicately poised mixture of satire, irony, parodic gothic and melancholy reflection on the modern world. The anti-climactic ending of this novel, like that of *The Mother's Recompense*, refuses the conventional death-or-marriage closure and leaves us with Nona Manford, still in her teens, finding herself so disaffected from the society in which she has been raised that she wishes to enter a convent, albeit 'a convent where nobody believes in anything' (p. 373). The anonymous reviewer for *The Observer* described *Twilight Sleep* as 'a problem-novel' and the writer L.P. Hartley noted, rather glumly, that it 'is not merely an indictment of the lives of a single group of rich people; it is a horrified forecast of what the world may be coming to'.[3]

Set entirely in the New York of the early 1920s, the novel's focus on the superficiality of modern America is sharp and unforgiving. In *The Mother's Recompense* (MR), Kate Clephane's desperate need, at the age of 45, to cling on to her 'youth and elasticity' (*MR*, p. 97) is presented with some pathos. In *Twilight Sleep*, however, the same language denotes

Pauline Manford's delight in her 'recovered youth and elasticity' (p. 25), but here in a novel littered with words beginning with 're', as a part of her quest to restore her mind and body to a previous condition – real or imagined – uncompromised by age and experience.[4] The rather disturbing reversal of roles in *The Mother's Recompense* – Anne Clephane's 'mothering' of the woman who abandoned her at the age of three and Chris Fenno's desire to marry the daughter after having had an affair with the mother – becomes translated into obviously dysfunctional relationships in *Twilight Sleep*. Nona takes on the cares and responsibilities of her family, while her workaholic father seeks escape from the boredom of marriage in an affair with his stepson's wife, and her mother rushes from pillar to post pursuing the latest fads, unaware that her family is malfunctioning around her. To drive home her point about inadequate parenting, Wharton also presents Kitty Landish and Amalasuntha as predatory parental figures who hope to make a fortune, respectively, out of Lita's and Michaelangelo's cinematic careers. In the world of *Twilight Sleep*, it is the conscientious and intelligent young people who shoulder responsibility for those around them, a generational distortion Wharton will pursue more obviously in the character of Judith in *The Children*. The strained mother–daughter relationship we see between Kate and Anne Clephane in *The Mother's Recompense*, in which silence about the past stunts the growth of honesty and love, is developed in *Twilight Sleep* into a mother–daughter relationship in which there is hardly any meaningful communication at all. Kate Clephane's resort to 'all the narcotic tricks of evasion and ignoring' (*MR*, p. 335) in order to cope with her sense of desolation becomes, in *Twilight Sleep*, a blanket rejection of pain by a whole culture, exemplified by the drug 'Twilight Sleep' (a compound of morphine and scopolamine) which banishes pain in childbirth.[5] Thus Lita was able to drift 'into motherhood as lightly and unperceivingly as if the wax doll which suddenly appeared in the cradle at her bedside had been brought there in one of the big bunches of hot-house roses that she found every morning on her pillow' (*TS*, p. 14).

This is a world in which babies are 'turned out in series like Fords' (*TS*, p. 15) and in which the opportunity to grow spiritually and emotionally through adversity is denied. The quick oblivion offered by 'Twilight Sleep', however, is not confined to privileged young mothers; it can also be induced by the mysticism of various theosophies, the use of drugs or alcohol, dancing, the frantic social life of New York and a very modern obsession with physical appearance. All such diversions work to prevent a profound engagement with pain, sorrow and death. As we shall see,

Wharton later becomes more insistent, in the Vance Weston novels, that pain is a necessary part of life, leading to wisdom and maturity, and in those works excoriates American society for trying to dispense with it. Thus, although to some readers *Twilight Sleep* has seemed a curious 'one-off' novel,[6] in fact it replays, in a heightened satiric key, several of the themes of *The Mother's Recompense* which will, in turn, be developed further in *The Children, Hudson River Bracketed, The Gods Arrive* and *The Buccaneers*. Once again Wharton departs from realism, tempering it with elements of the gothic mode in order to make distinct her satiric vision, the palimpsestic gothic plot offering a profound critique of modern life whilst the novel's surface uses satire and parody in order to entertain.[7] The result is a complex and layered novel: the narrative drive conjures the frenetic whirl of New York in the 1920s whilst the gothic element raises broad and disturbing questions about the nature of modern society more generally. If *Twilight Sleep* is 'overplotted',[8] it is so in the tradition of dramatic comedy, opera and the gothic.

The hybrid nature of *Twilight Sleep* has produced some interestingly partial interpretations. Whereas the gothic element of the novel has been neglected by critics, its humorous element seems to have divided them. Even those who have written perceptively and at length on *Twilight Sleep* often tend to ignore its comic dimension. Phillip Barrish, for example, in an illuminating essay on the novel, treats it almost as if it were a tragedy.[9] However, Naomi Royde-Smith, reviewing the novel on its publication, was quick to spot that its strength lay in its 'acid' satire and that its targets were of international relevance:

For Mrs. Manford, inexhaustibly rich, indiscriminately charitable, visiting her divorced husband once a week and completely failing to understand how horrid a mess she is making of her second marriage, is a thoroughly American type. And Mrs. Wharton has exposed her with a thoroughness that only just stops short of caricature...The book, it will be seen, is full of good, acid reading. And its satire will not be lost on London or Paris, where Mrs. Manford and her Inspirational Healers and Initiates have their counterparts. Mrs. Wharton is not telling that uncomfortable thing the Truth exclusively about American millionaires.[10]

In a sense, Barrish and Royde-Smith are both right in that this highly satirical novel includes a deeply melancholic strain as well as the sharp cynicism required of the genre. Wharton's satiric portrayal of the fraudulent language of cults and causes and the new languages of leisure and entertainment that mark affluent America in the 1920s, warns how such diversions will not fill the void left by moral disintegration and spiritual emptiness. Nothing effectively counteracts the sense of nihilism following the Great War: Christianity is moribund in the secular world of the novel (there is no equivalent of Dr Arklow in *Twilight Sleep*), as is comically illustrated by Pauline's secretary's assumption that the date for Easter is decided on commercial grounds: 'I never could see why they picked out such an awkward date for Easter: perhaps those Florida hotel people did it' (p. 7). Following the collapse of a traditional belief system and the values that went with it, the lure of other religions, represented by various charlatans, combines with heady pleasure-seeking and the rise of materialism to fill the void.

Wharton's use of satire during the 1920s was itself part of a larger cultural mood of postwar cynical detachment. She greatly enjoyed the work of contemporary satirical novelists such as Theodore Dreiser, Sinclair Lewis, Anita Loos, Aldous Huxley and Evelyn Waugh. In particular, she admired the work of Sinclair Lewis, whose novel *Babbitt*, dedicated to Wharton and published in 1922, strongly critiques the materialist values of modern America.[11] Indeed, in one sense *Twilight Sleep* can be seen as a response to Lewis's novel, the self-regarding disillusion experienced by Babbitt translating into Dexter's disaffection with his wife and his career. Wharton's novel, however, has a more problematic ending, replacing the sentimentally restored bond between father and son in Lewis's novel with a scene showing Nona wounded both physically and emotionally and still unable to communicate meaningfully with her mother. Several contemporary reviewers clearly recognised Wharton as part of this school, one linking her with Dreiser, Sinclair Lewis, John Dos Passos and Elliott Paul and another claiming that *Twilight Sleep*, written by 'an American Anthony Trollope' was 'a better "Babbitt", probably because it is of a woman by a woman'.[12] Wharton certainly foregrounds the female characters in *Twilight Sleep*, thereby raising questions about the lack of meaningful roles for women in modern America. In a society which still denies women access to most professions, Pauline's immense energy is neurotically dissipated across numerous causes while Nona, 'the cleverest girl in New York' (p. 72) and a putative novelist (as a child she 'wrote interminable stories', p. 10), gradually grows thinner and paler, sinking into disaffection and depression. Their very different forms of discontent result, Mary Suzanne Schriber has suggested, from inhabiting a 'domestic sphere that threatens atrophy of the mind rather than promises the mental stimulation James thought ideally possible there'.[13] *Twilight Sleep* can be seen then, as part of a new wave of postwar satirical writing in which a cynical loss of faith in the modern world combines with a dislike of 'jazz-age' morals and a desire to return to a more authentic code of values. Wharton was very happy to be included as a member of this postwar movement and in 1921 expressed her delight that an eminent critic had recognised her as a satirist: 'Mr. Ed. Wilson Jr. speaks words that are as balm to me, for it has dawned upon him that perhaps satire *is* my weapon!'[14] In this respect, Wharton's work in the 1920s can be seen as typical of late modernism which, in the words of Tyrus Miller, 'reopens the modernist enclosure of form onto the work's social and political environs, facilitating its more direct, polemical engagement with topical and popular discourses'.[15]

In *Twilight Sleep* we see a 'lost' younger generation to which Nona Manford, Jim and Lita Wyant (née Cliffe) belong: 'the bewildered disenchanted young people who had grown up since the Great War, whose energies were more spasmodic and less definitely directed, and who, above all, wanted a more personal outlet for them' (p. 7). Initially, Nona and Lita, linked through Lita's marriage to Nona's much-loved halfbrother, Jim, dance the nights away together (p. 9) and seem to enjoy the same activities despite differences in temperament:

> Lita had always been amiably disposed toward Nona. The two, though so fundamentally different, were nearly of an age, and united by the prevailing passion for every form of sport. Lita, in spite of her soft curled-up attitudes, was not only a tireless dancer but a brilliant if uncertain tennis-player, and an adventurous rider to hounds. Between her hours of lolling, and smoking amber-scented cigarettes, every moment of her life was crammed with dancing, riding or games. (p. 13)

The birth of her son constrains Lita's activities – however marginally – and she becomes eager to deny her motherhood, toying with the idea of accepting a contract from Serge Klawhammer, a Jewish movie director looking for new talent. Eventually she embarks on an affair with Nona's father, Dexter Manford, who has become infatuated with her and who blinds himself to Lita's proclivity for exhibitionism, blaming her faults on inadequate parenting by her aunt, Kitty Landish. Bent on fulfilling her own needs Lita has no scruples about pursuing any activity that will produce diversion and fun; indeed, all she wants is a place where she 'can dance and laugh and be hopelessly low-lived and irresponsible' (p. 300). Wharton uses Lita just as she had used Lilla Gates in *The Mother's Recompense*: as a straightforward representation of the selfishness and promiscuity of the postwar 'flapper' generation and its potential to produce social disintegration.

Nona's observation of Lita's careless immorality and of her father's furtive and inappropriate conduct, changes her profoundly. Intelligent, imaginative, sensitive and sensuous – she responds ardently to being kissed by Stan Heuston – she is also a young woman of scruples and moral responsibility. Able to empathise easily with others, she quickly responds to Maisie Bruss's anguish about her sick mother and is made deeply anxious by the culture of easy separation encouraged in New York society: 'It was one thing to theorize on the detachability of human beings, another to watch them torn apart by the bleeding roots' (p. 217). The suffering of the children of divorced parents particularly distresses her and she reflects that 'she could never have bought her happiness by a massacre of innocents' (p. 211). She prematurely takes on the role of responsible carer in a family whose adult members are morally short-sighted and driven by their own needs. Wharton has her wryly acknowledge the situation through her realisation that 'they all needed help, though they didn't know it' (p. 167) and her occasional philosophical reflections on the limits of responsibility: 'Where, for instance, did one's own self end and one's neighbour's begin?' (p. 220); 'Where...did one's own personality end, and that of others...begin?' (p. 237). Her problem lies in locating personal as well as social authenticity as she is clear-sighted enough to see that her family's behaviour is symptomatic of a broad cultural optimism that is almost incomprehensibly naive:

> There were moments when Nona felt oppressed by responsibilities and anxieties not of her age, apprehensions that she could not shake off and yet had not enough experience of life to know how to meet...It was as if, in the beaming determination of the middle-aged, one and all of them, to ignore sorrow and evil, 'think them away', as superannuated bogies, survivals of some obsolete European superstition unworthy of enlightened Americans, to whom plumbing and dentistry had given higher standards, and bi-focal glasses a clearer view of the universe – as if the demons the elder generation ignored, baulked of their natural prey, had cast their hungry shadow over the young. (pp. 47–8)

Wharton, in a manner typical of her writing in the 1920s and 1930s, here contrasts the abstract and the concrete, the mythic and the industrially produced, to illustrate the valorisation of the solution, the cure, over the process of learning something about the nature of the malaise.

The contrast between the 'demons' and 'dentistry' illustrates a technique deployed throughout the novel to signify the gothic dyad of the trappings of civilisation and the forces of darkness and unreason. Nona responds to the confusion around her by wishing that she had been born in the early 1880s (p. 43) instead of the first years of the new century, her disenchantment with New York society becoming so pronounced that she comes to view life with a 'desolate eye' (p. 210) and an 'uncanny detachment' (p. 237). Eventually she finds herself to be:

> more and more like one of the trench-watchers pictured in the wartime papers. There she sat in the darkness on her narrow perch, her eyes glued to the observation-slit which looked out over seeming emptiness. (p. 280)

This is the language of extremity, conjuring conflict, isolation and desolation. Aged 19 throughout the novel, the age at which many of those 'trench-watchers' would have met their deaths in the First World War, Nona comes to thinks of herself as much older than her years: '"I feel like the oldest person in the world, and yet with the longest life ahead of me..." and a shiver of loneliness ran over her' (p. 281). Youth, as in the Great War which is metaphorically recalled here, is sacrificed in this society.

Conversely, Wharton uses the character of Nona's mother, Pauline Manford, to encapsulate the heady naive optimism and unthinking 'busy-ness' of postwar America.[16] Whereas in *The Mother's Recompense* the older woman is presented sympathetically as dislocated from the modern world, in *Twilight Sleep* the older woman, in her unthinking embrace of every innovation or new fad, is shown as having helped create it. Pauline Manford is a woman who wishes to 'de-microbe life' (p. 60) and who is intent on banishing ageing and suffering, stating openly that 'We ought to refuse ourselves to pain', to which Nona replies sardonically, 'Did Christ?' (p. 325). Generous but not wise, she takes 'particular pains to avoid hearing anything painful or offensive' (p. 63); thus her concern for her secretary's mother, gravely ill with cancer, takes the form of paying for her treatment rather than a bedside visit. An excellent mother in many ways – 'whatever her faults, [she] was always good-humoured and usually wise with her children' (p. 127) – she needs, like Lita, to cram her life with activity in order to prevent it seeming meaningless. Her busy schedule renders her deaf to Nona's discreetly expressed concerns about her father's relationship with Lita, leaving her daughter to bear the knowledge of it alone. Pauline's quest is to join any organisation that will recognise her prominence and fill her day with activity that distracts her from a potential hiatus. She sees, after all, no contradiction in subscribing enthusiastically to the Mothers' Day as well as the Birth Control lobbies; her high profile in both organisations is supposed to fulfil the injunction of the Mahatma – one of Pauline's gurus – to strive for a pitch where 'all discords were resolved into a higher harmony' (p. 115). However, her near catastrophic error, beginning her Birth Control Speech at the Mothers' Day meeting, does at least bring a moment's pause to her blithe assumption that she is able to reconcile all such contradictions. Wharton reminds us of the comedic potential of the episode when she tells us that Pauline 'did not need her daughter's derisive chuckle to give her the measure of her inconsequence' (*TS*, p. 115). We see here an intense and driven woman, fending off the knowledge of an empty life by the application of high seriousness to often spurious moral, intellectual or spiritual causes. The comedy – bitter comedy though it is – derives from the expense of spirit in the pursuit of aims and ideals that could be attained so much more simply; as Dexter says, Pauline 'never walked upstairs, and then had to do gymnastics, and have osteopathy, and call in Hindu sages, to prevent her muscles getting atrophied...' (*TS*, p. 79).

The novel opens with a bleakly comic description of Pauline Manford's daily regime:

> 7.30 Mental Uplift. 7.45 Breakfast. 8. Psychoanalysis. 8.15 See Cook. 8.30 Silent Meditation. 8.45 Facial massage. 9. Man with Persian miniatures. 9.15 Correspondence. 9.30 Manicure. 9.45 Eurythmic exercises. 10. Hair waved. 10.15 Sit for bust. 10.30 Receive Mothers' Day deputation. 11. Dancing lesson. 11.30 Birth Control committee at Mrs. – (*TS*, pp. 3–4)

The comedy here has several sources, the most obvious being the nature of Pauline Manford's packed day in which a crowded schedule of meditation, massage, manicure and a Mothers' Day deputation leaves no room for a conversation with her own daughter, Nona. There is a clear irony in the fact that Pauline's 'psychoanalysis' session – that will no doubt deal in a fashionably Freudian manner with the dynamics of family life – is tightly scheduled for 8.00 until 8.15, whereas Pauline Manford's own daughter is given no time, no space at all by her mother. Indeed, Nona's renaming of her mother's boudoir as 'the office' signals her awareness of her mother as a public, rather than a private, presence. There is no dividing line between the domestic and the professional, a situation which

Wharton exploits for all its comic worth, as her picture of Pauline's idea of an intimate evening makes plain:

> Intimacy, to her, meant the tireless discussion of facts... In confidential moments she preferred the homelier themes, and would have enjoyed best of all being tender and gay about the coal cellar, or reticent and brave about the leak in the boiler; but she was ready to deal with anything as long as it was a fact. (*TS*, pp. 199–200)

Nona, however, having feelings rather than facts to discuss, has difficulty making direct contact with her mother – and instead has to liaise with her through her private secretary, Maisie Bruss, whose voice has become 'thinned and sharpened by continuous telephoning' (*TS*, p. 3).[17] It is worth noting here that the telephone itself plays a distinctive role in the buzzing New York world of *Twilight Sleep*. Like Evelyn Waugh, who used telephone conversations as a new way of presenting dialogue in the novel, Wharton was alert to the impact of modern technology on how people communicate and was interested in portraying this in her fiction. However, rather than enable communication, telephone conversations in *Twilight Sleep* seem more often to result in what John Mepham describes as 'distressed listening',[18] a state of emotional dislocation induced by bad news, unsatisfactory interchange or just plain insensitivity in one or other of the communicants. Of the dozen or so telephone calls featured in the novel, only one – that between Jim and Nona, prior to his telling her that Lita wants a divorce – has a satisfactory, albeit short-lived, resolution. All the others either bring bad news, delivered in 'remote and utterly indifferent' voices (*TS*, p. 187), or convey an impatient and agitated desire to be heard; what telephone dialogue actually signifies in *Twilight Sleep* is *failure* of communication.

The telephone is just one example, for Wharton, of how progress and late capitalism have resulted in a very sophisticated American lifestyle, but not a better quality of life. More might just, in some contexts, mean less. The emotionally unsatisfactory and complex social life of the Manford family is shadowed by a dysfunctionalism that is also evident in society at large. This dysfunctionalism expresses itself in rampant materialism, a fear of ageing and, in Dexter's case, workaholism. Fear of ageing combines with a cult of the body that, for older women such as Pauline, results in a neurotic desire to stay young – 'Rejuvenation! The word dashed itself like cool spray against Pauline's strained nerves and parched complexion' (p. 319) – and for younger women, such as Lita, produces eating disorders: '[Lita] either nibbled languidly at new health foods, or made ravenous inroads into the most indigestible dish presented to her' (*TS*, p. 36). The self in such a society is something constructed through surface activity in which even spirituality – 'silent meditation' – can be bought as a commodity and timetabled. Wharton's vein of satiric social observation here owes much, as do her other late novels, to authors such as Jane Austen, William Thackeray and George Meredith[19] and has its contemporary English parallel in the scathing society novels of Evelyn Waugh – in particular, the comic gothic *A Handful of Dust* (1934), in which parental emotional neglect results in the death of a child. However, whereas Waugh very obviously parodies gothic devices in order to achieve his ends, opening the novel in a mock gothic building and closing it with his hero irretrievably lost in a Brazilian jungle, condemned to read in perpetuity the novels of Dickens to the mad and illiterate Mr Todd, Wharton evokes and parodies the gothic mode more subtly. Playing with the boundaries between naturalism and the gothic, *Twilight Sleep* contains no supernatural presence, but it offers the proposition of gothic plots, tropes and conventions. This is an example of Wharton deploying the technique which she admired in the work of Proust, working as a 'renovator' rather than an 'unintelligible innovator'.[20] She saw the French author as great not only because he was stylistically experimental, but also because he 'was himself that far more substantial thing in the world of art, a renovator' – that is, he was part of, and owed much to, 'the great line of classic tradition'.[21]

One has only to turn to Wharton's collection of ghost stories and its preface to see how well-read Wharton was in the classic gothic tradition. In *Twilight Sleep* she uses gothic devices and references gothic texts in order to convey the emotional horrors underlying the smooth and sophisticated surface of New York society.

The novel's epigraph, taken from one of Europe's classic gothic texts, Part Two of Goethe's *Faust*, warns the reader that modern America's desire to outlaw sorrow and pain is arrogant and misguided. Pauline Manford's attempt to make Cedarledge, the family's country retreat on the Hudson, into a rural paradise equates to Faust's 'last great project', a desire to drain the sea in order to create 'an inland paradise'. Both are doomed to failure. Faust's plans are disrupted by the arrival of Four Grey Women representing Debt, Want, Need and Care ('Sorge'), demons he determines to exorcise from his kingdom. However, although Faust's power and wealth protect him from the first three, Care finds a way in through the keyhole. Warning him that 'All men's lives I tyrannize' and noting that 'Men live their lives in blindness', she actualises her observation by literally blinding Faust. Comically adapting this scene, Wharton has Pauline's rural retreat – recently 'improved' by the planting of 75,000 daffodils – horribly disrupted by 'care' in the form of familial violence. As we shall see, Wharton – like many European authors before her, uses the Faustian myth, as did Goethe himself – in order to satirise the overweening ambition and material greed of modern society in which any sense of the spiritual and the divine has been jettisoned in the pursuit of status, wealth and power. Indeed, Goethe's *Faust* functions as a moral and spiritual touchstone throughout her late novels.[22] Nona's sad observation, after discussing with Jim his failing marriage to Lita, that life has become 'a tortured tangle' (p. 220), is repeated when she describes her relationship with Stan and Aggie Heuston as 'such an inextricable tangle' (p. 237). This clearly echoes Faust's angry fear that the Four Grey Women will turn his life back into a 'dire/Chaotic nexus of entangling pain'.[23] However, whereas Nona at least gains insight into life through suffering, Pauline remains blindly optimistic, embracing travel abroad as escape and antidote to the possible impinging of reality on her carefully guarded sense of self and family at the end of the novel.

As well as referencing specific gothic texts such as *Faust* in *Twilight Sleep*, Wharton also adapts several tropes and devices characteristic of gothic fiction. Although Nona is not literally an orphan – unlike the heroines of many classic gothic tales and unlike the deadly Lita – her parents' embrace of New York values has *emotionally* orphaned her. It is not only her mother who is unavailable: 'her own father, Dexter Manford, who was so clever, capable and kind, [was] almost always too busy at the office, or too firmly requisitioned by Mrs. Manford, when he was at home, to be able to spare much time for his daughter' (*TS*, p. 9). It is significant, of course, that Jim – Pauline Manford's son by her first marriage – who invariably has time for Nona, is one of the few characters not caught up in the materialist values of modern New York. Jim, a kind but rather aimless young man, now working in an office to support his wife and child, is the only person with whom Nona feels at ease. It also appears that a relationship with the older Stan Heuston, a 'clever sensitive fellow' but also a 'disillusioned idler' (*TS*, pp. 210 and 211), who is even more detached and alienated from New York society than Nona, might offer an intimacy that would give meaning to her life. However, Stan's marriage to the pious and frosty Aggie stands in the way for Nona, the only woman in her set with any scruples. In this novel, unlike *The Mother's Recompense*, it is the younger woman who is blessed, or cursed, with principles. Nona is, indeed, the ethical touchstone of the novel; as – ironically enough – Dexter says, she is 'firm as a rock: a man's heart could build on her' (*TS*, p. 126). However, it is this very scrupulousness that deepens

Nona's sense of isolation and alienation as the plot develops. Like many gothic heroines, she feels alone, despite being surrounded by people, and becomes an acute observer of a society and family from which she feels more and more detached. As the narrative progresses so increasingly is the action focalised through her eyes.

Like Kate Clephane, Nona is disturbed by the transience of relationships in modern society. Indeed, Lita and Jim's state-of-the-art drawing-room strikes Nona as:

> very expressive of the modern marriage state. It looked, for all its studied effects, its rather nervous attention to 'values', complementary colours, and the things the modern decorator lies awake over, more like the waiting-room of a glorified railway station than the setting of an established way of life. Nothing in it seemed at home or at ease... (p. 30)

Lita and Jim have been married for only two years but it is evident from this description that Lita is already bored with her role as wife and mother. The 'early kakemono' and white Sung vase that adorn the drawing-room are fashionable aesthetic indicators of a wisdom and peace which have been completely destroyed by the New York rush of life, another example of the spiritual dimension being cancelled out by commodification. Lita's black boudoir 'with its welter of ebony black cushions' (*TS*, pp. 30–1) and its Cubist statue is taken straight from the pages of popular American magazines clearly reflecting contemporary taste in interior décor but also its inauthenticity.[24] Lita's insistence that, for the sake of effect, the aquarium is kept illuminated night and day, results in a form of piscine torture which soon turns the sleepless fish into scaly corpses. One suspects that for Lita, if not Jim, their six-month-old son is not much more than the final designer touch, an accessory, in a carefully composed ménage. Transgressive and quasi-incestuous desire is hidden within this glamorous and fashionable house and Nona, with her 'uncanny gift of divination' (p. 185) is the only character to intuit it at this stage. As Phillip Barrish notes, Wharton makes a great deal of 'darkness' in this novel in order to suggest the 'unheimlich' within the well-lit middle-class home.[25]

Such dark disturbances are ironically intimated, however, as are the many other potentially gothic elements in *Twilight Sleep*. For example, the weight of the past and the importance of ancestral lineage in the traditional gothic novel, which are often signalled through the family portrait,[26] are here reduced to comic self-delusion: 'Mrs. Manford would glance with pardonable pride at the glorious Gainsborough over the dining-room mantelpiece (which she sometimes almost mistook for an ancestral portrait)...' (*TS*, p. 11). Even the darkest gothic element of the plot, the quasi-incestuous relationship between Dexter Manford and his stepson's wife, Lita, is presented, finally, in somewhat farcical vein. The older man's pursuit of a younger woman – often his niece or his step-daughter or his daughter-in-law – is a common plot element of many classic gothic novels, and one which probably derives from Horace Walpole's *Castle of Otranto*, the first gothic novel in English, published in 1764. After the untimely death of his young son, the novel's villain, Manfred, Count of Otranto, pursues his son's fiancée, Isabella, abandoning his loyal wife of many years in the process. Assuming Isabella is secretly meeting a handsome young peasant named Theodore, he tracks her down and stabs her – or so he thinks. In fact, in the dark and the gloom he has mistakenly stabbed his own daughter, Matilda. The scene is written in a somewhat operatic style, combining horror with melodrama:

> Manfred, whose spirits were inflamed, and whom Isabella had driven from her on his urging his passion with too little reserve, did not doubt but the inquietude she had expressed had been occasioned by her impatience to meet Theodore. Provoked by this conjecture... he hastened secretly to the great church. Gliding softly between the aisles, and guided by an imperfect gleam of moonshine that shone faintly through the illuminated windows, he stole towards the tomb of Alfonso, to which he was directed by the indistinct whispers of the persons he sought. The first sounds he could distinguish were – Does it, alas, depend on me? Manfred will never permit our union. – No, this shall prevent it! Cried the tyrant, drawing his dagger, and plunging it over her shoulder into the bosom of the person that spoke – Ah me, I am slain! cried Matilda sinking: Good heaven, receive my soul! – Savage, inhuman monster! What hast thou done? cried Theodore, rushing on him and wrenching his dagger from him. – Stop, stop thy impious hand, cried Matilda; it is my father![27]

In Wharton's Notebook, '*Notes and Subjects' Jan. 1924–1928*, held in the Beinecke Library, Pauline and Dexter are given the surname 'Manfred'.[28] Throughout her notes, as the novel is plotted, the names 'Manford' and 'Manfred' alternate. Although in the final published version she opts for the former, it is clear that *The Castle of Otranto* is in her mind as she works out the plot of *Twilight Sleep*. In Wharton's novel, Arthur

Wyant, brought up in a 'tradition of reticence and decency' (p. 165), is driven to desperate extremes by his suspicion that his beloved son Jim has been sexually betrayed by Lita in her affair with Dexter Manford, at least thirty years her senior, and sets out to kill his ex-wife's husband while the family is staying at Cedarledge, their country home. Just as in Walpole's novel, the older man with a score to settle accidentally wounds his own daughter. With certain changes – for example, the sexual appetite and the violent nature of Manfred being split between two failed father figures, Arthur Wyant and Dexter Manford – the end of *Twilight Sleep* distinctly echoes elements of the above scene from Walpole's novel, including its combination of horror and farce:

> Pauline went in.
> All the lights were on – the room was a glare. Another man stood shivering and staring in a corner, but Pauline hardly noticed him, for before her on the floor lay Lita's long body, in a loose spangled robe, flung sobbing over another body.
> 'Nona – Nona!' the mother screamed, rushing forward to where they lay.
> She swept past her husband, dragged Lita back, was on her knees on the floor, her child pressed to her, Nona's fallen head against her breast, Nona's blood spattering the silvery folds of the rest-gown, destroying it forever as a symbol of safety and repose.
> 'Nona – child! What's happened? Are you hurt? Dexter – for pity's sake! Nona, look at me! It's mother, darling, mother – '
> Nona's eyes opened with a flutter. Her face was ashen-white, and empty as a baby's. Slowly she met her mother's agonised stare. 'All right...only winged me.' Her gaze wavered about the disordered room, lifting and dropping in a butterfly's bewildered flight. Lita lay huddled on the couch in her spangles, twisted and emptied, like a festal garment flung off by its wearer. Manford stood between, his face a ruin. In the corner stood that other man, shrinking, motionless. Pauline's eyes, following her child's travelled on to him.
> 'Arthur!' she gasped out and felt Nona's feeble pressure on her arm.
> 'Don't...don't...It was an accident. Father – an accident! *Father!*'
> (*TS*, pp. 354–5).

The attempted murder, the sobbing, the screaming, and the blood-bespattered garments of this scene evoke the mood and tenor of opera, the gothic and melodrama rather than that of realism or naturalism. For the scene *is* comic and farcical as well as deeply disturbing. Tragedy is averted; Nona does not die but survives to regard the world from a position of even more remote ironic detachment. Reputations are not shattered but preserved because Powder, the comedically tactful butler, is astute enough to invent a burglar as the perpetrator of the dastardly crime. The apocalyptic ending of *The Castle of Otranto* (in which the ghost of an ancestor appears to a clap of thunder as if 'the last day was at hand'[29]) is here replaced by what is described as 'an unnatural clamour, immense, mysterious and menacing'; no gothic force of retribution this, however, but 'the Cedarledge fire-brigade, arriving double quick in answer to their benefactress's summons' (*TS*, p. 356). This is the very fire-brigade that has already inspired Dexter's observation that Pauline (a 'Goddess of Velocity' in her husband's eyes) enjoys watching their uniforms, shiny helmets and drills 'as much as other women do love-making'(*TS*, p. 297). It is not surprising then, that, at this point, 'Pauline, bending over her daughter's face, fancied she caught a wan smile on it...' (*TS*, p. 356). Wharton's use of irony, bathos, anti-climax and gothic parody demands engagement with something other than the realist mode if we are to make sense of the shooting 'accident' in *Twilight Sleep*. As Nancy Bentley has noted, 'In a Wharton narrative... the accident is a violent symptom of modern conditions, which few characters can see or understand but almost all can feel'.[30]

As we suggested in our introduction, Wharton frequently uses gothic effects in her late novels to convey crises of identity in her female characters; experiencing themselves as 'ghosts', they find their environments unreal or suffocating. As Kathy A. Fedorko has remarked, 'Wharton's Gothic allows her to press the limits of rationality, to utter the unutterable about sexuality, rage, death and fear, and, especially, the nature of men and women'.[31] In *Twilight Sleep* gothic effects bubble under a surface of satire to suggest the destructive nature of such visceral emotions when they remain unchecked by any valid belief system or moral code; indeed, the novel is a good example of what we might call comic gothic or gothic satire.[32] In the tradition of American writers such as Herman Melville, Wharton uses gothic devices 'to articulate [a] more coded understanding of the darker underside of the new nation's optimistic surfaces'.[33] Wharton's use of parody in this novel nevertheless also conveys the characteristic gothic challenge: that is, a counter-narrative to the Enlightenment story that modernity, built on the tenets of reason and science, is always indicative of progress.[34] Fundamental to the optimistic narrative of Enlightenment philosophy is the idea that both the State and the family are benign and protective institutions. The gothic text gives us an alternative reading which presents the State as oppressive and the family as a unit of entrapment, particularly for women,[35] in which power struggles and perverted values can lead to abuse and emotional dysfunctionalism. The dysfunctionalism we see in *Twilight Sleep* results from the excesses of a postwar, increasingly materialistic society in which individuals have become entirely self-obsessed and incapable of deep engagement. Indeed, Pauline thinks to herself, 'an hour is too long for meditation – an hour is too long for anything' (p. 134); in this she is not unusual. However, we do glimpse moments of despair and disillusion in certain characters: for example in Dexter Manford's bucolic fantasy of returning to Minnesota where, earning his living as a farmer, he would be surrounded by 'all the healthy blustering noises of country life in a big family' (p. 81) and in Nona's desolate observation on returning home at four o'clock in the morning after a dance: 'What was it all for, and what was left when it was over?' (p. 91). As Helen Killoran has observed, both Nona and Dexter are associated with suicidal thoughts, the former through her reflections on suicide ('at the worst it will only last as long as I do; and that's a date I can fix as I choose' (p. 167) and the latter through his reading of Ingersoll's essay 'Is Suicide a Sin?'[36]

Blind to the idea that the New York society in which she lives is less than perfect, however, Pauline sees beyond it only to project whatever she finds offensive or unacceptable onto a 'primitive' Europe. In a reworking of the classic English gothic novel, in which the Catholic Church is usually painted as an agent of malevolent control within a corrupt and degenerate state,[37] and simultaneously re-playing overtly Henry James's portrayal of American naivety in the face of European decadence, Wharton presents Pauline as both appalled and impressed by her cousin's life in Italy. The fraudulent and frenetic society of New York is counter-pointed in Wharton's novel by the equally fake relics of 'old Europe' who find their way to the New World. Indeed, Pauline, whose 'ingrained Protestantism' makes her recoil 'in horror' from 'the sacrament of confession' (p. 133), congratulates herself on her tolerance in courting the attentions of the Cardinal and on her generous financial support of the Catholic Amalasuntha. However, this facade of open-mindedness does not need to be scratched very deeply before 'the old Puritan terror of gliding priests and incense and idolatry rise to the surface' (*TS*, p. 373). Beneath such hyperbole lies Wharton's interest in the tensions between various beliefs and how they guide human behaviour. There is clear conflict in the novel, for example, between Arthur Wyant, whose 'old New York blood' (*TS*, p. 11) manifests itself in a quaint chivalric code, and Pauline Manford, whose values are entirely 'modern' in that her spirituality is 'New Age', alternative and bought for hard cash. This tension is exemplified again by the contrast between the casual frequency with which divorce takes place in New York and Amalasuntha's admittedly strategic Catholic and Italian refusal to contemplate divorce at all. Indeed, the novel's flirtation with Italy, woven in through Amalasuntha's marriage to the Marchese Venturino de San Fedele, 'of one of the great Neapolitan families' (*TS*, p. 16), echoes comically the gothic tale's fascination with the foreign 'Other'.[38] It therefore comes as no surprise to find that Wharton took Pauline's Italian cousin's name from the history of the Ostrogoths.[39] In the classic gothic novel, Italy is usually associated with decadence, degeneracy, superstition, intrigue and mortal danger. Wharton, however, presents 'old Europe' through the eyes of Pauline Manford, whose cultural ignorance comically reduces it to a mixture of the glamorous and the primitive:

It's so dreadful – the wicked lives those great Roman families lead. After all, poor Amalasuntha has good American blood in her – ...but what is [she] to do, in a country where there's no divorce, and a woman just has to put up with *everything*? The Pope has been most kind; he sides entirely with Amalasuntha. But Venturino's people are very powerful too – a great Neapolitan family...' (*TS*, pp. 18–19)

Needless to say, her 'good American blood' does not stop Amalasuntha from pursuing the possibility that her feckless son might play Caesar Borgia to Lita's Lucrezia in Serge Klawhammer's forthcoming film – thereby earning them both a great deal of money. In this comic gothic novel, the poisonous intrigues of the Borgia family are to be translated into a celluloid romp and the threat of the Italian stiletto or the Spanish Inquisition is reduced at the level of plot to a means by which Amalasuntha can sponge off her quondam cousin. For 27 years Pauline Manford has been prepared to finance her ex-husband's relative's expensive tastes for the sake of being connected to the 'exotic lustre' (*TS*, p. 17) of old Europe since Amalasuntha is, by her own admission, still 'a useful social card' (p. 18). Against the sinister glamour of this old Europe there is the lure of the new America as represented not only by New Age cults and the emphasis on the body but also by Mr Klawhammer and his Hollywood opportunities. In her portrayal of Seth Starkadder's rise to fame through the 'silver screen' in *Cold Comfort Farm* (1932), Stella Gibson was similarly to lampoon the beginnings of the celebrity culture.

In this world of surfaces, cults and commodification, the law has become increasingly important. Notwithstanding the comic patina of *Twilight Sleep*, it is significant that Dexter Manford is a lawyer; as such, he represents not only a successful self-made American, but also that aspect of modernity concerned with public justice, transparency, accountability and control. However, in this role, he also represents the Law of the Father, in that both through his profession and what Barrish describes as his 'privileged sociocultural status as ruling-class white man',[40] he shores up the patriarchal values of America in the 1920s. The fact that Dexter specialises in divorce law adds to the novel's piquant focus on failed relationships; he has made a very profitable career out of what Wharton's narrator describes as 'the matrimonial quicksands of New York' (*TS*, p. 12) – one that allows his wife to indulge her taste for expensive houses and décor. Through Dexter Manford and his Protestant commitment to work –'he had been brought up to think there was a virtue in work per se, even if it served no more useful purpose than the revolving of a squirrel in a wheel' (*TS*, p. 6) – America is presented as fast becoming a work-obsessed and litigious nation. In encouraging the quantification of personal pain by way of financial reparation, the legal system allows yet another dimension of human life to become commodified. This is a rich, efficient and busy society but it is one that hides a great deal of turmoil and discontent. The emptiness of life in such a world drives several characters to seek fulfilment in the bizarre, the superficial and the merely charlatan – the 'Spiritual Vacuum Cleaning' (*TS*, p. 139) of Alvah Loft, 'the Busy Man's Christ' (p. 179), the 'eternal rejuvenation' (*TS*, p. 319) offered by Sacha Gobine, or the Mahatma's 'wonderful mystical teachings about Self-Annihilation, Anterior Existence and Astral Affinities...all so incomprehensible and so pure...' (*TS*, pp. 20–1; Wharton's ellipses).

The Mahatma, who runs the 'School of Oriental Thought' (*TS*, p. 46) at Dawnside, where he encourages his female disciples to wear loose and rather transparent Eastern dress (*TS*, p. 111), is a composite of several contemporary guru figures popular in America in the 1920s. Hermione Lee suggests Paramahansa Yogananda, a Hindu yogi, and 'Oom the Omnipotent' (alias Pierre Bernard) as possible models.[41] The Mahatma might also be based on George I. Gurdjieff. Gurdjieff set up 'the Institute for the Harmonious Development of Man' at Fontainbleau (just outside Paris) in 1922, establishing a centre 'for the study of consciousness' where activities such as 'Sacred Gymnastics' took place in pursuit of spiritual wholeness. Although based in France, Gurdjieff's influence was not limited to Europe and his tour of New York and Chicago in 1924 consolidated his 'considerable American following'.[42] Wharton burlesques Gurdjieff's emphasis on the body in Pauline's tribute to the powers of the Mahatma: 'it was certainly those eurythmic exercises of the Mahatma's ("holy ecstasy," he called them) which had reduced her hips after everything else had failed' (*TS*, p. 20). The pseudo-spiritual discourse of the Mahatma and the other substitutes for organised religion we see in the novel have their foundation in the practices and linguistic styles of actual 'gurus' such as Gurdjieff, Paramahansa Yogananda and 'Oom the Omnipotent'. The satiric portrayal of such cultish figures is an important part of Wharton's examination of the modern world; just as Eliot invokes Madame Sosostris in *The Waste Land* to highlight the loss of authentic faith, so Wharton employs the Mahatma and others. Every aspect of the spiritual life in *Twilight Sleep* is portrayed as fraudulent. It is no wonder, then, that by the end of the novel what Nona craves is 'spiritual escape' (p. 362).

Echoes of the gothic become more pronounced as *Twilight Sleep* draws to a close and the realisation of Dexter's incestuous desire – 'something dark and lurid, which had threatened to submerge them' (p. 256) – becomes more imminent. As R.W.B. Lewis commented in his review of *The Ghost Stories of Edith Wharton*, published by Constable in 1975:

> Edith Wharton...deployed the supernatural as a way of getting at certain aspects of human nature and experience – the aberrant, the perverse, the lawless, the violently sexual – which could not be dealt with in realist fiction and to which, consequently, her imaginative processes had until late in her life only limited access.[43]

Thus, after the gun shot rings out, Pauline runs down a 'shadowy corridor...skimming over the ground, inaudibly, like something ghostly, disembodied'; as 'sounds low, confused and terrified' come from Lita's bedroom, she hears herself 'scream "Help!" with the strangled voice of a nightmare...' (p. 353). Reflecting on the drama, the wounded Nona finds it curious how Pauline, reduced to a 'haggard and stricken apparition' and a 'dishevelled spectre' (p. 363) during the shooting episode, has so quickly been restored to her normal self. Such language is a clue as to how we should read the novel's ending. Conversely, those critics who have tried to read *Twilight Sleep* as a realist work have found themselves disappointed and irritated by its closure – Cynthia Griffin Wolff, for example, dismissing it as 'falling into dreadful melodrama'.[44] Indeed it is probably impossible to make much sense of the novel's last few pages without reference to the conventions and tropes of the classic gothic novel. In such a text the orphaned heroine invariably escapes from a convent or a castle, where she has been immured by a predatory older male, and – after many meanderings and adventures – marries the virtuous young hero. The last chapter of Radcliffe's *The Italian* (1797), for example, celebrates in an almost hysterically joyful manner the marriage between Ellena Rosalba (formerly incarcerated against her will in a convent) and Vincentio di Vivaldi. The effect of such closure should be compared and contrasted with the last words of Wharton's novel where the classic gothic plot is inverted. Rather than marry, Nona wishes to *enter* a convent – but a convent 'where nobody believes in anything' (*TS*, p. 373). If marriage as closure represents a positive re-engagement with society – and that is what the comic mode usually indicates – then Nona's rejection of marriage and her flippantly announced wish to become a nun in such a convent represent a state of intense alienation. Conversely, Pauline's attitude to life is seen as correlated with a modernity ushered in by a Puritanism that, for complex historical and social reasons, has hardened into a peculiar narrowness and intolerance. Such intolerance refuses, of course, to accept that the irrational or the questionable resides within oneself, instead – just as in the Protestant English Gothic novel – it is projected onto Italy, or old Europe, or the past. The locus of evil and folly is always somewhere else for Pauline Manford, not least in the 'wicked lives' led by people who reside abroad. For Wharton herself, however, the problem lay in the postwar 'new' America: as she wrote to Sally Norton: 'All that I thought American in a true sense is gone, and I see nothing but vain-glory, crassness, and total ignorance – which of course is the core of the whole evil'.[45]

Appropriately, *Twilight Sleep* ends with dusk closing in. Here twilight becomes synonymous with darkness and sadness, rather than with a medical compound. Before he leaves with his wife for their grand tour of far places, Nona's father comes to say goodbye:

> She wound her fingers into his, and they sat silent again. She liked to have him near her in this way, but she was glad, for his sake and her own, that the twilight made his face indistinct. (*TS*, p. 369)

The fragmented and incomplete conversation that follows articulates little but tells us volumes about what these characters cannot say. It speaks of evasion, compromise and sorrow and is quite unlike the ending Wharton originally planned.[46] In a novel in which appropriate intimacy is largely absent, this scene comes as a shock. It is ironic that such affection can be demonstrated only after Dexter has committed the hideous act of betrayal that led him to Lita's bed. Of course, the most memorable intimacy between father and daughter in Edith Wharton's writing is that between Beatrice Palmato and her father in the fragment that bears her name.[47] Their encounter brings the secret of transgressive desire out of darkness and into the light, out of silence and into words. On one level, the highly erotic episode between Beatrice and her father, featuring oral and penetrative sex, cannot be compared to the parting scene between Dexter and Nona.[48] However, the physical ambiguously haunts the emotional congress between father and daughter even here. The presence of his 'shadowy bulk' (p. 360) is both sinister and comforting: 'She felt a tremor of his shoulders as they pressed against her, and the tremor ran through her own body and seemed to loosen the fibres of her heart' (p. 37). Nona calls him 'Old Dad', attempting to retrieve a previous, more innocent version of her father, but also seeking to suspend her knowledge of her father's sexual relationship with his alternate daughter, Lita. She is glad that the dusk means she cannot see his face and, on his departure from her room, 'her heart folded like two hands around the thought of him' (p. 370). We have already learnt that, since the shooting, Nona can no longer sleep properly at night and that it is only by day that she can drift off. She is, quite literally, in a 'twilight sleep' when her father arrives to say goodbye. The phrase thus moves from signifying relief from physical pain at the beginning of the novel to connoting a moment's respite from the pain of emotional knowledge at its end. Nona, as the witness to, the victim of and the scapegoat in this shallow and dysfunctional world, is recompensed for her suffering by an understanding of 'the powers of darkness' (*TS*, p. 48) that increasingly alienate her from it. As Phillip Barrish points out, Wharton's use of the phrase 'powers of darkness' is significant here since she intended to use it as the title for a volume of tales which would include the 'Beatrice Palmato' story. In the context of her life and work the phrase therefore indicates the dark and lurid nature of incestuous desire, and perhaps alerts us disturbingly to the linguistic play between Nona's 'two hands' and the name 'palmato'.[49] The boundaries between the acceptable and the taboo that had been threatened by the affair between Dexter and Lita have apparently been reinstated through the novel's closure – at least at the level of plot. However, Wharton's use of language and allusion here renders those boundaries unstable once more. Nona now fully understands the fragility of goodness and the role of suffering in coming to maturity. However, there is no place in this society for her insight, her knowledge and her integrity – hence her desire for retreat from it, if only to a convent 'where nobody believes in anything'. The novel's uncertain and ambiguous ending is a far cry from the death of a beautiful woman as presented in *The House of Mirth*. Just as *Villette* is a more knowing and cynical reworking of *Jane Eyre*, so *Twilight Sleep* is a more sophisticated and cynical treatment of the destructive effects of modernity than that offered by *The House of Mirth*.

Such cynicism is reflected in the fact that *Twilight Sleep* offers us no viable point of reference for authenticity; even 'old Europe' is given to us only as a fantasy of the glamorous or the abject, a fantasy which is itself dependent on fictional and cultural narratives. It has no real presence as a preferable or superior space. Wharton has ceased, at this stage of her career, to seek such validity elsewhere. The satire of *The Custom of the Country*, which always seems to place America in comparison with France to the former's disadvantage, has become, to a large extent, *sans frontières* in *Twilight Sleep*. No one is safe from her irony here, although it is clear that Nona's sad and cynical detachment from her society will result in a new sort of female consciousness. However, whereas Evelyn Waugh's innovative use of comic gothic resulted in *A Handful of Dust* being canonised as a brilliant work of satire, Wharton's novel has been misunderstood and unjustly neglected precisely because her change of style and substance – focusing on the incest theme for example – made her work less palatable to an American readership. Disturbed by the psychopathology of everyday life in modern America, Wharton brings opposites together in this palimpsestic novel, mixing melancholy and pessimism with the acid wit of satire and the black humour of comic gothic. *Twilight Sleep* disrupts the American dream by revealing the emotional and spiritual vacuum at its core, thereby anticipating Freud's *Civilization and its Discontents* (1930). Writing in the 1920s, Wharton's funny yet melancholy appraisal of modernity resonates interestingly with Freudian thought, which conceptualises the 'bourgeois drama' being played out 'on the conscious stage of the psyche' as always inflected by 'a Greek tragedy...going on somewhere else'.[50] It is not surprising, then, that Nona Manford is not only described by the narrator as a 'bewildered little Iphigenia' (*TS*, p. 48) but also sees herself as a sacrificial figure in a world in which sacrifice no longer has any meaning. In a society in which the middle-aged 'ignore sorrow and evil', dismissing them as 'survivals of some obsolete European superstition unworthy of enlightened Americans' (*TS*, p. 47), it is the young whose innocence is abused – for they are left to bear 'the load' resulting from seeing, clear-eyed, 'the powers of darkness' (*TS*, p. 48). In effect, Nona's youth has been sacrificed by an older generation so caught up in the pursuit of pleasure and self-fulfilment that it has become blind to the needs of its children – a theme Wharton will pursue even more fiercely in *The Children*, as we shall see in the next chapter.

3
The Children

'the incurable simplicity of the corrupt'[1]

At the heart of Edith Wharton's 1928 novel, *The Children*, lies an unanswered and disturbing question: what happened to Doll Westway? The story of the Westway family appears tangential to the novel's main plot concerning Martin Boyne, Judith Wheater and Rose Sellars, but Wharton frequently returns to it, weaving references to the story of Doll's life and death throughout the novel. In so doing, she provides a fractured, incoherent vision of a fractured, incoherent life. As the wealthy, dysfunctional, rootless Westway family moved between one stylish European resort and another, we learn – through fragments of conversation and the pursed-lip utterances of those who watched but did not intervene – that 'poor Doll Westway', who was 'kicked about from pillar to post' (p. 149), 'committed suicide...at Deauville' (p. 153), a fashionable resort on the Normandy coast, the year before Judith Wheater comes into Martin Boyne's life. Her mother, Sybil Lullmer, 'is always chock full of drugs' (p. 153) and uses her remaining daughter, Pixie, as a handmaid; her father, Charlie, is described by Cliffe Wheater as 'a down-and-outer' and a 'blackguard' to whom 'no law-court in the world' would have awarded the custody of his children (p. 149). The family are never, however, permitted to fade from the novel: Wharton reintroduces them via Mr Dobree, who acted as a lawyer in the Westway divorce case and who, according to Rose Sellars, has 'knowledge of Judith's intimacy with that wretched drug-soaked Doll Westway'. He is also familiar with 'the horrible details that led up to the girl's suicide'. The novel's narrator continues:

> She and Judith were together at Deauville the very summer that she killed herself. Both their mothers had gone off heaven

knows where. Judith proclaims the fact to every one, as you know. (p. 202)

This skeletal story leaves several questions unanswered. What did Charlie Westway do to provoke such condemnation in a social set not conspicuous for its responsible parenting? Did he introduce his young daughter to drugs? Did he verbally abuse her? Did he sexually abuse her? How far was Sybil Lullmer complicit with her husband's behaviour?[2] What, in the end, drove Doll to shoot herself at the age of 14? Where was Judith – who had spent the whole summer with Doll – at the time? How much did she know about the Westways' degenerate lifestyle? How far did she share it? Wharton's elliptical and yet persistent references to the family prompt questions which, structurally, act as a counter-balance to Martin Boyne's idealisation of Judith's innocence. Judith is much more complex than Boyne wants to believe; in a text replete with words that express a fluctuating and fluid grasp of what a familial relationship or a proper manifestation of adult behaviour might constitute, she is a 'little-girl-mother' (p. 38) and, at 15 years, 'as old as the hills' (p. 61) with 'the writing of a child of ten' (p. 100). It is clear that this young woman might have followed in Doll's footsteps had it not been for her deep attachment to, and sense of responsibility for, her 'family' of siblings and stepsiblings.

In this novel Wharton attacks satirically the fetishisation of youth through her portraits of older women holding onto their currency in a very turbulent marriage market: Sybil Lullmer, Zinnia Lacrosse and, initially, Joyce Wheater. However, she also conducts a systematic critique – developed even further than in *The Mother's Recompense* or *Twilight Sleep* – of the male fixation on perpetual renewal in the form of the younger woman. Wharton is merciless in her exposure of the vanity of the older man in this text, from the loud, over-exposed Cliffe Wheater, lying beside the 'small sleek' (p. 153) Syb Lullmer on the beach 'like a raised map of a mountainous country' (p. 160), to her central protagonist, Martin Boyne, who over-determines Judith with his own unstable fantasies from the very beginning of the narrative: 'he was disappointed, for he was already busy at the masculine task of endowing the woman of the moment with every quality which made life interesting to himself' (p. 35).

This is not a novel about the deleterious effects of divorce on children, as most reviewers have assumed. Its focus is much broader, as it critiques the incoherent values of a decade that does not see the desire of an older man for a young girl as taboo. Blind to this aspect of *The Children*, one contemporary reviewer actually referred to the poignancy of 'the delicate romance of Martin and Judith'.[3] Such readings prompted Wharton, in a letter to Royal Cortissoz, written on 11 October 1928, to remark of the novel's critical reception:

> I had become passionately attached to my seven children, & the uncomprehending drivel (laudatory or other) that I have so far read about them had really plunged me in the deepest literary discouragement I have ever known. – I kept thinking: 'To have had such a vision, & be able to convey only *that* of it!' I know nothing more depressing than to see a book selling & selling, & feel that nobody knows what they're buying.[4]

In *The Children* Wharton explores both the personal and social costs of the cult of youth in a milieu crammed with the paradoxes of that cult: innocence and freshness are sought after by the ageing, but the authentically young, like the tragic Doll Westway, whose story weaves the faint but insistent narrative of corruption and death throughout the texture of the novel, are neglected and abused.

As in Louisa May Alcott's *Little Women* (1868) – where it becomes clear that the women of the title become 'little' once grown, being compelled, as adults, to fit into the very small spaces allowed for women in the society of the time – so it is clear from Wharton's *The Children* that the seven youngest characters are much less childlike than their errant parents. As Miss Scope says: 'Judith's never been a child – there was no time' (p. 26). Completely at the mercy of their appetites, apparently, the Wheaters and their assorted exes and currents are incapable, for the most of the narrative, of putting aside their own desires and cravings for sensation in order to make appropriate arrangements for their children. In such a context, the fact that Martin Boyne has some sense of his own unseemliness, even while showing an immediate preference for a woman upon whom he can imprint whatever yearning he currently feels, means that the only hope of a mature, intelligent relationship – that between Boyne and Rose Sellars – is doomed to failure. The novel is focalised through Boyne but his insistence that he is fully aware that Judith is only a child and that his feelings for her are fraternal or 'half-fatherly' (p. 245) is contradicted by his obvious (at least to the reader) sexual desire for her. This is apparent throughout the novel, from its very opening pages: 'Men of forty-six do not gasp as frequently at the sight of a charming face as they did at twenty; but when the sight strikes them it hits harder' (p. 4), throughout the narrative: '...he put his arm about her and bent his head to her lips. They looked round and glowing, as they did in laughter or emotion; they drew his irresistibly' (p. 269), to its end: '...he shrank from her touch, from the warm smell of her hair, from everything about her which he had to think back into terms of childhood and comradeship while every vein in his body still ached for her' (p. 310). Boyne is helpless in the face of his longing to possess Judith physically. He tries, sporadically, to deny his passion, but it is nevertheless conveyed to the reader not only through direct expression of his innermost desires, but also through Rose Sellars' perceptive appraisal of the relationship and Mr Dobree's acute observations on Boyne when he is in Judith's company.

The result is a complex and disturbing novel about sexuality and ageing and the 1920s obsession with the nymph figure as referenced, for example, in the figure of 'the girl-bride of the movies' as Rose Sellars puts it (p. 38). This cultural infatuation with the 'girl-bride' or 'nymph' derived from a particular trend in the film and fiction of the 1920s. In Scott Fitzgerald's *Tender is the Night*, first published in 1934, the narrator comments in a section entitled 'The Way Home 1929–30':

> The only physical disparity between Nicole at present and the Nicole of five years before was simply that she was no longer a young girl. But she was enough ridden by the current youth worship, the moving pictures with their myriad faces of girl-children, blandly represented as carrying on the work and wisdom of the world, to feel a jealousy of youth.[5]

Rose's wry comment and Nicole's jealousy are reactions to the craze for films made between 1910 and 1930 that featured vulnerable, often orphaned, young girls as heroines; parts frequently played by women at least twice their age. Mary Pickford excelled at such roles, playing the lead in *The Little Princess* (1917), *The Poor Little Rich Girl* (1917), *Rebecca of Sunnybrook Farm* (1917), *Daddy Long-Legs* (1919), *Pollyanna* (1920) and *Little Annie Rooney* (1925) when she was 25 (in all three 1917 films), 27, 28 and 32 respectively. Directors whose films featured girl-woman heroines included David Lewelyn Wark Griffith, known as 'The Father of Film', who made *Broken Blossoms* in 1919 in which the 26-year-old Lilian Gish played a girl of 12; and Erich von Stroheim, whose film *Foolish Wives* (1922) featured a lead male character who seduces a 14-year-old girl. As Graham Vickers points out, sometimes this cultural obsession with the child-woman was reflected in the private lives of film directors and actors. Griffith, who 'has the distinction of giving the movies their first recognizable prototype nymphet' 'took actress Carol Dempster as his mistress when she was seventeen or younger'; Erich von Stroheim was fascinated by little girls; Charlie Chaplin conducted several questionable relationships, initially with 'a fifteen-year-old girl called Hetty Kelly' before developing a crush on 12-year-old Maybelle Fournier, going on to make 14-year-old Mildred Harris pregnant and then fathering a child when he was 35 with 16-year-old Lillita Grey, whom he married in 1924 and divorced in 1927.[6] Whereas many would now categorise such behaviour as paedophilia, society turned a blind eye to it in the 1920s if the perpetrator was an artist or a man of some standing. Indeed when Chaplin's liaisons with young girls finally broke in the newspapers, the 'ensuing scandal was huge but only dented Chaplin's popularity'.[7]

By the 1930s, the fashion for young women playing nymphs had been superseded by child actors impersonating adults, among whom the most famous was Shirley Temple. There were few voices prepared to challenge this trend and when, in 1937, Graham Greene, in a review of *Wee Willie Winkie* (1937) in the magazine *Night and Day*, pointed out that Shirley Temple (aged 11 when she played the lead role in the film) displayed 'a certain adroit coquetry which appealed to the middle-aged man', noting how 'with dimpled depravity' she used 'her well-shaped and desirable little body' to seductive effect, a libel suit followed that bankrupted the magazine.[8] Eleven years previously, in 1926, Wharton had expressed her own amusement, apprehension – and perhaps irritation – at the nymph cult. In a letter to Gaillard Lapsley she refers to Robert Norton ogling the '150 ladies of the Hellenic Association grouped about the Castalian Fount in daring costumes' (they were on a yacht cruise at the time) and describes them as 'brawny nymphs in grass-green "Mother Hubbards" and Cubist sweaters'.[9] It is against this broad background of a cultural obsession with the child-woman and woman-child that Wharton wrote her novel. Although Martin Boyne seems at first an unlikely child seducer, his erotic desire for a girl more than thirty years his junior is deeply disturbing.

The novel also focuses on the deleterious effects of wealth and the consumer culture on a set of shallow Americans who put material things above emotional responsibilities. Included in the multiple targets for satire is the newly fashionable eugenics movement, represented in the novel by the ideas of the Princess Buondelmonte, which was to have such dire consequences a few years later when absorbed into Nazi ideology.[10] In this respect, *The Children* continues the debate, which featured regularly in many novels and literary journals during the 1920s, about the changing nature of Western culture and society after the First

World War. It is perhaps no accident that the Westways are thus named: they are moneyed but barbaric and are, in the novel, set implicitly against Rose Sellars' 'civilised' values deriving, in Wharton's usual shorthand, from old New York society. Miss Scope early corrects Boyne's description of his having come out of 'the wilderness' of the developing world: '"The real wilderness is the world *we* live in; packing up our tents every few weeks for another move...And the marriages just like tents – folded up and thrown away when you've done with them"' (p. 23, Wharton's ellipses). In this respect, *The Children* continues the strong satirical thrust of *Twilight Sleep*, published a year earlier and also focusing on the fate of the younger generation in such a world. In Rose Sellars, Edith Wharton creates a wiser and more intelligent woman than Pauline Manford and through her, develops the interest in mature female sexual desire that she explored so unflinchingly in *The Mother's Recompense*. The comedy of *The Children*, which derives not only from its obviously satiric elements but also from the outspokenness and rough-and-tumble behaviour of the seven children, is offset by the pathos of Rose Sellars' situation and, finally, by Martin Boyne's self-imposed exile. As Pamela Knights observes, in the three novels published between 1925 and 1928, Wharton anticipates 'the "depthless" spectacle of post-modernity', communicating a picture of a world where 'linguistic laxity', although sometimes comic, actually signals a 'wider moral and cultural collapse'.[11] *The Children* is funny but also despairing; it is, in Hermione Lee's words, 'a daring and profoundly sad book' over which hangs a strong 'sense of desolation'.[12]

The novel's humour derives from a combination of Wharton's affectionate portrayal of the children's antics and her biting use of satire, the latter directed mainly at the drifting, wealthy American expatriates who represent the materialism, consumer culture and unthinking amorality of the 1920s, the subject also of much of Scott Fitzgerald's fiction. In a world 'grown clockless and conscienceless' (p. 81), the women in this set compete for the latest exclusive designer clothes carrying the label 'Anastase' or 'Callot' and flaunt expensive jewellery. They all wish to be slim and youthful looking; ageism is an inevitable correlative of youth worship so these women cannot allow themselves to mature. The result is an uninspiring homogeneity which Boyne sees displayed to its full effect one evening at the Lido Palace hotel in Venice:

> Boyne remembered Mrs Sellars' wail at the approach of a standard-ised beauty. Here it was, in all its mechanical terror – endless and meaningless as the repetitions of a nightmare. Every one of the women in the vast crowded restaurant seemed to be of the same age,

to be dressed by the same dress-makers, loved by the same lovers, adorned by the same jewellers, and massaged and manipulated by the same Beauty doctors...from the movement of their lips, and the accompanying gestures, Boyne surmised that they were all saying exactly the same things as Joyce and Zinnie and Mrs. Lullmer. It would have been unfashionable to have been different; and once more Boyne marvelled at the incurable simplicity of the corrupt. (pp. 154–5)

Meanwhile, the men acquire expensive boats and consumer novelties such as Lord Mendip's new tent, which Lady Wrench (formerly Zinnia Lacrosse) describes as 'The very last thing. Sort of black Cubist designs on it. Might give Anastase ideas for a bath-wrap' (p. 157). The acquisitiveness of the Wheater set is not even redeemed by an interest in art or culture. They settle in Venice for the hotels and the climate, not for the history or the art. Education and culture are of little interest to them: at the beginning of the novel, Boyne remembers that Cliffe Wheater is 'reputed to be mainly interested in Ritz Hotels and powerful motor-cars. Hadn't he a steam-yacht too?' (p. 5). A little later Joyce tells Boyne that for Cliffe 'education has always just been college sports and racing-motors' (pp. 54–5) – in stark contrast to his frail eldest son, Terry, who is acutely intelligent, hungry for knowledge and desperate to have a tutor.

However, Cliffe Wheater's business interests, which Boyne recalls having run across 'even in the Argentine' (p. 5), represent more than just one man's situation in the novel. They are the result of a particular phase in American society and politics:

The election of Harding in 1920 marked the true beginning of the business era, most notably with the appointment of Andrew Mellon, a wealthy businessman, as Secretary of the Treasury. Mellon cut business and income tax and halved federal spending over the decade. While much of Europe rebuilt itself or experienced severe depressions and social turmoil, from 1922 economic activity boomed in the United States; having expanded industrial production during the war, it increased peacetime production to an unprecedented degree. As a result America became the most productive and prosperous nation in the world.[13]

The burgeoning of the American industrial base, as Susan Currell goes on to point out, became associated with materialism, anti-intellectualism and a philistinism from which many writers and artists retreated by fleeing to Europe.[14] Wharton, too, viewed this sudden American prosperity from the culturally conservative safety of France with much misgiving[15] and uses the Wheaters in her novel of 1928 to show how enormous wealth can stunt moral growth. Indeed, the adult Wheaters are described as if they are the children: 'The only trouble with them is that they're too rich. That makes them fretful: it's like teething. Every time your father hears he's made another million it's like cutting a new tooth' (p. 63). Wharton's title for her novel is clearly ironic: most of the adults in it – including Martin Boyne – are child-like in some ways, the inevitable result of a rich but dysfunctional society in which traditional values have broken down. 'The fact is, we're none of us grown up' (p. 247), Boyne reflects later in the novel. It is, of course, significant that none of the male characters in the novel were involved in the First World War:[16] their lives have been untouched by the horror and suffering that transformed some of their American contemporaries and many of their European counterparts.[17] The situations of Wharton's characters thus hint constantly at a wider scenario. As Nancy Bentley has noted:

> By linking money and mobility, by connecting continental and marital crossings, her stories of rich travellers who 'inter-married, inter-loved, and inter-divorced each other over the whole face of Europe' and beyond become a kind of index to the global powers that are otherwise missing from the surface of the fiction.[18]

The plot of the novel is driven by the emotional tangle that develops between the three main characters: Martin Boyne, Rose Sellars and Judith Wheater. It is no coincidence that Judith Wheater, aged 15, is just out of puberty whereas Rose Sellars, in her forties, is approaching the menopause. The novel is concerned with profound questions about sexuality: the sexual desire of a man who does not understand his own feelings; the sexual identity of the older woman trapped for many years in a passionless marriage; the precocious sexuality of an adolescent girl who has never been appropriately loved or nurtured. Martin Boyne, despite having travelled the world as a civil engineer and despite his love for Rose Sellars, finds himself, at the age of 46, gradually becoming besotted by the young Judith Wheater, whom he sees as a nymph figure: 'At such moments, Boyne thought, she was like a young Daphne, half emerging into reality, half caught in the foliage of fairyland' (p. 265).[19] From a twenty-first century perspective, it is tempting to see this as a crisis precipitated by the fact that the woman who was previously off limits because married has now become a widow and is therefore available and requiring a solid commitment. Martin Boyne, like Dexter Manford in *Twilight Sleep*, is confused both about his age and his loyalties; at times he feels simultaneously young and old, committed and uncommitted. Imagining his future life with Rose he reflects:

> Once they were married she would surely see that, for his soul's sake, and until the remainder of his youth was used up, she must let him go off on these remote exciting expeditions which seemed the only cure for – for what? Well, for the creeping grayness of age, no doubt. (p. 240)

But it is not just his age that makes Martin Boyne vulnerable at this point in his life. Although, as an early critic noted, Boyne might be 'solid, tender-hearted, an example of probity',[20] he is also a rather insecure, awkward and emotionally naive man, despite his worldly experience. He often feels that he has blundered or done the wrong thing when in the company of women: 'Oh, damn it, what had gone wrong again now? (p. 131); 'Decidedly, he was doomed to blunder in his dealings with women, even when were no more than little girls' (p. 191). The episode concerning the 'odd and exquisite and unaccountable' pendant (p. 188), bought for Judith, and the expensive but rather 'commonplace' engagement ring bought for Rose – and the recipients' astute interpretation of their significance – painfully reveals his emotional clumsiness as well as the subtle shift of investment of time and devotion to Judith from Rose.

Most importantly, Boyne is a man who does not really know himself; indeed, Helen Killoran suggests that the various allusions in the novel to 'Rip Van Winkle', 'Sleeping Beauty' and Browning's poem 'The Grammarian's Funeral' work to produce a picture of Boyne as an escapist and a fantasist who refuses to face the real nature of his desires.[21] Through various fictional devices, Wharton allows the reader to understand Boyne's emotions before he fully admits them to himself, although most of the novel is focalised through his character. His occasional thoughts of his charismatic great uncle Edward – 'whose travel-adventures were famed in the family' (p. 1) and who kept company with the celebrities and intellectuals of his age – produce a sense of inadequacy in Boyne; he also feels that, by comparison, adventure and excitement have eluded him. Indeed, at the opening of the novel he sees himself as 'a critical cautious man of forty-six, whom nobody could possibly associate with the romantic or the unexpected' (p. 3) – but it is at that very moment that he catches sight of Judith, who will change his life. His emotional confusion about his love for this girl-woman is signalled throughout the novel by a tension between his physical desire for her and his insistence on seeing her – and constantly addressing her – as a child. However, Rose Sellars and Mr Dobree – arguably the only 'adults' in the novel in terms of emotional maturity – recognise that his protective stance towards Judith in fact hides a sexual infatuation that blinds him to the inappropriateness of the relationship. Boyne's desire to hold and touch Judith is physically enacted throughout the novel: 'He slipped his hand through Judith's arm' (p. 34); 'He let his hand fall on hers with a faint laugh' (p. 35); there are constant references to their faces coming together; they hold hands 'ardently' (p. 184), he allows his arm to be taken 'captive' (p. 186), he lays 'a "grown up kiss"' (p. 210) on her hand, and 'his feet…seemed winged and the air elixir, because a girl's shoulder brushed his own' (p. 254). He is also seduced by the feeling of liberation that Judith and the children evoke in him: he finds their sheer energy delightful and their lack of sophistication (which produces some unwitting apercus) charming and refreshing. Whilst the widow Sellars is used goods, the children are, he convinces himself, in spite of their worldliness, fresh and innocent. But it is Wharton's constant focus on Judith's 'round red lips' (p. 6), the 'flame' of her mouth, her wild tousle of hair and her 'laughing eyes' (p. 119) that convey the erotic desire she arouses in Boyne even before he is able to connect it to his own emotional prevarications about Rose. Some of the most uncomfortable episodes in the novel concern this lack of awareness. Boyne's instant and noisy dismissal of Rose's first delicate suggestion that he loves Judith indicates his confusion, as does his protest 'This is ridiculous' when she later directly accuses him: 'Martin…but you *are* in love with her!' (p. 220). It is not until the picnic, organised by Mr Dobree (a man of 60), that Boyne begins to recognise if not admit the sexual nature of his desire for Judith. Asleep, 'her hat tossed aside, her head resting in the curve of an immature arm', Judith's small profile is enlivened by colour: 'A live rose burned in her cheeks, darkening her eyebrows and lashes, and putting a velvet shadow under her closed lids' (p. 205). Boyne suddenly finds himself thinking that 'she looks kissable' (p. 205) but, catching sight of Mr Dobree looking 'excited', his 'clear cautious eyes grown blurred and furtive', he immediately projects his own feelings onto the other man, realising, nevertheless, that 'he disliked Mr. Dobree the more for serving as his mirror…' (p. 206). It is not surprising, that, when later denouncing Mr Dobree to Rose Sellars – 'I never could stand your elderly men who look at little girls' (p. 215) – he becomes 'hot, angry, ashamed' (pp. 219–20) when Rose Sellars responds to his charge by revealing that Mr Dobree had assumed that Boyne was in love with Judith from the way he was looking at her.

When Boyne does, belatedly, begin to understand what he feels for the girl, it is often expressed as physical pain, almost as if he were experiencing the pangs of adolescent love complicated by the self-consciousness of the adult. He constantly justifies the change in his feelings as having literal representation in changes in Judith's age and maturity. As he is poised to ask her to marry him – 'in his new awe of her nearness – so subtly had she changed from the child of his familiar endearments to the woman he passionately longed for...' – she continues to thwart and elude him: '"Darling," she said again; then, with a face in which the bridal light seemed already kindled, "Oh, Martin, do you really mean you're going to adopt us all, and we're all going to stay with you forever?"' (pp. 308–9). He sees 'bridal light' (p. 309) but others, like Syb Lullmer, turning 'a meaning smile on Boyne' (p. 163) and, perhaps drawing on Doll's history, immediately see his interest in Judith as being far from paternal. In this text, however, there is no need to interpret from such nods and winks – the directness of Boyne's eventual admission of his desire for the 15-year-old Judith is a new departure for Wharton whose previous characters experienced intergenerational desire as something to be kept hidden.

It is worth here pausing to consider the portrayal of other sexual relationships between those of different generations in Wharton's work: Dexter Manford's quasi-incestuous affair with his stepdaughter-in-law in *Twilight Sleep* explodes overtly into the text only when Arthur Wyant tries to shoot him and it is never acknowledged in words; Kate Clephane's sexual jealousy of her daughter and her own former lover in *The Mother's Recompense* is stifled and repressed. In Wharton's 1917 novella, *Summer*, the narrative is focalised through the young woman, Charity Royall, whose account of her repudiation of the sexual advances of her guardian is, at first, authoritative and full of 'a deep disgust' as she blocks his entry into her bedroom and ignores his plea – '"Charity, let me in. ... I'm a lonesome man"'[22] – but then, of course, the novella ends with their marriage. Compared with her earlier work, Wharton presents inter-family, transgressive relationships very differently in her novels of the late 1920s – but she goes further in *The Children*. In *Summer*, despite his lapse of judgement, taste and decency in trying to force entry to her bedroom, Lawyer Royall is, in many ways a heroic figure and, in a letter to Bernard Berenson Wharton is emphatic about his dominant role: '...*he's the book!*'.[23] The novella is full of dark insinuations about 'the Mountain' (p. 125), from whence Charity came, where they never have '"...the minister up to marry them. And they never trouble the Justice of the Peace either. They just herd together like the heathen"' (p. 157). It is clear from the fluidity of the Mountain families that incestuous relationships are common but the fact that the elderly Lawyer Royall tries to force himself upon his ward and then marries her is rendered anodyne and is even excused by the honourable way in which he behaves at the point of marriage. Martin Boyne, apparently principled and decent, becomes fixated on a 15-year-old girl from the moment he sees her and he perhaps unconsciously prepares himself for the transition between viewing her as a child to thinking of her as a lover by early jumping to the conclusion that she is Cliffe Wheater's wife rather than his daughter (p. 11).

There is a shadowy and more sinister alternative reading of the story of Boyne's relationship with Judith which has its only expression in the fractured narrative of Doll Westway: that is, of a young girl as sexually vulnerable to an older man because of exposure to the wrong influences and absence of appropriate parental love and care. Cliffe Wheater calls Charlie Westway 'a blackguard' whilst being content to entrust his own children to a man he last saw when they were undergraduates together and who has spent his working life in the developing world, far from the 'old social dance of New York' (p. 5). Both Syb Lullmer and Mr Dobree – the only two people who feature directly in the text who have knowledge of the circumstances leading up to the death of Doll Westway – believe that Martin's motives for looking after the children are suspect; the pattern of his behaviour has clear resonances for them. Martin Boyne seems a more decent and responsible figure than Charlie Westway but his obsession with a girl of 15 is disturbing, as they rightly intuit. There are, as Helen Killoran points out, enough references in the novel to works such as Milton's *Comus*, Goethe's *Faust* and R.L. Stevenson's *The Ebb Tide* to justify a reading of Boyne as a self-deceiving predator whose surface respectability disguises a predilection for paedophilia: 'The image of him that emerges...shows him as...the Sorcerer who transforms people into animals and seduces virgins, a Faustian character in love with a child, the Satanic inhabitant of Morocco and other hot climes, and the insane ruler of a tropical island who plays God with the children's destinies'.[24] Such an extreme interpretation is actually moderated in the novel by Wharton's ameliorative portrayal of Boyne as confused and often well-meaning; the result is a complex and believable character whose surface respectability, however, is thrown into question by insistent references to literary texts that evoke lurid pictures of transgressive desire. In one sense, he is simply a product of a youth-obsessed culture in which adults strive to turn back their biological clocks and girls are prematurely sexualised, a culture that ignores parental neglect and turns a blind eye to paedophile tendencies.

It is only Joyce Wheater's late conversion to rectitude and frumpiness in the company of Mr Dobree that thwarts any plans Martin has for a future life with the children, although in Wharton's original plan for the novel he marries Judith. The language in which Wharton describes this marriage in the outline of the novel she sent to Appleton, her publisher, in February 1927, is all about reluctance. Judith:

> turns in despair to Boyne's sheltering and understanding love. She is now nearly 17, and she agrees to marry Boyne if he will let her adopt Beechy, Bun and Zinnie. He sees the folly of the marriage, and yet is so frightened by her loneliness...that, having obtained the consent of her parents, Boyne marries her – but as if he were taking a little sister home...The story ends on this note of quiet emotion, and yet hopeful.[25]

The language in which Wharton charts Boyne's growing sexual obsession with Judith as the novel proceeds, however, belies any suggestion of the benignity and self-sacrifice attained – at least at the end of the novel – by Lawyer Royall. The words in which Boyne actually acknowledges his feelings – at least to himself – are frank and visceral:

> What he wanted, at the moment, was just some opiate to dull the dogged ache of body and soul – to close his ears against that laugh of Judith's, and all his senses to her nearness. He was caught body and soul – that was it; and real loving was not the delicate distraction, the food for dreams, he had imagined it when he thought himself in love with Rose Sellars; it was this perpetual obsession, this clinging nearness, this breaking on the rack of every bone, and tearing apart of every fibre. (p. 323)

What then becomes unreal is the appropriate register, the appropriate relationship: that with Rose. As in *The Mother's Recompense*, Wharton uses images of ghosts and phantoms near the end of the novel to convey a sense of inauthenticity and emotional crisis. Pamela Knights has pointed out that the main characters in these problematic novels of the 1920s 'begin to experience themselves as becoming spectral; possible and lost selves become visible at their vanishing point'; finally they are haunted by 'phantom-forms of their relationships' and by 'shadow selves'.[26] It is not surprising, then, to find Boyne describing Rose Sellars to himself as a 'lovely shadow' (p. 259) and as a 'mirage [that was] now the phantom of a phantom' (p. 271) – or that he later admits to feeling 'like a ghost' (p. 319), even evoking Rose herself as one of many 'ghosts of good women...in the world of shadows' (p. 336).

In contrast to Rose's gradual metamorphosis into a 'phantom of a phantom', Judith's spontaneity and youthful sensuality are vividly presented throughout the novel, not least by Boyne, who interprets her frankness as childlike when it is more likely to be unmannerly. Boyne makes much of her vulnerability, as did some contemporary reviewers, who described her as 'an altogether lovable child', 'so completely innocent' and 'altogether unawakened'.[27] However, Percy Hutchison was sharper in his review, suggesting that Judith 'combines the sophistication of the serpent with the benign wisdom of the angels'.[28] Ill-educated and not at all interested in books or culture, occasionally shedding 'large childish tears' (p. 75), Judith is indistinguishable from women like Syb Lullmer in her combination of faux innocence and behaviour that is described as 'uncannily mature' (p. 42). The responsibility of keeping the children together sometimes lends her a 'wistful air of middle-age' (p. 57) and she is adept at handling her elders in complex emotional situations. Boyne is keen to note how, in the company of the children, she is 'instantly woman again – gay, competent, composed, and wholly mistress of the situation...' (p. 36). Yet he continues to think of her as a child with whom he can take physical liberties, like hand holding and kissing; in order to feel comfortable with such proximity, he rejects her precocity until he needs to acknowledge it to justify his proposal. Judith has been close witness to the vicissitudes of her parents' sexual and emotional relationships with each other and with their various lovers. Joyce Wheater describes her to Boyne as 'older and wiser than any of them' (p. 53) and reveals that because Judith had been her confidant during the break-up of her relationship with Buondelmonte she had seen, as in the case of Doll Westway, some horrors. Judith, Joyce confesses, is 'like a mother to me' (p. 54), indicating unwittingly the dysfunctional reversals her lifestyle has produced within the Wheater family.

Evidence of this 'knowingness' is an aspect of Judith's personality that Boyne finds difficult to accept, feeling 'his gorge rise' at Joyce's account of Judith's maturity (p. 54), contradicting as it does his need to view her as an innocent. He does not like hearing about Judith's chequered past and his tendency to close down her confessions prompts occasional outbursts from her in which she rejects his desire to infantilise her – 'I've seen a good deal more of life than Terry, and I've known other girls who've done what I did, and none of them ever went to prison' – that Boyne does not find at all 'reassuring' (p. 183). His irritable response to her awareness that her mother is about to conduct an affair with Gerald

Ormerod provokes a sudden fit of temper in Judith: 'She was on her feet in a flash, quivering with anger. "My age? My age? What do you know about my age? I'm as old as your grandmother. I'm as old as the hills"' (p. 61). He does not want her to behave like a woman but he cannot counteract the fact that she is a very adult 15-year-old: she flirts with him in French: 'Vous êtes encore très bien, mon cher' (p. 120), an act which is a reminder of the summer she spent in Deauville with Doll; she smokes[29] and she is not at all surprised that Gerald Ormerod wishes to marry her in preference to her mother. Her behaviour sometimes suggests a will that will not be brooked: 'Her strong young hands imprisoned him in a passionate grasp' (p. 181) and she can be both arch and artful. Indeed, her supposedly innocent question to Boyne, who is by this time no longer sure that he wishes to marry Rose Sellars – 'I'm sure you wouldn't marry just for position, or for money, or to regularise an old liaison; would you?' (p. 193) – seems calculated to throw him deeper into doubt. Her precocity, however, is finally turned to use as justification for his conduct as he moves into romantic rather than parental physicality. He recalls her apparently easy assumption that Gerald would rather marry her as justification for his own proposal: 'He remembered then that she had spoken to him with perfect simplicity of Gerald Ormerod's desire to marry her, as of the most natural thing in the world; and his own scruples began to seem absurd' (p. 312). The view that she is constantly veering between 'embittered shrewdness' and 'nursery simplicity' (p. 265), belongs to Boyne alone; others, including her mother and Miss Scope, seem clear that she has left childish things far behind.

Rose Sellars, on the other hand, is very much the older woman in *The Children*. A humorous and ironic person, she is in many ways the moral touchstone of the novel. Her name in New York acts as 'a synonym for cleverness and originality' (p. 39) and, unlike Boyne, she both understands herself and sees others clearly. Boyne finds her stability and consistency immensely attractive, although such features also prevent him from thinking 'of her as having been really young' (p. 39). In contrast to the colour red and the vitality with which Judith is associated, Rose Sellars is linked with words such as 'cool' and 'reason' throughout the novel. Her calm life of harmony and order is illustrated by the quiet beauty of her rented chalet in Cortina, which is far away from the 'blare of jazz and electricity' (p. 83) and which Boyne thinks of as 'Bethesda', a place of healing.[30] She is, throughout, associated with books and culture and her writing desk and writing duties are frequently mentioned. Like Halo Spear in *Hudson River Bracketed*, she wishes to introduce the man she loves to the writings of Goethe, whose work she so much admires.

Near the end of the novel, Boyne remembers how she had read aloud to him a passage from Goethe's *Faust* in which the Lemures, having just dug Faust's grave, describe life as something 'lent for a moment only' (p. 332).[31] Charged with a revived passion for Judith, however, whom he has not seen for some time, Boyne chooses to ignore the acknowledgement of mortality Goethe's lines convey and reinterprets them as the marvellous 'moment' he had when Judith was his companion. His distortion of the meaning of Goethe's lines is symptomatic of his tendency to misread both people and situations. Unlike Judith, whose unchecked energy and emotion draw Boyne to her, Rose Sellars appears to him often in abstract terms, reminding him of 'lovely Logic' (p. 172) and 'Milton's "How charming is divine philosophy!"' (p. 87) – a line that had particular resonance for Wharton, who cites it in her unpublished autobiography, 'Life and I', as expressing perfectly the illumination that reading François Coppée for the first time brought into her intellectual life. Rose's intelligence, perceptiveness and constancy provide the haven of the mind that Boyne craves in a confusing world but, confronted with the reality of her physical self, he no longer values what makes her unique. And, indeed, her wisdom in the face of Boyne's volatile emotions makes her appear older than him although she is much the same age. On hearing of his plans to take the children with him rather than see them separated, she remarks 'Then you're a child yourself, dear' (p. 137). Sharply observant, she quickly realises that Judith is not just a child, seeing her as 'already grown up' and 'a young lady with very definite views' (p. 177) who is 'very capable of fighting her own battles' (p. 171).

She has her own vulnerabilities, however; it is perhaps her acknowledged 'grief at being childless' (p. 100) that prompts her to suggest that she and Boyne might adopt Terry when the Wheaters separate (although this could also be read as one of the several devices she uses to test Boyne's commitment to her). Rose Sellars is, then, an immensely attractive character and, to begin with, Boyne endows her with young and 'springlike' (p. 115) qualities despite her widowhood – 'Freedom of spirit and of body had mysteriously rejuvenated her' (p. 85). But once his affections have shifted away from her there is much emphasis on the silver in her auburn hair; meeting her in Paris, Boyne notes her 'graying temples' and her face which 'looked changed and aged, like her hair' (p. 318). Also lurking behind the mysterious ageing of Rose, however, is Boyne's grimly humorous caricature of the older woman who surfaces in the novel both as 'the nervous spinster in the next room' of the hotel who bangs on the wall and calls out 'venomously' (p. 256) and as Scopy or 'Horror Scope' who – no doubt younger than

Mr Dobree – is described as 'gaunt and ravaged' and 'the Witch of Atlas' at one point (p. 112). Rose Sellars herself is fully aware of society's tendency either to marginalise or dismiss the older woman as extraneous or odd: in answer to Martin's suggestion that she might meet Judith, she ironically responds 'If you think she won't be too frightened of a strange old woman?' (p. 119). Increasingly associated by Martin with pallor, dusk and the evening chill, Rose Sellars' maturity becomes even more sharply contrasted with Judith's youth, both in his eyes and in those of the reader: 'She had caught at the last splinter of the rock of Reason still visible above the flood; and there she clung...with lips that pined and withered for his kiss' (p. 236). Reflecting the invisibility of older women in a youth-obsessed culture, she does indeed disappear from the pages of *The Children*; we know that she returns to New York to pick up the threads of her life there because at the close of the novel Boyne travels to Europe in order to avoid seeing her. In case the reader feels the same temptation to dismiss or forget her, however, Wharton reminds us that Rose Sellars is the real voice of integrity in the novel: 'All I care for is to know the truth', she tells Boyne (p. 233). It is this quiet wisdom and her alert sympathy – aspects of maturity that society ignores at its cost – that make her the book's moral touchstone.

Like Wharton's portrayal of wealth, however, the outcome of the painfully evolving relationships between Martin and the two women to whom he proposes marriage is presented not just as a personal tragedy but as a critique of a culture obsessed by youth – by nymphs and flappers. As indicated earlier, Rose Sellars responds early in the narrative to one of Martin's letters in the following way:

> I'm so much interested in your picturesque description of the little-girl-mother (sounds almost as nauseating as 'child-wife', doesn't it?) who is conducting that heterogeneous family across Europe, while the parents are jazzing at Venice....Luckily you'll be parting soon, or I should expect to see you arrive here with the girl-bride of the movies... (p. 38)

In fact, Wharton's subtle exploration of this 'want of decency' is her answer to Margaret Kennedy's *The Constant Nymph*, with which her novel was clearly in dialogue. Wharton wrote to Gaillard Lapsley on 14 February 1925, asking:

> Have you read 'The Constant Nymph' with which England echoes? I don't know whether Eddy Marsh launched it, but it's really a good

deal better than 'Lady into Fox'. In fact, it's rather like a much less-good 'Futility'. America rings with Edna Ferber's 'So Big' – good too, but (illegible) & inconclusive, rather. None of them have the gifts of Lewis.[32]

Margaret Kennedy's *The Constant Nymph*, published in 1924, is perhaps the most famous fictional example of the cultural craze for the girl-woman during the 1920s. Featuring a girl of 14 in love with an older man, it became instantly a bestseller in Britain and the United States and was made into a film with the same title which was released in 1928. Praised by Hardy, A.E. Housman, Galsworthy and William Gerhardie, the latter a friend of Wharton's whose opinion she valued highly, the novel was regarded as a classic in France and likened by Antonio Gramsci to Dostoevsky's *The Idiot*. Kennedy was even compared with George Meredith by a *New Statesman* reviewer.[33] Despite being set in the late Victorian period, the novel clearly offers a critique of postwar 1920s' behaviour and values. Wharton's deliberate appropriation of Kennedy's book is obvious even from a brief plot summary of *The Constant Nymph*.

Opening in the Austrian Tyrol, the novel focuses on the Sanger family, headed by Albert Sanger, a brilliant composer who chooses to lead a bohemian life. Their unconventional lifestyle leads to their being known as the 'Sanger's circus'. The seven children of this family derive from his marriage to three separate women: his first wife, Vera Brady, an opera singer, had two children but died in childbirth with the second; the second wife, Evelyn Churchill, a former pupil of Sanger and 20 years his junior, bore him four children before dying at the age of 30; his live-in mistress, Linda Cowlard, mother to his youngest daughter, is a sensuous but rather stupid woman who still shares his life in the large and rambling chalet in the Alps. Neglected by their father and his third wife, the children are poorly educated but have a knowledge of life and sexuality beyond their years. Antonia, the 16-year-old daughter, is like Wharton's Blanca in her sexual precocity and Caryl, the eldest child, is physically frail, rather like Wharton's Terry. Teresa (or Tessa), the 14-year-old heroine, equates to Judith in her sense of responsibility for her siblings and half-siblings and is something of a Heidi figure in her 'peasant dress of the country, a yellow frock, brief and full, with a square cut bodice and short sleeves'.[34] There are various subplots (Sanger's current wife has an affair with a visiting choreographer, Kiril Trigorin, and Antonia runs away with a wealthy Jew, by whom she is seduced) but the main story concerns Tessa's devotion to Lewis Dodd, a young rather arrogant avant-garde composer and follower of Sanger, who frequently stays at the chalet. Very fond of Tessa, but completely unaware of her love and devotion, Lewis becomes entranced by Florence Churchill, aged 28, Tessa's cousin (the daughter of Evelyn Churchill's brother), who comes to stay at the chalet. Other characters, however, are aware of Tessa's devotion to Lewis. Antonia informs Florence at one point that 'It's Tessa he belongs to...And, of course, Tessa's too young really to have a lover. At least, she's only just grown up, you know' (p. 130) and Tessa's uncle, Charles Churchill, later decides that Lewis and Tessa would have been ideally suited as man and wife, despite their age difference. However, Lewis and Florence become engaged and return to London, where Florence intends to use her contacts to further his career. Albert Sanger dies and the fate of the children is debated between various parties, including Lewis, Florence and Evelyn Churchill's brothers, Robert and Charles Churchill. It is decided that Tessa, Pauline and Sebastian should attend Cleeve College in England but Tessa's hatred of school and her subsequent residence in the home of Lewis and Florence begins to cause problems. Florence's ambivalence about Tessa: 'there was a sardonic turn about [her mouth], which Florence did not like to see in so young a girl' (p. 103), whom she sees as far from artless, evolves into jealousy and spite as she observes her husband's growing fondness for Tessa. Lewis, meanwhile, feels more and more distant from Florence, now seen as a 'domineering stranger' and begins to realise that he loves and desires Tessa, whom he realises he always saw as innocent and perfect. Lewis and Tessa (now 15) finally elope to Brussels, but before they can consummate their love, Tessa suddenly dies of heart failure in their boarding-house bedroom. Lewis, 'utterly bewildered' (p. 320), sends for Florence who is well aware of the legal implications of Lewis's elope-ment with a minor: 'It's going to be difficult. The whole thing looks so bad. She was under sixteen, you know. The law...' (p. 321).

The similarities between Kennedy's and Wharton's novel are very obvious and were noted by many of the reviewers of *The Children* on the novel's publication. Percy A. Hutchison in the *New York Times Book Review*, Rachel Annand Taylor in the *Spectator*, Tess Slesinger in the *New York Evening Post*, the anonymous reviewer in the *Times Literary Supplement*, Beulah Amidon in *Survey* and Arthur Maurice in *Mentor* all commented on the similarities between the two works, some rather dismissively, implying that Wharton's novel was merely derivative.[35] None of these critics, however, explored their similarities with any rigour nor did they comment on the differences between the two novels in any detail. The same has been true for more recent critics of Wharton's work.

Tessa, like Judith, is more complex than she appears at first and is perceived as both young and old, innocent and artful;[36] Lewis Dodd, like Martin Boyne, is rather emotionally immature despite, or perhaps because of, his enormous artistic gifts. Like Kennedy, Wharton uses a plot structure and themes reminiscent of Jane Austen's work – dinners, picnics, the symbolic significance of gifts of jewellery, a ball, the importance of primogeniture;[37] both authors use town and country – the Austrian Tyrol and London in one case, the Italian Tyrol and Venice in the other – to provide contrasting settings and suggest opposing values; both draw on literary allusions to sharpen their points; both frequently use the words 'savage' and 'civilised' to contextualise and evaluate the behaviour of their characters and social trends; both refuse marriage between the two main characters as closure. However, there the similarities end. Whereas Kennedy avoids the sexual implications of the relationship between Lewis Dodd and Tessa Sanger – displacing them onto the behaviour of Birnbaum, Trigorin and Sanger who all, as Billie Melman notes, 'prefer young women'[38] – Wharton exposes her main characters' emotions and desires only too painfully. Florence's comment is the only allusion to a sexual dynamic between Lewis and Tessa and it is ill-founded, given the fact that the relationship was never consummated and was never given physical expression. Florence's suggestion that he might have broken the law, however, gives her a form of emotional power over her errant husband. Entirely preoccupied with the novel as a metaphorical dialogue between 'high' modernist art, expressed through Sanger's avant-garde compositions, and popular culture, as he disdains the taste of the masses, with Tessa acting as an intermediary between the two – contemporary critics were either not interested in, or blind to, the sexual implications of the love between Lewis and Tessa. Wharton, on the contrary, meticulously explores, as we have seen, the psychology of the older man who falls in love with a 'nymph' and the resulting cost to himself, the girl and the rejected older woman. In that respect alone her novel is a fiercer and more critical engagement with the values and fashions of the time. As Nancy Bentley has noted, 'In *The Children*, the vicissitudes of travel not only figure for us a new distance between parent and child but also forge new intimacies that shade into the taboo of incest'.[39]

Nor does Wharton allow herself the indulgence of marriage or death as closure. Most modern readers, while enjoying Kennedy's portrayal of a bohemian lifestyle – apparently partly based on that of Augustus John – and the novel's lively characters, find the ending of *The Constant Nymph* bathetic. Despite the author's frequent hints in the novel that her heroine has an underlying condition that could prove serious, Tessa's sudden death seems evasive and sentimental. Interestingly, in a post-mortem on her novel which she wrote in the early 1930s, Kennedy diagnosed some of its weaknesses and commented on her difficulty in deciding how to end it. Originally she had intended that Tessa should be brought back to England after the Brussels elopement, dying nine months later:

> But I could not carry this thing out...I did not know how to manage anything so grim without resorting to rude violence. The unconscious callousness of Lewis would not take him to the point of deserting Tessa. So I let her die before even Florence got to Brussels.[40]

As Billie Melman notes, Kennedy 'was reluctant and, perhaps, unable to discuss openly the topic of feminine sexuality. Tessa's death is immensely revealing. Rather kill the heroine than bring the story to its logical conclusion'.[41] Her reticence, however, worked to good effect as far as the reading public was concerned. *The Constant Nymph*, as Melman points out, 'could be considered "clean" and "healthy". And any "uncleanness" in it could be attributed to the promiscuity of the Bohemian or "artistic" characters'.[42] There were, however, as Faye Hammill points out, a small number of critics who did voice reservations about whether a best-seller could also be a literary novel; some even expressed 'distaste at the novel's eroticizing of young girls or brand(ed) it as a deliberately commercial undertaking'.[43]

As already noted, Wharton also had a different ending in mind when she drafted the summary of the novel for Appleton but in the writing out of the love triangle she rejected the anodyne and asexual marriage she originally proposed and gave to Boyne a much darker and confused set of motives. Instead of the death of Terry, also originally proposed, the narrative closes after what Pamela Knights rightly describes as a 'casual reference to the death of a child – one of Wharton's bleakest and most blighted images'.[44] Chipstone's death, like many deaths of children in novels of this decade and the early 1930s, functions as a symbolic indictment of an irresponsible society. In the novel's final pages, however, we experience Judith's beauty and sensuality one more time through Boyne's eyes. Wharton skilfully uses images of natural ripeness and shades of pink and red to evoke yet again the erotic desire Boyne feels for her:

> He watched her with a passionate attentiveness. Her silk dress was of that peculiar carnation-pink which takes a silver glaze like the bloom

on a nectarine. The rich stuff stood out from her in a tier of flounces, on which, as she stood motionless, her hands seemed to float like birds on little sunlit waves....Her throat and neck were bare, and so were her thin arms; but a band of black velvet encircled one of wrists, relieving the tender rose-and-amber of her dress and complexion. Her eyes seemed to Boyne to have grown larger and more remote, but her mouth was round and red, as it always was when she was amused or happy. (pp. 346–7)

However, still trapped in the habit of counterpoint he cannot help but add: 'Or perhaps she was still a child, half frightened in the waking consciousness of her beauty, and the power it exercised...' (p. 347). Wharton's use of ellipsis here and elsewhere when Boyne seeks to occlude the logical conclusion of his thoughts, highlights his regression to seeing Judith as a child again even though he has already acknowledged his continuing passion for her: 'The pain of not seeing her was unendurable. It seemed to empty his world...' (p. 345). Just as Wharton appropriated and revised Grace Aguilar's *The Mother's Recompense* when writing her own novel of the same title, so she takes Margaret Kennedy's *The Constant Nymph* and develops its plot and themes in order to offer an explicit and damning critique of a youth-obsessed society that nevertheless fails to protect its young. Sharper, bleaker and braver than Kennedy's best-seller, it was, nevertheless, reviewed through the lens of the earlier novel; it is no wonder that Wharton felt that her readers did not know what they were buying if the reviewers simply sentimentalised Judith as innocent and Boyne's desire for her as noble. Wharton's own desire, like that of Rose Sellar, was to tell the truth, however uncomfortable – the truth about the implications and consequences of a cultural obsession with the figure of the nymph. In so doing, she chose to ignore the art and culture debate implicit in Kennedy's novel. However, in her next two novels, *Hudson River Bracketed* and *The Gods Arrive*, she was to turn her attention entirely to the role of the artist in the modern world.

4
Hudson River Bracketed

'Man errs, till he has ceased to strive'[1]

Edith Wharton continues her satiric portrayal of American society and its values in her last two completed novels, *Hudson River Bracketed* (1929) and *The Gods Arrive* (1932). However, making her main character a young aspiring author enabled Wharton to expand her critique beyond the usual targets to include aspects of modern literary culture. Drawing on her own experience as a writer, she charts the challenges and difficulties facing the gifted author from a newly middle-class background in a society which is increasingly concerned to commodify literature and which alternates between Philistinism and a slavish devotion to literary trends. Wharton had been trying to write a kunstlëroman for most of her literary career[2] and in the story of Vance Weston she embeds some of the intellectual vexations of her own background – her lack of a formal education and the hostile attitude of family and friends to writers and writing. However, she transplants these to the most culturally barren point of origin she can imagine, the Midwest, land of Sinclair Lewis's *Babbitt*.

In her last two completed novels Wharton also moves beyond the satirical dimension, attempting to show how cultural and moral redemption might lie in the figure of the artist whose vision and aspirations go beyond the material and the fashionable. To do this, she turns to the artistic templates found in the work of Goethe, her favourite writer, and A.J. Downing, an American landscape architect and horticulturalist whose agenda was moral as well as aesthetic. The values inherent in the text of *Faust*, invoked both directly and obliquely in *Hudson River Bracketed* and *The Gods Arrive*, together with Downing's enthusiasm for the architectural bracketed style (which represents craft *and* art, fitness for purpose *and* civilised living) are offered as a solution to the ills besetting a modern world that seems to have lost contact with nature, spirituality and any real sense of authenticity.[3] One of Wharton's problems, however, in *Hudson River Bracketed* in particular, is to find a mode in which to critique the shallowness of prior attempts to articulate the numinous while communicating the intellectual and aesthetic difficulties of doing so. Wharton is ultimately no more successful than her characters in her effort to express a sense of the supernatural that is also conceptually rigorous when trying to communicate the mysterious nature of creation. Notwithstanding such difficulties, Wharton emphatically sees it as the duty of the artist to recover a sense of integrity and continuity with the past which the modern world has forfeited in its pursuit of material wealth and status. The fact that her creation, Vance Weston, frequently falters in this quest does not mean that the quest itself is invalid.

Concerned to avoid what she saw as the self-conscious, directly autobiographical and stylistically pretentious nature of works such as Joyce's *A Portrait of the Artist as a Young Man* (1916), Wharton eschews time slips, the stream of consciousness technique and other literary devices that characterised certain novels published during the first two decades of the twentieth century as modernist. Indeed, in October 1928 she wrote to Desmond MacCarthy that she intended to write an article 'on this tiresome stream-of-consciousness theory which is deflecting so much real narrative talent out of its proper course'.[4] In her own portrait of the artist she adheres to a conventional chronology and a more traditional representation of inner thought, adapting and modulating the epiphany so that its significance becomes less anchored in the individual and more rooted in historical continuity. As a consequence, in some ways the two novels hark back to the nineteenth century both in structure and technique, although, as previously indicated, Wharton thereby creates difficulties for herself in having to rely in large part on the narrative strategies of realism in her attempts to communicate the spiritual. Her desire to create hybrid texts in this late stage of her writing career, however, does result in a quiet transformation of some of the traditional features of the kunstlëroman. In addition, *Hudson River Bracketed* and *The Gods Arrive* maintain, as Sharon Kim has noted, a constant dialogue with modernism, which in turn complicates a straightforward reading of Wharton's stated aversion to it.[5] Whereas the artists and writers in novels by Joyce and Woolf (such as Stephen Dedalus or Lily Briscoe) feel adrift in and alienated by the modern world, Wharton makes it clear that for Vance Weston to overcome his own limitations and to succeed as a writer, he must relate to history, culture and tradition. The key word in *Hudson River Bracketed* is 'continuity' in both the physical and (as Vance reminds his grandmother, Mrs Scrimser) the metaphysical sense: 'Couldn't she feel the beauty of continuity in the spiritual world, when the other was being pulled down and rebuilt every morning?'[6] For Wharton, as for T.S. Eliot, the link between tradition and the individual talent is vital – a belief she reiterates frequently in *The Writing of Fiction*. As she later reflected:

> the accumulated leaf-mould of tradition is essential to the nurture of new growths of art, whether or not those who cultivate them are aware of it. All the past seems to show that when a whole generation misses the fecundating soil stored for it by its predecessors its first growth will be spindling and its roots meagre.[7]

Furthermore, her excitement at the work of Marcel Proust, as well as demonstrating her unequivocal admiration for a leading modernist, illustrates Wharton's sharply individual assessment of the opportunities for fiction afforded by modernism. As we have seen, for Wharton, Proust exemplified a talent beyond the ability to innovate in being 'that far more substantial thing in the world of art, a renovator'.[8] Above all, Proust's profound engagement with the past elevated him for her above all other modernists: 'The more one reads of Proust the more one sees that his strength is the strength of tradition. All his newest and most arresting effects have been arrived at through the old way of selection and design'.[9] Where the novels show Vance Weston's excitement at engaging with the past they do so most effectively when Wharton follows Proust and harnesses that 'strength of tradition'. However, Wharton, like Vance, makes errors of judgement and falls into temptation along the way, unable to resist jibing at modernist writing, including the rather cheap shot at the 'me book' (p. 232) written by those caught in the 'after-war welter, with its new recipe for immortality every morning' (p. 392). Both Wharton and her creation strive for transcendence but the artist, despite all aspirations, is human and prone to distraction – 'Man errs, till he has ceased to strive', as Goethe puts it in *Faust*, a key text in *Hudson River Bracketed*.

In Vance Weston, as many critics have noted, we see the aspirations and frustrations of the young writer that Wharton knew from her own experience.[10] In both *Hudson River Bracketed* and *The Gods Arrive* Wharton counterpoints her frank and positive portrayal of the artist and his necessary egocentricity with a sympathetic portrait of a woman of fine discernment and wide education who determinedly embraces the role of helpmeet and, occasionally, muse. Halo Spear, constantly tried and tested by Vance from the day they meet and sexually betrayed by him in *The Gods Arrive*, is an attractive and complex character and, like Rose Sellars in *The Children*, her presence causes the actions and reactions of the putative hero, the artist, to be subjected to a different balance of judgements. Her self-renunciation – a trait that relates her to several of George Eliot's female characters – seems to contradict the capaciousness of her intellect and emotions. However, in this relationship between two complex characters, Wharton was also working out her thoughts about gender and creativity in a way that aligns her with artists whose contiguity she resisted – such as Virginia Woolf. Rachel Vinrace in *The Voyage Out* (1915), Sally Seton and Clarissa Dalloway in *Mrs Dalloway* (1925) and Mrs Ramsay in *To the Lighthouse* (1927), for example, are all women whose artistic potential has not been fully realised and who, confined within the domestic arena, translate their talents into private piano playing, the art of flower arranging and orchestrating beautiful meals. Even Lily Briscoe, the gifted and innovative painter of *To the Lighthouse*, assumes that her masterpiece will be 'hung in the attics' or destroyed.[11] Although such parallels are obvious to the modern reader, Wharton herself identified more readily with a previous generation of writers. There are indeed many points of comparison to be made with George Eliot in particular.[12] Like George Eliot, Wharton was aware that she was the exceptional woman in a society that privileged male talent and creativity and she chose to portray in her fiction the lot of most women, rather than that of the extraordinary woman. It is worth noting that Wharton championed Eliot's work, often linking her with Goethe, even though George Eliot's fiction was critically neglected at this time.[13] It is also worth noting, however, that Wharton made central to her argument about Eliot's work that which she considered a faultline between her personal and professional life: 'If George Eliot had been what the parish calls "respectable," her books would have been a less continuous hymn to respectability'.[14] With the exception of her very public divorce in 1913, Wharton kept her private life private. However, she had no such inhibitions in her art; her characters in her late novels live as George Eliot and George Henry Lewes lived. Halo and Vance spend the majority of *The Gods Arrive* in unmarried cohabitation and a baby is conceived out of wedlock – and this from a writer who was denounced when her heroine of 1905 took tea unchaperoned in a bachelor's apartment.[15] The subversive nature of Wharton's late fiction, examined in earlier chapters, brings into sharp focus here the masculine sensibility, talents and fortunes of Vance Weston and the consequential sorrows of Halo Spear, who bears the social stigma of their transgressive relationship. Between the two novels Wharton offers not only an alternative portrait of the artist as a young man and an agenda for artistic and cultural renewal, but also an analysis of the social and historical forces that shape the interaction of gender, creativity and inequality.

Edith Wharton's aim in writing *Hudson River Bracketed* is to be found in her brief summary of the novel, written for Appleton, her publisher:

> I want to try to draw the experiences of an unusually intelligent modern American youth, of average education and situation, on whom the great Revelation of the Past, which everything in modern American training tends to exclude, or at least to minimize, rushes in through the million channels of art, of history, and of human beings of another and richer civilization.
>
> I cannot give more details yet. But the canvas will be broad and full of figures. Vance Weston becomes a writer – literary critic and novelist – and dies young, full of the awe of [*sic*] the world's wonder and beauty.[16]

A set of notes for the novel, written between 1924 and 1928, has Vance Weston fathering a child by his first wife, Laura Lou, and – after their deaths – having another child with his second wife, Halo Spear. The notes also refer to the 'Literary crowd in N.Y.' and to Vance's death following the publication of his finest novel.[17]

However, the origins of the novel and its companion, *The Gods Arrive*, lie earlier in Wharton's writing life, in the 1913–14 semi-autobiographical project 'Literature', a fact which Wharton acknowledged in a letter to Elsina Tyler when thanking her for her praise of *Hudson River Bracketed*: 'I had begun it before the war, but in our own milieu, & and the setting of my own youth. After the war it took me long to re-think it & transpose it into the crude terms of modern America'.[18] The experiences that she had related as formative in the life of Richard Thaxter, the artist portrayed in 'Literature', were her own. However, it is clear that by the 1920s Wharton had come to regard semi-autobiographical writing with some ambivalence. Noting in *The Writing of Fiction* that 'the autobiographical gift does not seem very closely related to that of fiction', she distinguishes between the subjective nature of what she calls 'self-confessions in novel-form' and the 'objective faculty' required to write a good novel. Autobiographical writing, she suggests, will always be the lesser form since:

> The subjective writer lacks the power of getting far enough away from his story to view it as a whole and relate it to its setting; his minor characters remain the mere satellites of the principal personage

(himself), and disappear when not lit up by their central luminary... the autobiographical tale is not strictly a novel, since no objectively creative effort has gone into its making.[19]

The wise Frenside in *Hudson River Bracketed* is shown as sharing such reservations when Halo anticipates his views on the dangers facing Vance in not 'arriving at an attitude of detachment from his subject' (p. 231). Wharton is absorbed, throughout the Vance Weston diptych, with questions of authorial distance but this is complicated by her desire to draw on her own experience in portraying the connections between self and art while avoiding the pretentious or the trite. She recognised with some admiration that Goethe managed to avoid this pitfall in *Werther*, a work which drew on the German author's own life while going beyond autobiography:

> Every page thrills with the dawning gift of creation. The lover has not been too much absorbed in his own anguish to turn its light on things external to him. The young Goethe who has noted Charlotte's way of cutting the bread-and-butter for her little brothers and sisters, and set down the bourgeois humours and the sylvan charm of the ball in the forest, is already a novelist.[20]

Werther, for Wharton, is 'the link between the real novel and the autobiography in novel-disguise'.[21] Given her probable plundering of Walpole's hybrid creation *The Castle of Otranto* when writing *Twilight Sleep,* and her life-long admiration of Goethe's work, it is not surprising that Wharton sought to emulate the hybridity of *Werther* when writing *Hudson River Bracketed.* At a time when autobiography and the novel were viewed as entirely separate art forms, this was both a bold step for her and continuation of a tradition she much admired. The structural and symbolic importance of Goethe's work in this novel and its sequel, to be discussed more fully later in this chapter and the next, cannot be over-stated. Indeed, the literary context of the book – its relationship with works by Wharton's contemporaries as well as with important predecessor texts, such as *Faust* and *The Confessions of St Augustine* – open it up to much more complex readings than would otherwise be possible.

It is clear from the outline that Wharton gave her publisher that she originally intended to write just one novel about a young gifted American writer and that it would end with his death. Circumstances conspired against this, not least among them Wharton's eventual sense that the issues she wanted to address about creativity, art and society could not be encompassed within one book. By July 1929, she had fallen out with Oscar Graeve, the editor of the *Delineator*, who had – without her permission – begun to serialise the novel six months in advance of the agreed schedule. Horrified by this, then falling ill for some months, during which time any work on the book became impossible, Wharton returned to it determined to abandon her original outline. Her decision to end the novel in the form we now have it allowed her to escape the clutches of the *Delineator*'s editor, whose reactions were entirely negative,[22] and to bring her themes and preoccupations to a satisfactory conclusion in the sequel which was to become *The Gods Arrive*.

The limitations of 'modern American training', the materialist values of modern America, the claims of modernism and the commercial nature of the literary market-place are all subject to Wharton's satiric vision in *Hudson River Bracketed*. As in *Twilight Sleep* (*TS*), the most offensive feature of modern life is its facile use of language, illustrated in that novel by Lita's linguistic laziness and Pauline Manford's susceptibility to sound over substance: 'whenever she heard a familiar word used as if it had some unsuspected and occult significance it fascinated her like a phial containing a new remedy' (*TS*, p. 138). In *Hudson River Bracketed*, the drive toward 'universal simplification' (*TS*, p. 226) is analysed for its effect on art as well as religion. The supposedly reactionary values implicit in Wharton's late works have been attributed to her growing conservatism and to her nostalgia for the past, as well as to a dislike of 'the newly fashionable breed of younger novelists'.[23] But this does both the late novels and Wharton something of an injustice. After all, she thought well of many of the 'younger novelists' – for example, Aldous Huxley, Evelyn Waugh, Sinclair Lewis and Anito Loos – whose *Gentleman Prefer Blondes* Wharton described as 'the great American novel'.[24] Rather, *Hudson River Bracketed* and *The Gods Arrive* demonstrate, as Stephanie Lewis Thompson has argued, 'the complex intersections between modernist aesthetics, middlebrow culture, and gender politics that constitute her argument with modernism'.[25] Indeed, in the well-known letter to Bernard Berenson in which she describes Joyce's *Ulysses* as 'a turgid welter of pornography (the rudest schoolboy kind) & unformed & unimportant drivel', she went on to write: 'I *know* it's not because I'm getting old that I'm unresponsive. The trouble with all this new stuff is that it's à thèse: the theory comes first, & dominates it' – and then, citing Goethe, 'Grau ist alle Theorie'.[26] It is thus not surprising to find that the novelists she admired most (with the exception of Proust) were satirists rather than 'high' modernists. Wharton made clear her reservations and scepticism about the many claims of modernism in *The Writing of Fiction* (1924) attacking, for example, the supposedly stylistically innovative nature of the 'stream of consciousness' and asserting that it was simply a version of 'the slice of life' technique used by early French realists such as Maupassant, Zola and the Goncourts.[27] Her scorn for those who do not recognise literary continuities is expressed in *Hudson River Bracketed* mainly through her portrayal of a New York literary coterie whose members have not even heard of Zola, who dismiss great nineteenth-century authors such as Thackeray out of hand and whose values are those of the market-place with prizes for authors who best pander to the newest forms of patronage (p. 386). Her own reservations about modernist writing are frequently voiced by Vance Weston, who responds to praise of Gratz Blemer's new novel as 'gorgeously discontinuous, like life' with the bitter reflection that it is merely 'a drunken orgy of unrelatedness...'. 'Life's continuous', he asserts obstinately in the face of the fashionable opinions adopted by 'The Hour' fellows (p. 386). Even Blemer, who has opportunistically adapted modernist techniques, warns Vance against the excesses of modernist writing in what is clearly a jibe at Woolf's 'The Mark on the Wall', published in 1917:

> See here, young man, don't you go and read the Prophets and get self-conscious about your work, or you'll take to writing fifty pages about a crack in the ceiling – and then the Cocoanut Tree'll grovel before you, but your sales'll go down with a rush. (p. 419)

In more comical vein, Wharton shows how the discontinuities encouraged by modernism in art and literature can degenerate into absurdity:

> Somebody had started to paint maps of the four quarters of the globe on the bare walls, but had got bored after Africa, and the fourth quarter was replaced by a gigantic Cubist conundrum which looked like a railway junction after a collision between excursion trains, but was cryptically labelled: 'Tea and Toast for One'. (p. 383)

The business of literary prizes and the celebrity cult it engenders is pilloried in the novel in Wharton's transformation of the Pulitzer Prize into the Pulsifer Prize, an event which, designed to gratify the sponsor's vanity and catch her an artist husband, repels Halo 'with its half-confessed background of wire-pulling and influencing' (p. 345). However, Wharton's desire to chart the aspirations and failures of a gifted young writer in a culture that seemed to have lost its way goes beyond an attack on literary fashion; it was, in part, a response to a general unease about fiction and the role of the artist in society that followed on the heels of the First World War and articulated itself in much cultural debate on both sides of the Atlantic during the 1920s.

Hudson River Bracketed was for Wharton the culmination of many years of thought about how best to portray the American artist, just as *Faust* was a project that preoccupied Goethe throughout his adult life (it took him 60 years to complete the drama). However, when the novel was published the reviews were mixed. A few critics thought well of it: Mary Shirley commented that it compared 'favorably with the finest work [Wharton] has ever done' and V.S. Pritchett, despite his reservations, championed it as 'a good old-fashioned novel of huge proportions'. Percy Hutchison, however, lamented the fact that Wharton's new novel 'had not the flashing irony of many of her books', while Herschel Brickell dismissed the characters as 'shallow' and Vance Weston as 'childish'. Gilbert Seldes, in turn, described *Hudson River Bracketed* as 'one of her "off-year" novels'.[28] In 1977, Cynthia Griffin Wolff dismissed both *Hudson River Bracketed* and *The Gods Arrive* as 'a tremendous disappointment'.[29] More recent readers have also seen the novel as a worthy failure. 'The difficulty Wharton sets herself in the figure of Vance is that he has to carry so much' Lee notes,[30] while for Beer, writing in 1990, Vance Weston seemed 'insufficient to carry the weight of authorial investment in the subject of what makes an artist'.[31] Despite Wharton's confidence that *Hudson River Bracketed* was her 'best book',[32] many readers find Wharton's straining for significance in her evocation of the past and her rather overblown literary style in this late novel irritating rather than uplifting.[33] R.W.B. Lewis, one of Wharton's most perceptive and positive readers, describes *Hudson River Bracketed* as a 'laborious and unsure' novel, 'much too long...its most suggestive themes...stretched thin, and often lost sight of, over large distances of narrative'.[34] Pamela Knights, however, has recently insisted that the Vance Weston diptych, in a late writing period 'full of concerns about how to give meaning to a "drifting, disorganised" existence and how to shape a story towards an ending', is an 'epic', albeit an epic which is 'painfully episodic and peripatetic', where 'any sense of "arrival" seems fragile'.[35] In order to understand why Wharton might have been drawn to 'epic' writing during the last phase of her writing career, it is useful to consider the wider literary scene of the late 1920s and early 1930s.

Three types of fictional writing dominated the 1920s; the novels of the 'lost' generation (Ernest Hemingway, Scott Fitzgerald, John Dos Passos, Sherwood Anderson, John Steinbeck); the work of the 'high' modernists (Virginia Woolf, James Joyce, Gertrude Stein, Djuna Barnes, Dorothy Richardson) and the satirical novel (Theodore Dreiser, Sinclair Lewis, Anita Loos, Aldous Huxley and Evelyn Waugh). Although different in style, many of these novels are marked by a postwar loss of idealism and the iconoclasm and cynicism that resulted from it; they also often featured wounded or ineffectual male characters. The First World War had triggered a widespread sense of crisis about the modern age and the integrity of the modern subject. Aldous Huxley, for example, wrote to his father explaining that *Antic Hay* (published in 1923) was:

> written by a member of what I may call the war-generation for others of his kind; and that it is intended to reflect – fantastically of course – but nevertheless faithfully – the life and opinions of an age which has seen the violent disruptions of almost all standards, conventions and values in the previous epoch.[36]

This articulation of purpose is not distinctly different from Wharton's rationale for recapturing the past, as expressed in *The Age of Innocence* (1920), her autobiography, *A Backward Glance* (1934) and her essay 'A Little Girl's New York', published in *Harper's Magazine* in 1938, from which the following is taken:

> Everything that used to form the fabric of our daily life has been torn in shreds, trampled on, destroyed; and hundreds of little incidents, habits, traditions which, when I began to record my past, seemed too insignificant to set down, have acquired the historical importance of fragments of dress and furniture dug up in a Babylonian tomb.[37]

Despite the violent, almost visceral language which Wharton uses here, she managed to convert her angry pessimism about the nature of American society to interesting and creative effect in the novels of the 1920s, turning to satire to express her dismay – Taylorism, Fordism, materialism and their consequences becoming the butt of her humour in the novels *Twilight Sleep* and *The Children* in particular. Indeed, as noted in Chapter 2, recognising their shared agendas, Sinclair Lewis dedicated *Babbitt* (1922) to Wharton, who greatly admired his *Main Street*. She also described Huxley's *Brave New World* as 'a masterpiece of tragic indictment of our ghastly age of Fordian culture' and was delighted that he thought she had 'put the case already' in *Twilight Sleep*.[38] These writers felt themselves to be kindred spirits. It is not surprising, then, to find that the new novels she enjoyed most during this decade were not by Faulkner, Hemingway, Woolf or Joyce but by the satirists mentioned above. In several ways *Hudson River Bracketed* engages directly with these novels but it also tries to go beyond them, seeking to offer both a remedy for America's material and shallow culture and a 'cure' for the loss of idealism and spiritual values that marked the 1920s on both sides of the Atlantic.

The materialistic world of real estate development, so sharply depicted by Sinclair Lewis in *Babbitt*, had already been portrayed by Wharton in her 1913 novel, *The Custom of the Country*. The story of the men whose fortunes were built on land and water deals – Abner Spragg and Elmer Moffatt – provided a template for this later generation of novelists; Wharton's dialogue with Lewis is continued in the opening of *Hudson River Bracketed* – Vance Weston's father has made his money in real estate. Like Babbitt, the parents of Vance Weston measure out their lives not in coffee spoons but by the number of modern appliances they acquire. The place names in *The Custom of the Country* – Apex and Opake – are followed by Lewis's Zenith and Floral Heights which in turn transmute into the false utopias of Hallelujah, Euphoria and Advance in *Hudson River Bracketed*. Vance's parents serve 'their trade like a religion' (p. 9) just as Babbitt holds the Second National Tower in awe as 'a temple-spire of the religion of business'.[39] But whereas Babbitt comes to understand the cause of his misery and restlessness only in middle age – 'I've never done a single thing I've wanted to in my whole life'[40] – Vance Weston escapes the confines of Euphoria when young and soon discovers his vocation as a writer. Wharton's focus is on the next generation, son of Babbitt. She was aware that she would need to move beyond the emptiness of Main Street if *Hudson River Bracketed* were to offer anything new for, by the mid-1920s, critics had come to find literary attacks on American materialism somewhat predictable. Having described Sinclair Lewis as 'a cynical chronicler of the immediate American moment', the English novelist Hugh Walpole, in an article entitled 'A Note on the Modern American Novel', commented that 'Mr. Mencken started some years ago the cry that America was crude, materialistic, and unaesthetic, and almost every American novel since has followed in his track'.[41] In 'The Great American Novel', published in 1927, Wharton noted that *Main Street* itself was in the same tradition as Robert Grant's *Unleavened Bread*, Frank Norris's *McTeague* and Graham Phillips's *Susan Lenox*. Ironically, the success of *Main Street* had led the American novel into a sort of provincialism, down a literary cul-de-sac, because the great reading public largely missed the fact that Lewis was a satirist and so took his assertion that 'Main Street is the climax of civilization'[42] in his Preface to the novel at face value. Wharton, despite her admiration for Lewis's work, could not but regret the effect that it had had on American letters:

> 'Main Street' has come to signify the common mean of American life anywhere in its million cities and towns, its countless villages and immeasurable wildernesses. It stands for everything which does not rise above a very low average in culture, situation, or intrinsic human interest, and also for every style of depicting this dead level of exist-ence, from the photographic to the pornographic – sometimes inclu-sively...the conditions of modern life in America, so far from being productive of great arguments, seem almost purposely contrived to eliminate them. ...It is because we have chosen to be what Emerson called 'mixed of middle clay' that we offer...so meagre a material to the imagination. It is not because we are middle-class but because we are middling that our story is soon told.[43]

Wharton's anxiety that the American novel itself was becoming 'standardized'[44] in this way explains why, although she opens *Hudson River Bracketed* in the Midwest, in order to fulfil her higher ambitions, she quickly moves, through the imagination of Vance Weston, into the realm of the transcendent, the spiritual and the numinous – what she called 'the inner life' of the writer, taking him, in *The Gods Arrive*, to Europe as well as to the north-east of America in order to allow the long humanised landscape sensuously to penetrate his essential being. For Wharton, no matter how isolated the conditions of existence for the protagonists of any novel, successful writers will always relate them to something greater than themselves. This is her epic vision, this is the grandest subject she can conceive of; the 'Great American Novel' is the narrative that depicts the drama of consciousness that makes the artist. It is both a strength and a weakness, as already noted, that Wharton knows the lexis that cheap-ens the attempt to express the sublime at the same time as struggling to find an alternative. As Vance constantly laments, the freighting of lan-guage with brilliance, originality and significance requires a superhuman effort to reach and evoke '"The Mothers" – that mysterious Sea of Being of which the dark reaches swayed and rumoured in his soul...perhaps one symbol was as good as another to figure the imperceptible point where the fleeting human consciousness touches Infinity...' (p. 449, Wharton's ellipses). In order to differentiate Vance from those she would satirise, Wharton simultaneously engages with a key theme of many satirical novels of the 1920s: the failed or ineffectual writer. Huxley's *Crome Yellow*

(1921) features an anti-hero, Denis Stone, an indecisive character who envies men of action and who is (and remains) a failed writer. Stella Benson's *The Poor Man* (1922), which Wharton described as 'the most brilliant & fatiguing "Jazz" book I've yet come across',[45] focuses on the adventures of another anti-hero, Edwards Williams, who is both an inadequate man and a failed author. Huxley's *Antic Hay* (1923) features as its main character Theodore Gumbril, who pretends to be a mysterious poet (in order to seduce women) and who fantasises about his future as an author. It also contains a pretentious and unsuccessful artist called Lypiatt. The novel closes with a pointless taxi ride round London, an apt conclusion to a story of failed art, failed relationships and aimless lives. There is a sense that such failure and loss of purpose is endemic in the postwar world: 'Good; good? It was a word people only used nowadays with a kind of deprecating humorousness. Good. Beyond good and evil? We are all that nowadays. Or merely below them, like earwigs?' thinks Gumbril.[46] These figures are represented in *Hudson River Bracketed* by the authors who frequent the Cocoanut Tree and by Chris Churley and Octavius in *The Gods Arrive*, wherein, like Wharton's contemporary, Bay Lodge, they fail to rise above the role of 'connoisseur and dilettante'.[47]

Contemporary critics and readers reacted to this transatlantic wave of cynicism and satire in literature with both condescension and alarm. Edwin Muir, in one of a series of articles on contemporary writers, dismissed Aldous Huxley's importance as a novelist: 'Mr. Huxley has intelligence, fancy, and wit, but little imagination: and he has chosen the prose form in which imagination is most indispensable'.[48] Reviewing eight new novels in 1928, Raymond Mortimer described Waugh's *Decline and Fall* as 'extraordinarily clever and amusing' and as 'a fanciful satire, in the Oxford manner' before warning the reader that 'people who like their humour to be wholesome should steer clear of "Decline and Fall".[49] A year later, in the same journal, Storm Jameson, in an article entitled 'The Decline of Fiction', lamented the lack of authenticity in current fiction, claiming that it was responsible for the growing popularity of biography, which seems (unlike the novel) to 'get at the truth of life'.[50]

The 1920s also saw an anxious debate about the world of publishing and the future of young writers. F. Sidgwick (of what was to become Sidgwick and Jackson), responding to an anonymous journalist's claim that publishers were exploiting their authors, wrote in a letter to *The Athenaeum* that they relied on successful novels in order to subsidise promising young authors. Such novels, he claimed, were few and far between.[51] Michael Sadleir contributed a long article entitled

'The Publisher and the Public' to the same journal in 1924 in which he lamented the fact that 'the conception of the publisher as a blood-sucking tyrant is not an author's conception only; it is shared by many members of the public who, while not themselves writers, are perhaps friends of writers or are readers and buyers of books'.[52] In the same year and in the same journal, Leonard Woolf's article 'The Making of Books', provoked a letter in defence of publishers, whose 'costs have doubled, while their returns have not'.[53] The decade saw growing unease at the prospect of publishers transforming themselves from benign patrons of the arts into businessmen who needed to make a profit out of their writers in order to survive. Wharton's own belief that the success of a novel might come to depend on its marketability and be inexorably linked to current literary fashions is expressed in the pressure Dreck and Saltzer exert upon Vance Weston to produce another and longer version of his previous success, *Instead*. Her anxiety about the growing hold publishers had over their writers is conveyed by the 'ring of possessorship' (p. 415) sounding in the voice of an alternative publisher with whom Vance discusses the possibility of working. Lewis Tarrant, who considers himself Vance's benefactor, having provided him with a three-year contract, thinks of Vance's work as belonging to him (p. 492) rather than to the author – at least when Vance is in favour with him. Like an inconsistent and capricious parent, Tarrant wants the credit for discovering Vance when things go well but palms him off as Halo's or Frenside's protégé when they don't.

It is against this background of failing authors in fiction and widespread concern about the actual world of publishing that Wharton's attempt to write an 'epic' novel in *Hudson River Bracketed* should be read. However, like all Wharton's late novels, it is a complex and many-layered text and its backward reach also refers to the foundations of Wharton's own formative reading. Wharton notes in 'Life and I' that '*Faust* was one of the "epoch-making" encounters for me'.[54] Several critics have noted her debts to Goethe, Jane K. Brown, for example, remarking that 'Goethe remained her favourite poet and *Faust* her favourite work until her death...the Mothers from *Faust II* are a leitmotiv in *Hudson River Bracketed* and the hero is advised to read Goethe's masterpiece...Wharton knew her Goethe chapter and verse...'.[55] In her biography of Wharton, Hermione Lee records that:

> Above all, she was influenced by Goethe, whom she had been reading and marking up since she was fifteen. Her cruise diary had an epigram from *Faust* – his expression of longing for a magic cloak that

would carry him into unknown lands... *Wilhelm Meister* gave her one of her favourite sayings (which she used as one of the epigrams for *A Backward Glance*), 'Kein Genuss is vorübergehend': 'No pleasure is transitory'.[56]

Fluent in German from adolescence, Wharton read Goethe's works in their original language and his writing remained a vital touchstone for her. Indeed, Kenneth Clark, who became a warm friend of Wharton during her last ten years, noted that 'to the end of her life she revered Goethe more than any other author'.[57] Lee comments that Wharton's own copies of Goethe's works 'are some of the most heavily marked of all her books;...his influence stretches from *The Valley of Decision* to *The Gods Arrive'*.[58] Wharton wished her last two completed novels to be regarded as her magnum opus, in the way that *Faust* Parts One and Two are regarded as Goethe's finest achievement. As Lee notes, 'More than any of her other novels, they are philosophical attempts to examine how creativity works, how the "indestructible inmost self" is made and what integrity it can sustain'.[59]

Wharton's admiration for Goethe is crucial to a proper understanding of what she was trying to achieve in *Hudson River Bracketed* and *The Gods Arrive*. As well as drawing on *Werther* and *Wilhelm Meister*, she modelled the themes and preoccupations of the two novels on *Faust*. In Part One of Goethe's play, Faust frequently turns to Nature, declaring at one point that 'as great Nature rules my mind', he will 'Discover the inner psychic force,/ The spirit speaking to its kind!' (*Faust*, pp. 16–17). A Romantic, he experiences intense joy in a sublime landscape:

> 'let's...then climb the rocky heights!
> Look how that stream pours down perpetually:
> The walk's worth while to see such sights.
> The birch-trees are all touched by spring
> Already, even the pines revive;
> Do our limbs too not come alive?' (p. 122)

As David Luke has noted, Goethe's Faust (unlike Marlowe's) 'exists not in a Christian but in a pantheistic frame of reference' (p. xvi). Vance Weston also searches for regeneration and for the sublime in nature; his first encounter with the sea is epiphanic and his thirst for transcendence grows ever more insistent while at the same time he is also driven by physical and sensual appetites. This sense of wanting to experience the extremes of both the sublime and the sensual is expressed by Faust – in words that became Wharton's favourite lines from Goethe[60] – as a self divided:

> In me there are two souls, alas, and their
> Division tears my life in two.
> One loves the world, it clutches her, it binds
> Itself to her, clinging with furious lust;
> The other longs to soar beyond the dust
> Into the realm of high ancestral minds. (pp. 35–6)

Vance Weston, like Faust, is a soul divided: he is a sensual young man, driven by his sexual desire for women as much as by his lofty literary ambition. He is easily seduced, either sexually by precocious young women such as Floss Delaney and Esmeralda Cran or emotionally by the superficial prettiness and neediness of virginal girls such as Laura-Lou. But he is also the thinker and writer who longs to transcend the boundaries of ordinary knowledge and experience. Not surprisingly, then, *Hudson River Bracketed*, like *Faust*, is marked by extremes – physical, emotional, spiritual. Taken literally to the heights when he visits Thundertop with Halo, Vance's imagination soars as he is inspired with the desire to create some sort of aesthetic unity from his experience. But he also knows that he must sink into the depths of his own mind and unconscious in order to tap the true sources of creativity.[61] The images of height and depth (particularly plumbing the depth of the seas) express a potentially infinite realm of truth and meaning which lies outside the illusory fixities of social 'truths'. This is what the artist, like Faust, must strive to reach, despite the dangers such a journey presents.

Wharton's rather curious description of Vance's psychic voyage into the deeps draws heavily on Mephistopheles' description of the sphere of the Mothers in Goethe's *Faust Part Two*; they are, he says uneasily, a matter of 'high mystery', goddesses 'Enthroned in solitude', 'No place, no space around them, time still less…They are the Mothers' (*Faust Part Two*, p. 51). As Lee has noted, Wharton 'is haunted by the moment when (as she puts it in an essay of 1902), "Mephistopheles tells Faust that, to evoke the phantom of Helen, he must descend to the Mothers, the hero shudders at the mysterious word, and the reader feels the recoil of the shudder". This passage sounds all through the story of Vance'.[62] In order to acquire full power and knowledge, then, Faust must search for the Mothers. 'Go to the depths to seek/ Their dwelling!' Mephistopheles tells Faust, adding that to find them, he will have to follow 'A path untrodden/ Which none may tread; a way to the forbidden/ The unmoved, the inexorable' and adding, as a warning, that during the journey Faust will experience intense solitude and desolation (*Faust Part Two*, p. 51). Coming across the passage about 'the mysterious Mothers' in *Faust* at the Willows, Vance responds dramatically to that sense of their 'moving in subterranean depths among the primal forms of life' (p. 336). '"That's it", he shouts – "the fellows that write those books are all Motherless!"' (p. 336) – his bathetic and excited outburst damning all those writers who have, in his eyes, only scraped the surface of life. Struggling with the novel that will develop into *Instead*, Vance becomes haunted himself by images of depths, rejecting the 'brilliant verbal gymnastics' of a modernism that leave him feeling a sense 'of an immense emptiness underneath, just where, in his own vision of the world, the deep forces stirred and wove men's fate' (p. 335). He decides that if he cannot express the power of those 'deep forces', he will abandon writing. 'The real stuff', he thinks to himself, 'is way down, not on the surface' (p. 336).

Like Faust, then, Vance Weston is by nature an overreacher and a striver who, as the epigraph to this chapter states, is bound to err and fail at some point. Both Faust and Vance experience acute despair, the two characters contemplating suicide early in Goethe's play and Wharton's novel respectively. Again like Faust, who is both terrified that 'life's mess/ Of trivial impediments' will destroy his 'active soul's creativeness' (*Faust Part One*, p. 48) and yet full of confidence – in Part One he announces to a supernatural presence 'It is I, Faust! You and I are the same!' (p. 19) – Wharton's hero is both insecure and sublimely arrogant. Mephistopheles warns Faust that 'such totality/ Is only for a god; perpetual light/ Is God's alone' (p. 54) but Faust is driven by a superhuman search for total understanding and knowledge beyond the normal. However, he is distracted from his quest (and from his desire for Helen of Troy) by Margareta, a poor girl who describes herself as 'just a child' (p. 102) and who attracts Faust because, as David Luke notes, she is everything that he is not; whereas he is an intellectual, she is naive, intuitive and innocent (p. xviii). Vance, too, craves transcendence and is drawn to a woman who is everything he is not; mistaking his sudden raging sexual desire for Laura Lou, a poorly educated and childlike young woman, for love, he comes to realise the power of communion beyond the physical between a man and woman only when he works with Halo on the writing of *Instead*. Both Faust and Vance feel desire for these young women and experience a need to protect them but then quickly feel trapped by the ensuing relationships. Vance's relationship with Laura Lou is purely physical; as long as his intellectual and creative hungers can be fulfilled elsewhere, she 'satisfied the rest of his nature' (p. 337); their 'groping for one another through the troubled channels of the blood' (p. 433) suggests a sexual compatibility that to some extent compensates for the absence of a like-minded lover. *Hudson River Bracketed* closes with the death of Laura Lou, leaving Vance free to pursue this other love, just as *Faust* closes with the death of Margareta. It is important to remember, however, that the two works are similar in ways that go beyond plot and character. In de-Christianising the story of Faust, Goethe created a myth of European Enlightenment as well as a myth of his own poetic development. Thus *Faust* can be read as a dialogue between romantic idealism (represented by Faust) and cynical nihilism (embodied in Mephistopheles); as David Luke notes, '[Goethe] gives us, not so much the drama of a human soul's salvation or damnation, as confrontation of opposite visions of the world' (p. xxx). In *Hudson River Bracketed* and *The Gods Arrive*, Vance's restless idealism is in constant tension with modern material values and the sophisticated cynicism of literary coteries, whether in America or Europe. It is Halo who provides the emotional ballast Vance needs as he ricochets between conflicting states of mind although it is not until the end of *The Gods Arrive* that he recognises this.

Hudson River Bracketed is then – on one level – Wharton's renovation of, and tribute to, Goethe's greatest work. It is also a classic kunstlëroman in which she draws on her own experiences as an author in order to examine the growth of the creative mind, while seeking to go beyond what she called the 'me-book'. Like the first part of *Faust*, Wharton's novel explores the driven and restless nature of the artist; it presents the quest for knowledge, understanding and achievement as both noble and flawed; it charts the cost of such a quest in human terms while attempting to convey the epiphanic and sublime experiences involved; it sets the intense joys of life on this earth against moments of utter despair; it reveals the limitations of sensual pleasures; it depicts life as a series of temptations and distractions as well as gifts and opportunities. The humour and authorial distance employed by Goethe in portraying his Faust 'as if the poet were looking back tolerantly at the "confusion", the "mist and murk" of his own youth' (Luke, p. xxxi) is echoed in Wharton's ironic and frequently distanced portrayal of Vance Weston. While the satiric element of both novels has attracted the majority of critical responses, Wharton's rich engagement with *Faust* in *Hudson River Bracketed* and *The Gods Arrive* – and all that it meant to her in terms of vision, transcendence and growth to maturity – is the key to a more profound reading of both novels, one which properly acknowledges the contribution she made to modernism.

Vance Weston's flights of mind are artistic rather than diabolic but they mark him out early as a potential visionary. His adolescent interest in his grandma Scrimser's evangelical Christianity suggests a latent longing for transcendence; they share an inclination for the numinous, although her descent into cliché dismays him both in private and public. He also finds himself strangely seduced by beautiful language: he is disarmed by Harrison Delaney's ability to use 'good English words, rich and expressive, with hardly a concession to the local vernacular, or the passing epidemics of slang' (p. 15) and one of the first things to strike him about Halo Spear is her unusual use of language. (As already noted, Wharton's verdict on American culture and society in the 1920s focuses sharply on the use and abuse of language.) Much as he respects his family's material success, Vance Weston senses that 'as a diet for the soul' the shallow materialism that surrounds him is 'deficient in nourishment' (p. 17). In *The Gods Arrive* Wharton has Vance say 'Words are too beautiful to be walked over in that way, with muddy feet, like the hall oil-cloth' (p. 39) – an image she had been desperate to use, following Henry James's extended riff, in his lecture to the graduating class at Bryn Mawr College in June 1905, on 'speech' as 'so many yards of freely figured oilcloth' upon which 'the vast contingent of aliens' trample in the process of assimilation to America.[63]

It takes the physical trauma of a grave illness and the epiphanies that follow from it to alert Vance Weston to a calling that will offer him a particular kind of transcendence: that of writing. Structuring the early part of the novel in this way, Wharton is able to combine elements of the nineteenth-century novel with a critique of modernist kunstlëromans, such as Joyce's *The Portrait of the Artist as a Young Man*. Vance's grave typhoid-like illness, for example, has two functions. It points to the inevitable outcome of a social system based purely on acquisitiveness and greed, as Vance contracts the disease through drinking water in Crampton when visiting his grandparents. Wharton is here re-using a scenario from *The Custom of the Country*, where Mr Spragg's fortunes are directly tied to his concern, after the death of two of his three children in a typhoid epidemic, 'that no Apex child should ever again drink poisoned water', with the result that 'out of [his] disinterested impulses, by some impressive law of compensation, material prosperity had come'.[64] In *Hudson River Bracketed*, a local doctor notes that Crampton water is 'rank poison' and that it results in several cases of the same disease each year. It transpires that an investigation into the poor state of the water was stymied by a deal between Vance's father and the Euphoria morning paper (ironically entitled 'The Free Speaker'), which enabled Mr Weston to buy a new Buick. Only his son's grave illness prompts Mr Weston to reconsider the possibility of supplying Crampton with cleaner water from Euphoria. Wharton thus uses Vance's illness to expose the corruption that results from an ideology based purely on financial gain. But she also uses it, in the spirit of Dickens and Charlotte Brontë, to plunge her main character into a spiritual, as well as a physical, crisis. In *Great Expectations* Pip arises from his sick bed a changed man, aware that he has wronged Joe through his aspirations to become a gentleman. Lucy Snowe, in *Villette*, comes to understand herself only through a near-death experience: 'And in cata-lepsy and in a dead trance, I studiously beheld the quick of my nature'.[65] Similarly, something crystallises within Vance during the course of his month-long illness. Coming out of his crisis, he feels an 'awful sense of loneliness' (p. 30) – a state that will forever be associated with the need to write – and he begins to draft a short story, for the first time able to project his own feelings onto a fictional character:

> He began hastily, feverishly, the words rushing from his pen like water from a long-obstructed spring, and as the paragraphs grew it seemed to him that at last he had found out a way of reconciling his soul to its experiences. (p. 32)

Vance's development as a writer is accelerated by several shocks to his system, the first being the sight of his grandfather, still a handsome womaniser, clutching Floss Delaney – to whom Vance was once loosely engaged – in a passionate embrace. The taboo nature of this secret relationship both repels Vance and shocks him out of his conventional understanding of human desire. For the reader, it resonates with the inappropriate age relationships portrayed in *The Mother's Recompense*, *Twilight Sleep* and *The Children*. The episode also represents an emotional rite of passage in that it teaches him the nature of pain: 'that when the soul is smitten deeply enough it seems to become one with the body, to share all the body's capacity for suffering a distinct and different anguish in each nerve and muscle' (p. 23). The second shock Vance undergoes is the backwardness of Paul's Landing on the Hudson River, where he goes to convalesce with his aunt's family. Appearing to him 'like something in a film of the Civil War' (p. 38), with its lack of modern conveniences (his cousin fetches him from the station in a horse and buggy rather than a 'neat Ford'), it challenges his preconceptions about how people should live and what constitute the important needs in life. Still seeing himself at this point as an ambitious young man, the area initially puzzles him:

> Paul's Landing was like a place that enterprise of every sort had passed by, as if all its inhabitants had slept through the whole period of industrial development which Vance West had been taught to

regard as humanity's supreme achievement. If Euphoria's values were the right ones – and he had no others to replace them with – then the people who did not strive for them were...as repugnant to the religion of business as the thief and the adulterer to the religion of Christianity. (p. 43)

In journeying to Paul's Landing, Vance has travelled not only East, but also back in time. For Vance, the past itself – particularly the history and culture of Europe – comes to constitute a challenge to modern American values. However, Vance's most important glimpse into the past and other worlds occurs during his first visit to the Willows and his magical encounter there with Coleridge's poem 'Kubla Khan'. His response to the poem constitutes an epiphany – a vision into or showing of another world beyond the quotidian and the material. It is yet another challenge to everything Vance has known and been brought up to respect.

The Willows, then, constitutes a sort of sacred space for Vance. The last occupant of the house was a disappointed spinster, Miss Emily Lorburn, who was distantly related through an inappropriate (in terms of class) and therefore largely unmentionable marriage to Mr Tracy. As the current owner, a Lorburn nephew, is largely uninterested in the house, it falls to the existing Tracy family – and to another branch of the Lorburn family (the Spears) – to keep an eye on the place. Framed by two ancient willows, the facade of the house 'suggested vastness, fantasy and secrecy' (p. 57). Vance is enchanted: he has never seen such an old house; nor has he come across a private house containing a library before. When he steps into the Willows, he steps into another land and he intuitively understands this; his time in the library lifts him 'to other pinnacles' (p. 152). The Hudson serves for Alph, the sacred river; the Willows for the 'stately pleasure-dome' and Héloïse Spear merges with 'A damsel with a dulcimer': 'he became conscious of her presence as of something alien, substantial, outside of his own mind, a part of the forgotten world of reality' (p. 64). Coleridge's poem is a world away from the work of Ella Wheeler Wilcox, Whittier and Longfellow, the writers Vance has been brought up on: it is 'what his soul had been alight for' (p. 63).

The house, it transpires, was built in about 1830 in the architectural style described by A.J. Downing, 'the great authority of the period' (p. 69), as 'Hudson River Bracketed'. It is indeed marked by numerous brackets:

The shuttered windows were very tall and narrow, and narrow too the balconies, which projected at odd angles, supported by ornate wooden brackets...A sort of sloping roof over the front door also rested

on elaborately ornamented brackets...An arcaded verandah ran across
[the] front, and all about it, and reaching out above it from bracket
to bracket, from balcony to balcony, a wisteria with huge distorted
branches like rheumatic arms lifted itself to the eaves... (p. 58)

For Laura Lou the house is full of ghosts but for Vance it is a place of
'elusive mystery' (p. 62). For a reason he cannot explain, it reminds
him of the Roman Catholic church that tolls its bell in the middle of
the night in Euphoria: 'He felt in the age and the emptiness of it something of the church bell's haunting sonority – as if it kept in its mute
walls a voice as secret and compelling' (p. 59). It provides a revelation
of almost religious significance to him: '"Why wasn't I ever told about
the Past before?"'(p. 62) – a question so naively ludicrous that it actually
manages to effect one of Wharton's aims – to show how the idea, the
felt meaning, is often failed by individual expression. The door of the
Willows is a door into the past and tradition, the house itself providing
continuity with earlier minds and visions.

Although Wharton cites A.J. Downing's *A Treatise on the Theory and
Practice of Landscape Gardening, Adapted to North America* as her inspiration for the Willows, the description of the Hudson River Bracketed
architectural style that she gives in her novel of the same name actually comes from Downing's *Cottage Residences: or, a Series of Designs
for Rural Cottages and Adapted to North America*. It is probable that the
two works had merged in her memory, particularly as she incorrectly
gives the date of the former as 1842 (it was actually published in 1841
whereas Downing's *Cottage Residences* was published in 1842). Wharton
also seems to have taken some artistic licence with Downing's work;
renowned for his architectural designs for 'bracketed' cottages and villas
along the Hudson River, he never actually used the phrase 'Hudson
River Bracketed' which in fact derived from the work of the American
architect Alexander Jackson Davis (1803–92). Whereas Downing does
indeed discuss a number of architectural styles in his book on landscape
gardening – including the Chinese, the Grecian, the Roman, the Italian,
the Gothic, the Tudor, the Rural Gothic and the Swiss – he nowhere
describes the 'bracketed' style that she attributes to this volume. For
that, one has to turn to the pages of Downing's *Cottage Residences*,
which includes a chapter entitled 'A Cottage Villa in the Bracketted [*sic*]
Mode' (pp. 99–123) containing a description of such a dwelling:

The strongly marked character which it has, is derived mainly from
the bold projections of the roof, supported by ornamental brackets,

and from the employment of the brackets for supports, in various other parts of the building...the unity of design should be further preserved, by carrying out the boldness of character in all portions of the building, by projecting the roofs, verandahs, porches etc. in a proportionate degree...[66]

Downing's explanation of the 'bracketted' style is accompanied by a plan showing the pride of place given to a library on the ground floor, described as 'a cool, airy apartment, shaded by the verandah that surrounds it on three sides' (p. 100). It seems clear that this passage provided the inspiration for the Willows. However, Wharton would also have been aware of the moral and aesthetic significance Downing attributed to his architectural designs. 'To reproduce the beautiful in this manner, and to infuse spirit and grace in forms otherwise only admirable for their usefulness, is the *ideal* of architecture' he wrote in his preface to *Cottage Residences*, adding that 'The principle of Unity, a principle of the highest importance in all works of art' should inform architectural practice (pp. 25 and 26). 'Unity is the principle of Oneness', he noted in the same passage. His architectural philosophy is made even clearer in the article 'On the Moral Influence of Good Houses', published six years later. Here he states:

a house is...an expression of the intelligent life of man, in a state of society where the soul, the intellect, and the heart, are all awake, and all educated...in this country, where integrity and industry are almost always rewarded by more than the means of subsistence, we have firm faith in the moral effects of the fine arts. We believe in the bettering influence of beautiful cottages and country houses – in the improvement of human nature necessarily relating to all classes, from the possession of lovely gardens and fruitful orchards...[67]

This agenda is absorbed into Wharton's novel, in which the architectural metaphor is used to revalidate previous spiritual, imaginative and intellectual 'constructions'. Reflecting on what he comes to see as his grandmother's 'religious emotionalism' (p. 464), Vance thinks:

Couldn't she feel the beauty of continuity in the spiritual world, when the other was being pulled down and rebuilt every morning? Couldn't she see that, ninety-nine times out of a hundred, it was sheer ignorance and illiteracy that made people call things new – that even the brick and mortar world that was being forever pulled down and rebuilt, the old materials and the old conceptions had to be used again in the rebuilding? Who wanted a new religion, anyhow, when the old one was there, so little exhausted or even understood, in all its age-long beauty? (p. 465)

The architecture of the Willows, then, stands for more than just the past; it stands for continuity *with* the past and a particular kind of integrity. Continuity, here represented by the old house, becomes a metaphor for continuity in the realms of the religious, the spiritual and the artistic. The building is for Vance a place of moral re-education, just as Mansfield Park is for Jane Austen's Fanny Price: 'His long hours of study and meditation at the Willows had made any kind of intellectual imposture seem the lowest form of dishonesty' (p. 467). This re-education derives from a deep engagement with the past, which he finds in the Willows: exposure to 'what used to be called a "gentleman's library"' (p. 68) provides 'that great nutritive element' necessary for the writer to grow and mature (p. 498); he is born again in the '"caverns measureless to man"' (p. 64) as surely as one of Grandma Scrimser's converts at a revival meeting.

Given the importance of the past and of continuity with the past in the novel, it is not surprising to see Wharton reworking the epiphany in *Hudson River Bracketed*. As Sharon Kim has noted, Wharton could see the importance of the epiphany in contemporary writing but she found its use in the work of authors such as Joyce and Woolf dislocated and ahistorical. In *Hudson River Bracketed* and *The Gods Arrive*, claims Kim, Wharton develops a new kind of epiphany that 'combines the aesthetics of modern epiphany with a subjective and historical continuity that has its roots in an older, perhaps more female, source of creative production'.[68] A good example is Vance's vision (for that is what it becomes) of the apple tree near the end of the novel:

Just outside the cottage window an apple-branch crossed the pane. For a long time Vance had sat there, seeing neither it nor anything else, in the kind of bodily and spiritual blindness lately frequent with him; and now suddenly, in the teeming autumn sunlight, there the branch was, the centre of his vision.

It was a warped unsightly branch on a neglected tree; but so charged with life, so glittering with fruit, that it looked like a dead stick set with rubies. The sky behind was of the densest autumnal blue; a solid fact of sky. Against it the shrunken rusty leaves lay like gilt bronze, each fruit carved in some hard rare substance. It might have been the very Golden Bough he had been reading about in one of the books he carried off when he and Laura Lou left New York.

Whatever happened to Vance on the plane of practical living... there still came to him this mute swinging wide of the secret doors... As usual with him now, the sudden seeing of the apple-branch coincided with the intensely detailed inner vision of a new book. (pp. 506–7)

This visionary moment arises directly from Vance's aesthetic sensibility but it takes on greater significance, both for him and the reader, because it resonates with Virgil's *Aeneid*. In that epic, Aeneas's descent into the underworld – where he will learn what the future holds for his people – can only be undertaken safely if he has with him the Golden Bough, a tree branch with golden leaves. The bough was said to be sacred to Proserpina (Persephone), the queen of the underworld, and was associated with the goddess Diana. Vance is, as already proposed, the heroic figure in the only epic Wharton aspired to write – the story of the growth of the artist's mind and creative capacity. Vance's vision of the branch also serves the same purpose as Homer's description of Aeneas's shield in the *Iliad*: contained within it is past, present and future, an allegory of the interaction of creativity with the solid facts of nature – sky and tree – and with art – carving and gilding, literature – the books. But also, crucially, in a coming together of craft and nature, the 'dead stick set with rubies' is transformed into the 'inner vision of a new book'. The dark depths inhabited by the Mothers are invoked here in slightly altered guise, lifted into epic mode by Wharton's encompassing of past precedent, present experience and future potential: the sudden desire to write is prompted by an epiphany in which the sensual and the mystical, the aesthetic and the spiritual, tradition and the individual talent, all combine to produce a fresh insight, a new vision of life. 'True originality consists not in a new manner but in a new vision' as Wharton stated in *The Writing of Fiction* (p. 17).

Hudson River Bracketed teems with passages and episodes like this which evoke earlier texts. For example, Vance's argument with Lewis Tarrant is followed by his seeing a pedlar beating his horse in the street, an episode which recalls Raskolnikov's dream of watching, as a child, some peasants cruelly beating a tired old mare and his rushing in to try to save the horse in Chapter 5 of Dostoyevsky's *Crime and Punishment*. However, it also references Dante's *Inferno* through Vance's exclamation 'Lasciate ogni speranza!' as he falls upon the pedlar ('All hope abandon', Canto III, line 9). The vision of a kind of hell – mankind's potential for cruelty and exploitation – is thereby obliquely evoked. Wharton's dense use of such intertextuality is based 'on the Goethean principle that "those who remain imprisoned in the false notion of their own originality will always fall short of what they might have accomplished"', as she puts it in *The Writing of Fiction* (p. 28). She is, as Kim points out, writing 'in harmony with a literary tradition, her theory of fiction representing a continuation instead of a departure' (p. 155). The structure and 'building' of her own novel, then, successfully illustrate the theories she expounds in *The Writing of Fiction*. Bearing in mind Goethe's warning that 'Grau ist alle Theorie', however, she seeks to translate her intellectual ideas into 'illuminating incident(s)'[69] and renovates the epiphany for her own ends.

The complication, in terms of the portrayal of the artist's re-education, is the influence of Halo Spear, who is Vance's mentor and his mediator of high culture. In the library, Vance plunges into Marlowe, Beddoes and Milton and feels awed by 'all those books about him, silent witnesses of an unknown and unsuspected past' (p. 120). Guided by Halo, he discovers a 'new world...a world of which he must somehow acquire the freedom' (p. 123). The relationship which seems to be promised here – one which will combine both physical and intellectual attraction – is contaminated, however, by Vance's refusal to be guided or judged by a woman. Wharton builds into her portrait of the artist a deep misogyny – perhaps inevitably since she is portraying a writer whose calling will inevitably keep him remote and isolated, even from those he loves dearly: 'he wondered if at crucial moments the same veil of unreality would always fall between himself and the soul nearest him; if the creator of imaginary beings must always feel alone among the real ones' (p. 559). This description of the apparently necessary egotism of the creative genius is to be echoed in Wharton's later comment on Proust: 'the fundamental cause of his isolation [was] that the only thing that interested him was the drama of the soul'.[70] But here it also sounds an ominous note for Vance's future relationship with Halo, which is played out in *The Gods Arrive*. Vance Weston's encounter with the Willows and his love for Halo Spear in *Hudson River Bracketed* comprise the first part of Wharton's attempt to fulfil a lifetime's ambition to communicate the heights and depths, the fractures and fissures, the sublimity as well as the bathos that go into the making of the artist. For Wharton, who never ceased to ponder and write about her own inspiration, her relationship with language – both hers and that of her predecessors – was the most challenging subject matter of her writing career, requiring the framework of epic. When she wrote in her unpublished autobiography, 'Life and I', of 'the sensuous rapture produced by the sight and sound of the words' of Macauley's *Lays of Ancient Rome* and Tennyson's poetry, she described these words as 'visible, almost tangible presences, with faces as distinct as the persons among whom I lived'.[71] The challenges of representing adequately the 'theme that I have carried in my mind for years',[72] as she described it to Elisina Tyler, became more and not less difficult over the course of Wharton's career. *Hudson River Bracketed* is, then, the first half of Wharton's epic kunstlëroman project. It is also a work made complex by a wandering authorial eye caught by the challenge of delineating a creative trajectory both sustained and disturbed by a relationship with a soul-mate. That soul-mate, Halo Spear, is one of Wharton's most interesting and perplexing female characters.

5
The Gods Arrive

'He who strives on and lives to strive/ Can earn
redemption still'[1]

The Gods Arrive, Edith Wharton's last completed novel, revisits and explores
many of the issues, thematic and stylistic, with which Wharton grappled throughout her career. This book, placed alongside *Hudson River
Bracketed, The Custom of the Country, Summer* and *The Children* was one
of her five personal favourites[2] – more dear to her than the novel that
made her name, *The House of Mirth*, or *The Age of Innocence*, which won
her the Pulitzer Prize. *The Gods Arrive* was a final word, a finished word
with which she was apparently content.

The novel opens with a skilful reprise of the salient facts from the
prior narrative of *Hudson River Bracketed*. As they sail from America for
Europe, Vance Weston and Halo Tarrant leave more than the New York
skyline behind. In the first three pages Wharton effortlessly commu-
nicates details of physical location, class and marital status, family
history, informing antecedent texts, and shibboleths to be confronted
and defeated. We are reminded of the importance of the sea to Vance,
of European heritage to Halo, of Goethe's *Faust* to the thematic strains
of the novel and, also, of the importance of locating a language vital
enough to communicate a new way of being in the world – all before
leaving port. Halo – like her artist lover – struggles to find words that
rise to the occasion of their exceptionality: looking back on the repres-
sive regime of her marriage to Lewis Tarrant, she thinks how 'quaint
and out-of-date it all sounded'.[3] Looking backward, yet also forward,
Wharton's prose here economically delivers the necessary information
from the recent past but is also proleptic in terms of its clear sighted
appraisal of the coming difficulties of their unconventional union: 'If she

were not Vance Weston's for always the future was already a handful of splinters' (p. 4).

The language of the two Vance Weston novels, especially when essaying the heights and depths of the artistic consciousness, can seem somewhat florid and sometimes stilted, but what Wharton is seeking here is nothing less, in the final assertion of her own modernity, than a review of her life's work. Her attempts to communicate the mysteries of creation lead her to include in the text casual references to her own artistic practice, formative influences on her work, dialogues with other artists and critics – both positive and negative – as well as allusions to her own novels and stories. Her friend and sometime rival, Henry James, haunts this text, but silently and amusingly, unlike Goethe who haunts it in a loud and sombre key. James's advice to the young Wharton – 'Do New York!'[4] – is reworked in Churley's outburst to Vance: 'I'm in rather a difficulty about you American novelists. Your opportunity's so immense, and...well, you always seem to write either about princesses in Tuscan villas, or about gaunt young men with a ten-word vocabulary who spend their lives sweating and hauling wood. Haven't you any subject between the two?' (p. 180). In relation to language itself, Wharton's borrowing of James's metaphoric oilcloth is used to conjure a vision of the English language as trampled upon in America. As Vance and Floss Delaney take tea in the garden of Brambles and Vance repeats '"Summer afternoon – summer afternoon"' (p. 299) there is another, double reference to James. The first is to the tea ceremony in the grounds of Gardencourt at the opening of *The Portrait of a Lady*;[5] the second is to Wharton's recollection of James's pronouncement on afternoon tea, soon to be included in her 1934 autobiography, *A Backward Glance*: 'James turned to me and said solemnly: "Summer afternoon – summer afternoon; to me those have always been the most beautiful words in the English language"'.[6] In addition, the cadences of James's own speech, and in particular, his well-known hesitancies and refusals to say anything definitive about his work are referenced in the occlusions – both physical and linguistic – of the speech of Octavius Brant, local literary guru:

No – no; I won't yield to the temptation. The lovely creature is there, swimming to and fro in the deepest deeps of my consciousness, shimmering like a chamaeleon, unfolding like a flower. How can you expect me to drag it up brutally into the air, to throw it at your feet, limp and discoloured, and say: 'This is my book!' when it wouldn't be, when I should be the first to disown it? (p. 285)

Details of Wharton's own memories and creative processes also pepper the text: Vance has to write on used wrapping paper (as the young Edith once did), when there is no other paper in the Lake Belair camp (p. 416) and the Furies (to whom Wharton habitually referred as her own demons) taunt Vance as he undergoes disillusion upon disillusion in his relationship with Floss Delaney: 'It was dreadful, the way old memories of pain fed their parasitic growth on new ones, and dead agonies woke and grew rosy when the Furies called...' (p. 407). Wharton's own critical pronouncements are reflected in a range of comments, from the steady stream of references to James Joyce's *Ulysses* ('The clever young writers he had known in New York had read only each other and "Ulysses"' (p. 47)), to a condemnation of modernist writers who 'substitute the cold processes of the laboratory for the lightening art of creation' (p. 393), to the inclusion of some of her most dearly held artistic tenets, especially those that assert 'the magic power of continuity' (p. 416).

Even more substantial, however, than the references in the text to people, opinions and incidents from her life, are the allusions to her own writing – in particular, *The House of Mirth*. For example, when describing himself, Chris Churley, soon to take his own life in the final acknowledgement of his failure as a writer, says: '"The fact is, I was meant to be a moment's ornament, and you all insist on my being a permanent institution"' (p. 248). Wharton here seems almost to be passing comment on her whole career as she harks back to the idea of Lily Bart as she might have appeared in a novel which was, at one stage, to bear the name 'A Moment's Ornament'. However, it is young men like Chris who seem now to be fragile, extraneous and disposable, not the women. This is, Wharton implies, what has happened in American society between 1905 and 1932. The trajectory of her writing career has seen women like Floss Delaney (more ruthless than Simon Rosedale or Elmer Moffat in the pursuit of financial security through marriage to a decorative but useless spouse) or Jane Meggs and her friends (independent women who live with men rather than marry them) gain some kind of salience, some kind of power. This is not presented, however, as a triumph of feminism but, in the spirit of Wharton's later parodic style, as women apeing the worst of men's lives rather than fighting for an equalisation of opportunities for women. Just as Undine Spragg imitated the rapacious behaviour of her father when closing the deal on her next husband, so Floss Delaney moves things on a step further when she triumphs simultaneously in financial and marital negotiations. The 27 years between the creation of Lily Bart and Halo Tarrant, however, yield more interesting developments in Wharton's work than the caricatures of women such as Floss and Jane. The female narrative line that began with Lily Bart ends with Halo Tarrant, who is still a victim of her class and her upbringing and who is too diffident to fight for her man or to assert her own identity as an artist or critic. She does, however, have the courage to invent a new way of being and seeing. The baby that Lily dies believing is nestling in her arms becomes a reality in Halo's life; her decision to have the child alone is an almost unimaginable step for a woman of her kind to take at this time but it is a decision through which Wharton makes an important statement about women's lives, their sexuality and their fertility.

In this novel Wharton switches adeptly between focalisers: the first chapter is Halo's, the second and third are Vance's, the fourth Halo's and so on. This means that even while Halo and Vance are together, their voices and feelings never converge completely; they have harmonious moments but in general Wharton's narrative technique ensures that they are seen as sharing little intimacy, either in intent or understanding. Vance is on a quest which is reflected in the restless wandering that takes him from America to Spain (Cordova, Granada, and Cadiz), France (Paris, Oubli-sur-Mer, Cannes, Nice), Monaco (Monte Carlo), England (London, Hindhead) and back to America (New York, Euphoria, Wisconsin, Chicago, Paul's Landing). It is, of course, significant that his final halt, where he is reunited with Halo, his first guide and mentor, is the sacred space of the Willows, a house that holds in its library the best in literary and historical writing. On a symbolic level, Vance's journey is elevated in the novel by Wharton's continual reference to great epic quests. His wanderings are frequently linked with those of Odysseus, Dante and Faust and the modernist text which haunts the narrative is, of course, the parodic quest of Joyce's *Ulysses*. However, any possible ennobling of Vance's quest or his character through such references is held in constant tension with Wharton's often distanced and ironic portrayal of him, expressed through the dual focalisation of his own and Halo's account of their relationship as well as through his crass lack of self-awareness. 'His apprentice days were over' (p. 16) he thinks cheerfully to himself at the beginning of a novel which goes on to reveal how deeply immature and inexperienced he is. Vance is a flawed hero but he is accepted as such by a sensitive, intelligent woman who bears with him through his most important quest: the painful journey towards emotional, moral and spiritual maturity.

On another level of his journey, Vance's desire to seek out 'the Mothers' – to plumb the depths of the mind in order to write with authority, originality and power – is gradually replaced in this novel by a retreat into self-doubt, darkness and solitude. The Mothers as abstract, mythic and symbolic figures, which can be annexed by the male, are finally replaced by the loving presence and greater wisdom of Halo.[7] His lonely sojourn in the forests of Belair in Wisconsin, where he reads *The Confessions of St. Augustine* is, for him, a dark night of the soul in which he plumbs the depths of himself rather than those of any mythological sphere. Out of this experience he emerges able to see Halo afresh and determined to redeem himself before attempting to commit himself to her fully. In the novel's last few pages we see him transformed from the utterly egocentric individual who set sail for Europe into a being who can at least acknowledge that he needs to work hard to pay proper attention to others and who recognises that it is 'The depth, and not the tumult, of the soul' that is valuable, both in art and life.[8] Like Goethe's Faust, he is saved not by God but by the development of his own humility and right-mindedness; he redeems himself, with some assistance from St Augustine. 'He who strives on and lives to strive/ Can earn redemption still' as Goethe puts it in Part Two of *Faust*. Faust's quest for God 'whether he recognizes it as such or not, is through the earth, through earthly Nature and earthly experience';[9] the same holds true for Vance, although it is not so much God he is seeking as the fountainhead of beauty, truth and meaning. Vance's quest is realised finally through a rejection of all that has previously seduced him – shallow male companionship, fame, literary coteries, Floss Delaney – and through physical retreat into the hemlock forests of Wisconsin where he engages with texts written many centuries ago. Appropriately, then, the last part of *The Gods Arrive*, with its quasi-mystical emphasis on the seasons, resurrection and the coming of a child, reaffirms the 'Goethean celebration of cyclic Nature and the process of eternal Becoming'.[10] The Gods arrive only at this moment; everything before, it is implied, was a world of 'half-gods': 'when half-gods go/The gods arrive' as Emerson put it in 'Give All to Love', the poem which provided Wharton with the title for her last completed novel. 'Oh me, how thankful I am to remember that, whether as to people or as to places & occasions, I've *always* known the gods the moment I met them', Wharton was to write in the last year of her life.[11]

The Gods Arrive, then, gives the reader a hero who regularly stumbles and falls and who, even at the close of the novel, is still struggling to eat 'the Food of the full-grown' (p. 418). Contemporary responses to the novel and its flawed hero and suffering heroine were mixed. Percy Hutchison, while praising the book in the *New York Times* as an interesting 'problem' novel that grappled with a postwar world of 'reduced stability', nevertheless noted that many readers 'may feel that any Vance Weston in real life would be deserving of having his neck wrung, as at best an unstable weakling, and at worst something of a cad'.[12] R. Ellis Roberts in *The New*

Statesman and Nation, suggested that Vance is 'not only more selfish, more inconsiderate, more stupid and less attractive than one's noble self: he is lower than any except the most vulgar nit-wits of one's acquaintance'.[13] In 1987, embracing a Second Wave Feminist perspective, Marilyn French described Vance as 'adolescent, self-involved, brusque, inconsiderate, childish, using people as means instead of ends and seeking above all not to suffer'.[14] All this and more is true; in Wharton's design Vance's many faults are deliberately foregrounded by the contrast his egocentricity, capriciousness, arrogance and volatility form with the selflessness, steadiness, humility and stability of Halo Tarrant. Wharton's critique of Vance, however, is implicit rather than explicit. As readers we must bear in mind that in both *Hudson River Bracketed* and *The Gods Arrive* the stereotyping of women occurs where Vance is the focaliser: his constructions of Laura Lou Tracy as child-wife, Floss Delaney as vamp and Halo Tarrant as mother-figure all derive from patriarchal assumptions that both contemporary and more recent readers have found jarring. As Diana Wallace has astutely suggested, however, Wharton's portrayal of Vance's often misogynistic attitudes to women is meant to expose 'masculinity as constructed and contingent, thus undermining its traditionally universalized and normative status'.[15] Wharton is here drawing attention – as she did in *The Mother's Recompense* and *The Children* – to how traditional, patriarchal cultural constructions of masculinity and femininity still haunt the modern mind in the 1920s and 1930s, despite the huge social changes prompted by the First World War and the winning of female suffrage. Rather than endorsing such stereotypes, she reveals in her last completed novel how they impede or even destroy men's emotional maturity and result in suffering and a lack of agency for women. When Vance decides, in the middle of his last, doomed pursuit of Floss, that 'Intellectual comradeship between lovers was unattainable; that was not the service women could render to men', he is uttering sentiments we know to be completely ill-founded, and indeed, risible – if for no other reason than that this particular pronouncement is followed by his determination that he will 'make [Floss] see that they belonged to each other, that they were necessary to each other, that their future meetings could not be left to depend on chance or whim. He meant to plead with her, reason with her, dominate her with the full strength of his will...' (pp. 390–1). We also know that 'intellectual comradeship' with Halo is waiting for him, which confirms that Wharton is here presenting him in the full light of her ironic gaze.

While continuing the thread of satire which informs most of the fiction Wharton wrote in the 1920s, *The Gods Arrive* offers a corrective to modern materialism and shallow living in its emphasis on the inner life and is particularly insistent on the role of pain in coming to moral and emotional maturity. In that respect, it is perhaps her most spiritual work – or at least it asks the questions that increasingly she felt to be essential in order to arrive at an understanding of life as authentic and meaningful. Vance's encounters with something numinous in various holy spaces are staging posts on his quest for a deeper understanding of life, one that has nothing to do with worldly success or material values.

These holy spaces are of two types: they are either religious buildings such as the Mezquita at Cordova and the church outside Paris where he witnesses a thunderstorm; or immense forests such as Fontainebleau in France and Belair in Wisconsin – although, as we shall see, the characteristics of each are somewhat interchangeable. It is these places that provide Vance with what Wharton calls elsewhere 'the illuminating incident',[16] during which he senses the infinite and the eternal, coming closest to those primal forces that, after Goethe, he describes as 'the Mothers'. On the other hand, the city locations in the novel, while they provide Vance with both stimulation and fashionable distractions, allow Wharton to exercise her satiric wit on literary patrons such as Mrs Glaisher and Lady Pevensey and on ersatz literary lions like Octavius Brant. Sylvia Beach – who published Joyce's *Ulysses* in 1922 after it had been refused by several other publishers – and her bookshop in Paris, 'Shakespeare & Co.' – are rather vindictively portrayed in Lorry Spear's partner, Jane Meggs, who is said to run 'a mysterious bookshop in the Latin Quarter' (p. 77). Wharton takes the opportunity here to have a joke with her contemporary readers, who would have instantly seen the parallel between Lorry's partner having changed her name from Jane Meggs to Violet Southernwood and Sylvia Beach having changed hers from Nancy Woodbridge Beach. The badinage of the Parisian artistic circles he encounters in the novel is eerily reminiscent of conversations in the Cocoanut Tree in New York, for both Vance and Halo as well as to the reader. The London literary scene is no different. Like their American counterparts, these European metropolitan avant-garde writers, artists and designers completely reject the past, of which they are deeply ignorant.

Wharton also revisits the figure of the failed writer and the dilettante in Alders and Chris Churley – both of whom are denoted in the kind of language Wharton reserved in her autobiography for acquaintances like Bay Lodge, who existed in a 'rarefied atmosphere of mutual admiration, and disdain of the rest of the world'[17] –with the result that they never actually achieve anything. Alders, who likens himself to Matthew Arnold's 'the Scholar Gipsy' (p. 45) but whom Halo thinks of as a 'dawdling Autolycus' (p. 48),[18] secures his future and an entrée into the fashionable set by becoming secretary to Mrs Glaisher. Chris Churley's life comes to a tragic end when he falls in front of a train at Toulon; his death, as his life, is without point and meaning. The fact that Vance feels himself partly responsible for Chris's death, having decided at the last minute to attempt to see Floss Delaney again rather than travel with his friend, is only one of several episodes that briefly cause him pain and remorse which are, however, all too quickly forgotten in his pursuit of self-gratification. Both Alders and Churley are parodic versions of Vance himself. Like Alders, he is easily lured away from his focus on one topic by other people and places, always convinced that he would be able to write better if he were somewhere else and, like Churley, he is self-obsessed, easily distracted from his current project and all too prone to spontaneous decisions which privilege immediate gratification over long-term commitment and effort. Alders and Churley are impressionable young men who, through their excited talk about art and literature, are permitted by Vance to sabotage his concentration on his own work and ideas; Vance's fundamental insecurity about his impoverished educational background and his dislike of learning anything from the lips of a woman, combine to render him susceptible to the 'cheap enthusiasms' (p. 87) they espouse. Halo's opinions are doomed to fall on deaf ears; before she even hears the first chapter of Vance's new novel, *Colossus*, she knows that it will be a disappointment since: 'Vance had been too much influenced by the stream-of-consciousness school which Jane's group proclaimed to a bewildered public to be the one model for modern fiction' (p. 108). Vance only recognises that she is right when the novel is published, the consensus being that 'it was much too long, nothing particular happened in it, and few people even pretended to know what it was about' (p. 355).

Wharton took a considerable risk in presenting the reader with such a flawed character as Vance Weston for her hero. She offsets his many faults, however, by giving him a capacity for imagination, vision and creativity. Because Vance is a writer we experience, vicariously, in Wharton's last two novels, the extremes of artistic experience that accompany the creative process: the restlessness, the struggle to make meaning out of life, the dissatisfaction with one's own work, the failure to realise one's vision, 'the poverty of all words' (p. 26) in the face of love and the sublime – but also the ability to experience the numinous and the infinite through the imagination and thus to transcend the ordinary, the banal and the merely material. Despite the 'tumult' he undergoes, Vance feels himself blessed as a writer: 'as always in the full tide of invention, he felt himself possessed by a brooding spirit of understanding, some mystic reassurance which sea and sky and the life of men transmitted from sources deeper than the reason' (p. 187). As Penelope Vita-Finzi has pointed out, the language that Wharton uses to describe Vance's experience of inspiration – 'divine', 'dream' 'vision', 'soul', 'spirit', 'mysteries', 'mystical' – echoes that which she uses to describe her own; the 'nature of...artistic experience defies direct description and can only ...be conveyed through the language of the spirit, and through suggestion and symbol'.[19] For a novelist trying to document such experience, however, this conundrum poses real problems, as we have noted earlier and in the previous chapter.

Wharton's detailed descriptions of Vance's four visionary experiences, or epiphanies, in *The Gods Arrive*, are meant to convey to the reader something of the mystical nature of inspiration. If we fail to grasp the significance of these, then we have failed to read the novel imaginatively, since nature and culture combine at such moments to provide Vance with inspiration and renewed energy. Wharton here inverts her language, using images of architecture to describe nature and images of nature to describe the architectural spaces where Vance has his visions, in an attempt to convey to the reader the intensity of his experience. In effect, she melds nature and culture in order to communicate a sense of the mystical just as she had years earlier when discussing the impact of Turner's 'Road to Orvieto' on the traveller who, later viewing the actual landscape, 'pausing by the arched bridge above the valley loses sense of the boundaries between art and life, and lives for a moment in that mystical region where the two are one'.[20] In addition, the metaphors deriving from building and architecture that informed *Hudson River Bracketed* are developed in this novel to suggest not only Vance's soaring aspirations but also the concentration on form and structure necessary to bring any artistic impulse to fruition. The author must be craftsman as well as visionary and must appreciate the craft of others – whether human or divine.

Accordingly, en route to Cordova (now known as Cordoba) and its Mezquita, Vance sees the Spanish sky as 'full of cloud-architecture', the 'cloud ramparts' resting 'like marble stairways on the hills' (pp. 20–1) as the sun sets. Vance's reflection on these cloud formations as like the ladders that 'Jacob's angels went up and down' prepares the ground for his experience in the Mezquita as mystical and sublime, marking him as one able to experience the transcendental in the here and now.[21] Many readers, including several American critics, have taken Wharton's use of the word 'cathedral' at a limited and limiting face value in this part of the novel. In fact, although the sacred space which Vance and Halo explore has officially been a Christian church for some centuries, the cathedral at Cordova is housed within one of the most magnificent mosques in the world, itself refashioned from a Christian Visigothic church begun in 600 AD which, in turn, was built on the site of a Roman temple. The mosque was begun in 784 and completed in 987, its outer courtyard, full of orange trees, designed to extend architecture into nature and vice versa. When the mosque, originally unwalled, was used for prayer during the period of Muslim dominance, the intense Spanish sunshine would filter through from the courtyard so that the 784 interior columns of its 19 naves took on the appearance of an infinite vista of palm trees. The capture of Cordova from the Muslims in 1236 resulted in the mosque being reclaimed as a Christian church, but the most significant alteration was made during the reign of Charles V, when a Renaissance cathedral nave was built in the middle of the structure. However, the building is dominated by its Muslim character and is still known as 'the Mezquita' by the inhabitants of Cordova.

Like the Willows, then, the Mezquita of Cordova literally embodies different ages and aspects of the spiritual, this time sacred rather than secular, making it another version of 'the palimpsest of later impressions' which Wharton uses in her unpublished autobiography, 'Life and I' to signify the accretions of ages and events.[22] The Mezquita takes Vance into a sacred space and a far distant past; in an attempt to understand its sublime nature, he likens its interior to both an ocean and a sky (p. 21). But it is the 'dim network of architectural forms' that creates this experience, art creating the illusion of nature. For a moment, in which the arabesques of Muslim architecture become conflated with the depths in which one finds the Mothers, Vance is completely overwhelmed: he 'felt as if he had dropped over the brim of things into the mysterious world where straight lines loop themselves into curves' (p. 21). There is no possibility of becoming distracted by the figurative, excluded as it is from the decoration of sacred Islamic monuments, so that Vance and Halo become temporarily disorientated by the repetitive, mesmerising beauty of the Mezquita, and Vance 'remembered a passage in the Second Faust which had always haunted him: the scene where Faust descends to the Mothers. "He must have wound round and round like this", he thought' (p. 23). Still lost in the labyrinth of pillars, Vance thinks:

> of the Cretan labyrinth, of Odysseus evoking the mighty dead, of all the subterranean mysteries on whose outer crusts man loves and fights and dies. The blood was beating in his ears. He began to

wish that they might never find the right door, but go on turning about forever at the dark heart of things. They walked and walked. After a while Halo asked: 'Are you really tired?' like Eurydice timidly guiding Orpheus back to daylight…and he thought: 'How funny that she doesn't know what I'm feeling!' He longed to sit down at the foot of one of the glimmering shafts and let the immensity and the mystery sweep over him like the sea. (p. 23)

Wharton is clearly trying here to express in fiction '*how it is all* done, and exactly what happens at that "fine point of the soul", where the creative act, like the mystic's union with the Unknowable, really seems to take place'.[23] Moreover, the references to Jacob, Faust, Odysseus and Orpheus, coming thick and fast in this chapter, seem to elevate Vance's quest to the level of epic; his journey, here presented without irony, is both physical and metaphysical. Such references also set him apart from Halo who, well-educated and well-organised, does not want him to have a partial education or to misunderstand, and so defaults to the guidebook: 'the choir, the high-altar, the Christian cathedral built inside' (p. 22). No matter how much they love each other and how much they share, Halo and Vance perceive place, self and others in ways that are profoundly different and therefore fatally separate. Halo finds that 'the bright confusion of his mind sometimes charmed and sometimes frightened her' (p. 41) and gradually realises that 'in throwing in her lot with Vance's she had entered into an unknown country' (p. 42) – a country that encompasses not only a sense of the numinous but also beings who are awkward with clever or socially adept women. Vance is content with the random, the unpredictable and the precipitate; the fact that he makes mistakes does not bother him or haunt him; remorse and regret are alien to his nature. The quest that Halo has embarked upon, whether she realises it or not, is to leave behind those aspects of her femininity that make her weak and vulnerable. She needs, in order to come to terms with life with Vance Weston, to become more like him, to think and behave more like a man: she has to dispense with self-doubt, with guilt and with shame. Early in the novel she tries to redefine what constitutes the shameful when thinking about her life with Tarrant: 'Now it was her past that she was ashamed of, not her present; there were lyric moments when her flight with Vance seemed like an expiation' (p. 34) – but she gets no support in this from him and she understandably falters. She also has to learn how to take control of her sexuality – and she eventually does so in the interview with Lewis Tarrant in Paris after Vance has returned to America and, most importantly, when she asserts her right to live in her own way with her child at the Willows. Wharton makes it clear that Vance's sensibility is that of the artist: intense and acute, it both sets him apart and yet also makes him susceptible to the power of the superficial. Wharton makes him reverberate to both the sublime and the ridiculous and Halo – who cannot supply either – is forced into the background. Having experienced the sublime, Vance emerges from the Mezquita, feeling 'like a disembodied spirit coming back to earth' (p. 23). What he felt in the Mezquita is described by Wharton elsewhere as 'the most precious emotion that such a building inspires: reverence for the accumulated experiences of the past', a moment in which 'enfranchisement of thought exists in harmony with atavism of feeling'.[24] Such accumulation takes place on a more personal level when, later in the evening, the branches outside the hotel remind Vance of the apple boughs that had produced a visionary moment when he was nursing Laura Lou. This rich 'leaf-mould' of personal memory and of cultural history – described by Wharton as 'essential to the nurture of new growths of art' – results in Vance feeling a fresh wave of inspiration.[25]

The differences between Vance and Halo are illustrated again by her organisation of a trip – 'a kind of spiritual honeymoon' (p. 79) – to the Cathédrale Notre-Dame de Chartres in northern France. Constructed on the site of the old cathedral of Chartres, its building began in 1205 and took 66 years to complete. Halo assumes that this magnificent Gothic edifice, renowned for its stained glass windows, will have the same emotional impact on Vance as did the Mezquita in Cordova. However, it does not: 'when at last he was face to face with the cathedral, he couldn't see it. He stood there, a little lump of humanity, confronting a great lump of masonry' (p. 80). Vance's mind is 'full of his new book' (p. 81); he is 'lost in the visionary architecture of his inner world' (p. 205) and is therefore blind to the immediate architectural beauty about him. Resistance to the guidebook experience also becomes, sadly, resistance to Halo; her eagerness to ensure that Vance experiences the best and the brightest, the highlights of her childhood tours of Europe with her wandering, impecunious parents, becomes a stick with which Vance can beat her once he decides that what he needs is not culture but the 'dark raptures' that he imagines Floss Delaney's all too corporeal body will yield to him. However, a month after the fateful visit to Chartres, a chance trip with Tolby and Savignac results in another mystical experience for Vance. Driving fifty miles out of the French capital for a day in the countryside so that his friends might do some fishing, they are forced to stop by a sudden thunderstorm. While Tolby and Savignac drive the car to a local garage for a quick check, Vance takes the opportunity to take

shelter in a small and seemingly unremarkable church. His thoughts are, once again, 'all tangled up in his new novel' (p. 82) but this time nature clashing with culture seizes him by the throat:

> a flash illuminated the walls of glass, and celestial fields of azure and rose suddenly embowered him. In another instant all was dark, as if obliterated by the thunder following the flash; then the incandescence began again – a flowering of magical sky-gardens in which every heavenly hue blossomed against a blue as dazzling as sunlight; and after each flowering came extinction.
>
> Vance sat among these bursts of glory and passages of darkness as if alternate cantos of the Paradiso and the Inferno were whirling through him...To his companions he said no word of it; he did not even ask the name of the town. (pp. 82–3)

This sudden and unexpected fusion of extreme weather and art – the lightening illuminating man-made stained glass and the moment itself infused with lines from Dante – gives Vance a 'fragment of heaven torn from the storm in the unknown church' (p. 83). As Penelope Vita-Finzi notes, in these late novels, 'Art and life become one in contemplation of a scene familiar from a painting, or when the scene is illuminated by reference to art'.[26] He has, he thinks to himself, 'secreted treasures unsuspected by [Halo]' (p. 83); like Wharton, who described her imagination as her 'secret garden',[27] Vance's creative inner world is his alone, he is insistent that she stays outside it. Like Proust, he chooses a necessary isolation; as in Goethe's *Faust*, the word 'treasures' refers not to actual riches but to moments of insight and creative inspiration.

The forest at Fontainebleau provides the next sacred space. On a sudden impulse born of a desire to escape the city and people, Vance takes a train from Paris one evening and finds accommodation in a small inn on the edge of the forest where he sleeps 'the dreamless sleep of the runaway schoolboy' (p. 113). Like Faust's transportation to ancient Greece during Walpurgis Night in Part One of Goethe's play, however, Vance's adventure here is also a flight from reality.[28] The next day he roams in the forest, feeling his way into the past through the ancient trees whose branches are 'heavy with memory' (p. 113). Wandering through areas of bracken, rocks, birch trees and oaks, he begins to feel healed by the 'endless' forest: 'In its all-embracing calm his nervous perturbations ceased. Face to face with this majesty of nature...he felt the same deep union with earth that once or twice in his life he had known by the seashore' (p. 114). Alone with his thoughts, Vance comes to realise that the current orthodoxy concerning the novel – that 'in fiction the only hope of renewal was in the exploration of the subliminal' (p. 115) – is misguided:

> The fishers in the turbid stream-of-consciousness had reduced their fictitious characters to a bundle of loosely tied instincts and habits, borne along blindly on the current of existence. (p. 116)

As previously noted, the novel is laced with sentiments that resonate strongly with Wharton's own pronouncements, not least in *The Writing of Fiction* where she remarks that, in reacting against the dominance of plot, contemporary authors:

> have gone too far in the other direction, either swamping themselves in the tedious 'stream of consciousness', or else – another frequent error – giving an exaggerated important to trivial incidents when the tale is concerned with trivial lives. (p. 102)

Wharton endows Vance with her own desire both to adapt the techniques of modernism while simultaneously imbuing the 'average man' with integrity and purpose, pitting him 'against the petty chaos of Jane Megg's world' (p. 116). The title of his new book, *Colossus*, is – unlike, of course, Joyce's *Ulysses* – 'not wholly ironic' (p. 116), since in it Vance will reject the nihilism and cynicism to be found in much contemporary writing. In another reference to her favourite author, Wharton has Vance think dreamily about Faust's Walpurgis ride while he rests after lunch in the forest. Goethe's odd and comic-satanic scenes, 'A Walpurgis Night' and 'A Walpurgis Night's Dream', in Part One of *Faust* contain a number of satirical references directed at several figures of the German literary scene, probably comprehensible only to the inner circle of his contemporaries.[29] The reader is reminded, then, both of previous cliques and sets whose misguided ideas were influential and of the parallel between Goethe's Faust – the visionary and immature idealist – and Vance Weston. But it is his visionary nature that enables Vance to recognise the beauty and mysterious depths of the forest as healing: 'what he needed was this tireless renewal of earth's functions, the way of a forest with the soul...' (p. 117). And, indeed, his visual and verbal imagination have already been rekindled by his time in the forest through a mixture of received and felt experience: 'He thought of purple grapes on hot trellises, of the amber fires of Poussin's "Poet and the Muse", of Keats's mists and mellow fruitfulness, and the blue lightening-lit windows in the nameless church' (p. 117).[30]

It is at this moment when, lost in the forest, he comes across a beautiful young woman, 'as sunlit and mysterious as his mood' (p. 117), asleep on a bank. Here Vance changes from being the subjective focaliser of the scene to becoming an object of Wharton's ironic scrutiny. Poetically idealising the girl, he sees her as a mythical creature, as a dryad whose 'slim arched feet...looked as if feathers might grow from them when she stirred' (p. 117) and as Diana, to whom he would play Endymion.[31] Despite her vulnerability and beauty, Vance dismisses the temptation to think of her sexually for 'she must remain a part of his dream, a flicker of light among the leaves' (p. 118). As he turns away, he sees approaching a 'stoutish common-looking young man with a straw hat tilted back on his head, and a self-satisfied smile on a coarse lip...' who 'walked jauntily, swinging his stick' (p. 119) – no doubt the young woman's boyfriend. For Vance 'the world of earthly things re-entered the forest' and, while not resenting the young man's presence, he feels a sense of bathos, for 'he wanted something rarer in his memory of the forest', to preserve his 'mysterious goddess of the cross-roads' (p. 119) in mythic form. Wharton's description of the boyfriend perhaps slyly evokes not only Joyce (who was often pictured wearing a straw hat and swinging his walking cane, or stick) but also Joyce's alter ego, Stephen Dedalus – for Vance's chancing upon a beautiful young woman clearly resonates with the end of Section 4 of *A Portrait of the Artist as a Young Man*. In this episode of Joyce's novel, Stephen, wandering on the seashore, thinking himself alone, comes across a beautiful girl, wading in the water. Joyce's language suggests both divine and erotic qualities in the young girl, whose beauty Stephen finds ecstatically inspiring: 'To live, to err, to fall, to triumph, to recreate life out of life! A wild angel had appeared to him...'.[32] The chapter ends with Stephen resting in a sandy nook of the dunes where, Joyce's language suggests, he masturbates before finally leaving the beach. Wharton, it seems, has reworked Joyce's scene, rejecting its erotic dimension and implying, perhaps, a critique of Joyce's 'schoolboy' vulgarity. Taking his inspiration where he often unexpectedly finds it, the artist – Wharton here implies – must strive to transform the stuff of life into art, rather than reducing it to the trivial, the vulgar or the banal. Like Faust's 'Mothers', his concern must be metamorphosis and rebirth: 'Formation, transformation,/ The eternal Mind's delectation' (*Faust Part Two*, p. 53). And like Faust himself, who is revitalised spiritually and physically by his sojourn in Greece during Walpurgis Night, Vance leaves Fontainebleau uplifted and realises that 'the girl in the forest' (p. 121) will form the subject of his first chapter in the new book. He spends the next day writing feverishly, feeling that he has plunged 'into the depths' (p. 122). Yet, on returning to Halo, he sees *her* as the girl in the forest: 'Do you know I could have sworn I saw you yesterday in the forest, asleep under a white umbrella?' (p. 124). Later the girl also becomes confused with Floss: 'Floss Delaney's brown shoulders flashed like the dryad's in the Fontainebleau woods' (p. 239). Wharton's purpose here is to show how Vance's masculine poetic sensibility derives from a cultural mythicising of women that blinds him to their individuality. We do not, of course, hear Halo liken either Vance or any of their male acquaintances to Apollo or Dionysus.[33] As Dianne L. Chambers has noted, 'Wharton asks her readers to attend carefully to her male narrators, who appear heroic but, ultimately, define and inaccurately portray female protagonists... Wharton's consistently ironic voice sets up a kind of double text that both tells a story and comments on that story simultaneously'.[34]

Such blindness is another aspect of Vance's immaturity, albeit one culturally and historically endorsed by a society in which male artists still tended to see women either as muse or mere subject matter.[35] We are therefore also invited to read the curious episode of the girl in the forest ironically. For Vance, despite his conflation of Halo and later Floss with the sleeping young girl and his lofty Puritan-in-France ideals, is easily sexually aroused by beautiful women, not least the sultry Floss, with whom he betrays Halo. Floss's seductive sexuality and voluptuous 'indolent beauty' (p. 212) are communicated through Wharton's constant emphasis on her body with its 'warm dusky pallor...[and] glints of red under skin' (p. 209). She is always associated with heat – her arms are frequently described as 'warm' and 'brown' (p. 223), looking like 'sun-warmed marble' (p. 241) or 'like amber in the moonlight' (p. 264) – and Vance's sexual desire for her is made clear: 'her nearness burned into his flesh' (p. 299). Intriguingly, the early, sexually active Floss, the young woman physically aware and almost feral in her appetites – sleeping with Vance's predatory grandfather (who had nothing of material advantage to offer her) as well as with Vance, and leaving Euphoria for another man, 'the fellow who kept her at Dakin' (p. 405) – disappears from view. Floss teases Vance but she is always too tired or too busy to respond to his expressed desires. All her sexual energy is channelled into her newly discovered entrepreneurial drive; as her own father says: 'You think she's all impulse, do you? Well...you wait and see her stow away those impulses if they interfere with any of her plans. Sometimes, you know, I think the inside of my daughter is a combination of a ticker and a refrigerator' (p. 234). However, it is not until she reveals that she has blackmailed the Shunts that Vance ceases to be mesmerised by her physical presence. By contrast, Halo – who is about the same age as Floss – assumes an ascetic and older appearance in Vance's consciousness: 'Halo had fine lines, but was too thin, the bones in her neck were too visible' (p. 212). Floss, like Halo, wants freedom above all else but for her this has nothing to do with emotional independence or integrity and everything to do with money and power. Vance's mistake is not merely erotic, however; he misconstrues her for an 'archway to the infinite' (p. 210) and a source of energy, 'a dark night, a hurrying river' (p. 302). He even sees his powerful desire for her as something that will deliver the authenticity he so craves: 'Vance knew there were selves under selves in him, and that one of the undermost belonged to Floss Delaney' (p. 264). Wharton could not be clearer than she is in *The Gods Arrive* about the self-deluding sophistry upon which many of her male characters base their actions: Vance finds himself torn between the two women, at one point even hoping 'to make [Halo] understand that a man may love one woman with all his soul while he is perishing for the nearness of another' (p. 265). Like Martin Boyne, beguiled into thinking that Judith Wheater wants him for a lover not a father, or Dexter Manford, so puffed up with hanging onto his youth and sexual attractiveness he forgets that the shallow young woman in his bedroom is his stepson's wife, Vance casts aside the real and invests in the fantasy woman. Goethe's lines 'In me there are two souls, alas, and their/ Division tears my life in two' (*Faust Part One*, pp. 15–16) resonate in more ways than one in *The Gods Arrive*.

As already mentioned, Wharton focalises over half of the novel through Vance's consciousness, using this technique as a vehicle to examine not only how a man's understanding can so easily become constrained by cultural constructions of women but also to explore how the writer's imagination works – including the frustrations of authorship and the drive to translate experience into language. And, despite all his failures, the reader remains interested in Vance because of his energy, his striving, his commitment to art, his capacity for experiencing the spiritual, his vision, his imagination. The psychological questions that David Luke sees as raised by Goethe's *Faust* also form the agenda of Wharton's novel:

How does a complex and creative human psyche achieve maturity? What are the integrative, relaxing, 'epic' processes of growth in an exceptional and developing personality? What kind of poetic or spiritual journey (an *epic* journey, comparable to that undertaken by Dante in the *Divine Comedy*) must be made by this new explorer? (Luke, *Faust Part Two*, p. xviii)

Like Faust, Vance is an explorer; he is complex and creative but a part of his exceptionality is his childishness, his still developing personality. In creating the character of Vance Weston, Wharton draws on much of her own experience as a writer. However, she also uses him to offer a critique of the culture that produced him, which she considers both patriarchal and shallow; this is a culture that encourages men, especially male artists, to denigrate women and to refuse to accord them equal status intellectually and creatively – to see them as either sex object or as a nurturing mother figure. As in *The Children*, where Wharton invoked the girl-woman socially constructed as nymph and therefore key to the sexual reinvigoration of the older male as a fatal distraction from the love of a mature and sensitive woman, so her male artist Vance sees women in a bifurcated way and, in so doing, still cannot take responsibility for his own feelings. Here he vaunts celibacy as the only alternative to the erotic life:

Two women people these agitated vigils; the one that his soul rejected and his body yearned for, the other who had once seemed the answer to all he asked of life...The whole question of woman was the age-long obstacle to peace of spirit and fruitfulness of mind; to get altogether away from it, contrive a sane and productive life without it, became the obsession of his sleepless midnights. All he wanted was to be himself, solely and totally himself, not tangled up in the old deadly nets of passion and emotion. (p. 414)

Yet Vance does not free himself from this sense of the split or helpless self until – at the very end of the novel – he is able to accept Halo as a separate being and as a soul-mate. The fact that Halo is still willing to accept Vance and even collude with the very values which Wharton critiques ironically in the novel is bewildering only if she is seen in isolation from Wharton's other most significant women protagonists. The line of descent from Lily Bart has already been noted but there are others who contribute to her eventual declaration of autonomy and strength – not least Kate Clephane from *The Mother's Recompense*.

In *Hudson River Bracketed* (*HRB*) Wharton presented Halo Spear positively as a complex young woman whose weaknesses – including a forgetfulness that sometimes caused pain to others – were a part of her charm. One of Wharton's most attractive female characters, Halo is generous, compassionate, witty, good-tempered, imaginative and idealistic, qualities that do not diminish as she ages. For her, 'Books have souls, like people...' (*HRB*, p. 119). Her romantic nature sometimes combines with spontaneity to produce impulsive behaviour that seems somewhat reckless to her family and friends but attractive to the reader and to Vance. She has an intense love of nature and, given her sensibilities, it is not surprising that Halo finds a kindred spirit in Vance, realising that 'here was someone with whom [her treasures] might be shared' (*HRB*, p. 88). She sees 'a latent power under his unformed boyish manner' (*HRB*, p. 91) that she finds deeply attractive. As the novel progresses, Halo acquires an additional wisdom and quiet dignity that make her seem considerably older than the novel's hero and, indeed, she frequently thinks of him as much younger than herself. The emotional relationship between the older woman and the younger man that Wharton explored in *The Mother's Recompense* and *The Children* is here played out in a different key but with results that make the woman less a victim and more the mistress of her own destiny.

The 'little thrill of feminine submission' (p. 6) with which *The Gods Arrive* opens is partly, Wharton intimates, due to Halo's upbringing but it is also an assertion of her own powers of discrimination and taste. Vance is the real thing for her, his resilient ego is one of his attractions as she no longer has to spend her time tiptoeing around the insubstantial, fragile and spoilt Lewis Tarrant. Despite an intellectually and aesthetically rich home environment, Halo has been subject to certain limitations; her parents' assumption that 'a Lorburn woman might be beautiful, or masterful, or distinguished, but never anything so ambiguous as "clever"' (*HRB*, p. 79) suggests that even in liberal American circles at this time certain gender expectations were still upheld. In addition, Halo's rich husband provided the means whereby her parents could be kept in the manner to which they aspired. The intellectual constraints are recognisably those that Wharton herself had to confront when growing up in the world of Old New York and that she documents in many of her fictions. Lee notes that when she was writing *Hudson River Bracketed*, Wharton was corresponding frequently with Zona Gale, whom she never met, but who was also writing about the limitations on the lives of American women.[36] Although Halo is financially independent at the start of *The Gods Arrive* – a cousin's legacy having made her 'a free woman' (p. 10) – she is not 'free' in the deepest sense of the word. She discovers that 'free love was not the simple experiment she had imagined' (p. 84), especially when her relationship with Vance brings social disapproval; she is 'cut' by Mrs Glaisher in

Paris, admonished by her own brother and rejected by Mrs Churley in Oubli-sur-mer because she is living with Vance while still married to Lewis Tarrant. She is also far from free psychologically. Having decided to 'serve the genius' (p. 30) of the man she loves, she even experiments with a little fantasy about Vance as 'strong and decided' which involves seeing herself, as they sail for Europe, as 'the weak inexperienced one' (p. 6). The events of the novel, however, prove otherwise, despite Halo's anxiety about sliding into the role of 'the blindly admiring wife' (p. 41). Her efficiency, practicality, generosity, dignity, insight into character, stoicism and wisdom become more and more evident as Vance travels from one place to another and turns from one person to another in his restless search for inspiration and understanding. 'Beauty, order and reasonableness' (p. 85) remain important for Halo throughout the turmoil of their relationship and, left alone, she comes to realise 'how deeply rooted in her were the old instincts of order and continuity' (p. 312). Such priorities clearly echo those of Wharton herself, who chose to have Thomas Traherne's 'Order the beauty even of beauty is' reproduced on the title page of *The Writing of Fiction*. Indeed, in the face of Vance's misjudgements, inner confusions, betrayals and irresponsible behaviour, Halo keeps order and stays remarkably calm while acknowledging to herself that she has sacrificed her own needs on the altar of his 'genius':

> everything had been done not for herself but for Vance. She had no longer cared to make her life comely for its own sake; she thought of it only in relation to her love for Vance. (p. 104)

During Vance's liaison with Floss Delaney, when he cruelly shuts Halo out of his life and she is left alone in the French Mediterranean village of Oubli-sur-mer, she turns to gardening (another of Wharton's passions) as consolation and is thereby linked with growth and nurturance, despite the lonely sadness of her situation – 'The seeds she had sown in the spring – phlox, zinnia, larkspur, poppy – contended in a bonfire of bloom' (p. 309). But Halo, like the father of her child, also grows through suffering. She does not find it difficult to resist the temptation offered by Lewis Tarrant, still legally her husband, to resume her marriage and thereby secure material comfort and social approbation for herself and her unborn child; in fact, her resistance signals the new strength she has found in acknowledging both her sexual and reproductive capacities. In this state of emotional crisis, Halo sees herself as not only ageing – '"I'm an old woman," she thought' (p. 330) – but, again like Kate Clephane at the end of *The Mother's Recompense*, as also ghostly and insubstantial – she has no place in the society she derives from; she is a truly new woman. She announces to Lewis that she wants to reclaim her freedom and independence: 'I want to be alone; to go my own way, without depending on anybody. I want to be Halo Spear again – that's all' (p. 368). It is also at this point that Halo – anticipating Grandma Scrimser's dying words 'as if being happy was the whole story!' (p. 375) – accepts the necessity of pain:

> Don't we all make each other unhappy, sooner or later – often without knowing it? I sometimes think I've got beyond happiness or unhappiness – I don't feel as if I were made for them anymore. (p. 368)

Ironically, then, it is only when she and Vance are able to break free of each other that they finally reach emotional maturity and recognise the nature of their life together. This period of separation and withdrawal, however, is linked for both characters with a deathly coldness. Halo is described frequently as experiencing physical coldness ('her cold hands', p. 357) and feeling ghost-like (pp. 313 and 358) and Vance retreats to the 'stark woods and frozen waters' (p. 412) of Wisconsin in order to reflect on his life.

It is Grandma Scrimser's dying words that prompt the necessary change in Vance. Her refusal to ratify mere romance or desire and her insistence on the importance of marriage – 'it's the worries that make married folks sacred to each other' (p. 374) – echoes Frenside's advice to Halo that marriage 'shapes life...prevents growing lopsided or drifting' (p. 317). And Grandma's Scrimser's final words to Vance – 'Maybe we haven't made enough of pain' (p. 409) – affect him deeply and set him on the final lap of his quest: 'Those last words of his grandmother's might turn out to be the clue to his labyrinth' (p. 411). And, indeed, it is only when he reads *The Confessions of Saint Augustine* in the cold landscape of the hemlock forests that Vance realises that accepting pain and responsibility are part of what it means to be adult: 'he felt that at last he was ready to taste of the food of the full-grown, however bitter to the lips it might be' (p. 419). The bout of pneumonia that follows this epiphany, like his illness at the beginning of *Hudson River Bracketed*, acts as a rite of passage. Rising from his sick-bed and walking gingerly in the weak spring sunshine, he feels he now has 'eyes cleansed by solitude', that allow himself to see 'a new world' (p. 419). He emerges from his retreat at Belair with a determination to return to the Willows and to rethink himself and his life. This last section of the novel, redolent with biblical language and images of resurrection, also reflects something of Goethe's *Faust*, in which '[t]he doctrine of transformation as being vital to development, of dying in order to become, of self-obliteration in the interest of something higher, is fundamental...'.[37] *The Gods Arrive*, as well as addressing the nature of creativity, also carries a spiritual dimension that marks it as one of Wharton's final works, the product of her last few years, during which she became increasingly drawn to the Christian faith and, in particular, to Catholicism.[38]

However, as we have seen, the novel does not only explore the difficulties facing a young male writer born into a materialistic culture and an educationally impoverished family background, but also probes the social and psychological constraints imposed on a gifted young woman during the 1920s and 1930s. The character of Halo Spear did not arrive in Wharton's last two completed novels without antecedents and Wharton herself is as important an antecedent here as Lily Bart, Kate Clephane and Rose Sellars. Like Wharton, Halo was taken to Europe as a child and as a consequence became rather detached from America; like Halo, Wharton had a wealthy aunt (Elizabeth Schemerhorn Jones) 'who lived alone in the ugly "Hudson River Gothic" house of Rhinecliff';[39] both feel great frustration at the inadequacy and narrowness of the American education system; both brim with ideas and works that remain unfinished;[40] both are fluent in German and see Goethe 'as a model for reading European culture';[41] both marry men with whom they are not really compatible; both are dedicated gardeners and have the ability to create domestic order wherever they live; and, like Wharton, Halo wishes above all to be independent. Unlike Wharton, however, she has no faith in her own creative talents. Halo Spear, then, is what a woman like Edith Wharton might have become had she not fulfilled her potential as a writer. It is perhaps no coincidence that Halo's full name, Héloïse, recalls Rousseau's famous novel *Julie, ou la nouvelle Héloïse* (1760), in which the heroine marries yet continues to love another man. Wharton's oblique reference to Rousseau might also remind readers of his thoughts on the education of men and women in Book V of *Emile: or, On Education* (1762), in which the author stipulates that Sophie is not to be educated in the same way as Emile, since 'The education of women should always be relative to that of men. To please, to be useful to us, to make us love and esteem them, to educate us when young, to take care of us when grown up, to advise, to console us, to render our lives easy and agreeable; these are the duties of women at all times, and what they should be taught in their infancy'.[42] This aspect of Western intellectual thought is played out fully in Halo's apparent self-renunciation in *The Gods Arrive*.

While Vance is suddenly endowed with the qualities of a remorseful disciple and putative great writer, Halo's emotional generosity, in taking him back after all that has happened, is transformed by Wharton into the spiritual grace of a Madonna:

> He raised his eyes to her, and she moved across the room and stood before him. With a kind of tranquil gravity she lifted up her arms in the ancient attitude of prayer.
>
> For a moment his brow kept its deep furrows of bewilderment; then he gave a start and went up to her with illuminated eyes.
>
> 'You see we belong to each other after all', she said; but as her arms sank about his neck he bent his head and put his lips to a fold of her loose dress. (p. 439)

Readers have found various ways to resolve their discomfort at what seems here to be Wharton's reaffirmation of gender stereotypes and her need for a quasi-religious – some might say sentimental – conclusion to her last completed novel. Abby H.P. Werlock, for example, sees Halo as a portrait of Wharton herself and Vance as based on Morton Fullerton. She develops this *roman à clef* approach into an argument that 'Not Vance but Halo is the dominant figure...The Faustian mothers to whom Vance refers repeatedly as the source of poetic inspiration, but whom he has been unable to call forth, [become] instead embodied in Halo, pregnant, at the novel's end'.[43] Julie Olin-Ammentorp, on the other hand, turns to Kristevan theory to retrieve Halo from her 'secondary' status. Drawing parallels between Kristeva's comments on the nature of the Virgin Mary in her essay 'Stabat Mater' and Wharton's portrayal of Halo, Olin-Ammentorp argues that 'Vance's embrace of the symbol of religious and literal maternality signifies...his return to the preverbal, the unarticulated', or what Kristeva calls the semiotic realm. This, she concludes, is Vance's real return to 'the Mothers' for whom he has been searching all along.[44] There have been other conciliatory readings, of course, including the idea that Wharton imbues both Vance and Halo with aspects of herself and that the child Halo is carrying and the book in Vance's mind become interchangeable at the end of the novel. Vance's belief that the novel is 'a live thing that's got to be carried inside of you before it can be born' (p. 49) and Halo's 'praying for that next book as lonely wives pray for a child' (p. 88) certainly make such an interpretation viable. This fusion of artistic creativity and actual birth can also be seen as Wharton symbolically reconciling the conflicting selves within herself that go to make up the writer.[45] Indeed, for Stephanie Lewis Thompson, the very form of *Hudson River Bracketed* and *The Gods*

Arrive, and particularly their dual focalisation, 'reiterates that Vance and Halo are two halves of a creative personality'.[46] She also sees Wharton's positive portrayal of Halo as challenging 'the pervading assumption that a masculine modernist aesthetic offered a positive alternative to a degraded, feminized, middlebrow culture' although she concedes that Halo's 'revolutionary potential [being] ultimately linked to her maternity also reminds us of Wharton's uneasiness about the position of the woman in the modern world, an uneasiness that resounded earlier in the fate of Charity at the end of *Summer*'.[47]

However, it is also possible to read Wharton's *The Gods Arrive* as, in part, a response to Annie E. Holdsworth Hamilton's novel, similarly entitled *The Gods Arrive*, published in 1897, just as *The Mother's Recompense* was in part a response to Grace Aguilar's earlier novel of the same title. Hamilton's work is a weak, blatantly anti-New Woman novel, both reactionary and sentimental, particularly in relation to rural life and traditional roles for men and women. Her heroine, Katherine Fleming, an intelligent, forceful and energetic young woman who has been educated at Newnham College, Cambridge University, grows thin and neurasthenic while working as a successful journalist in London and campaigning on behalf of the Labour Movement. Her enforced return to the family farm in Hampshire restores both her health and her femininity, despite various family crises and the suicide of her younger brother's girlfriend (who, as a woman of spirit and an independent horse-trainer, is clearly bound to come to a sad end). Separated by a series of misunderstandings from the man she loves, Richard Franklin, also a political activist in London, Katherine embarks on a book entitled *The History of the Labour Movement*, only to suppress it when she finds out that he has written a pamphlet with the same title. Abandoning her desire to be a published author of an important historical work, and handing over the management of the farm to her brothers, she devotes herself to philanthropic work in the village, concentrating on the women and children. Her reconciliation with Franklin in the novel's last few pages is redolent with biblical imagery, meant to suggest a profound transformation in both herself and her relationship with him:

> The temple she had built should be a home for the People...
> A great light shone on her face.
> Franklin stopped...She had recognised him! ...No, not yet. Her eyes gazed beyond him as if the saw a vision of angels.[48]

Several similarities between this novel and Wharton's suggest that perhaps Wharton had read the earlier work: Hamilton has Franklin quote from Emerson's poem in the first chapter and the narrator refers to the 'half-gods' and the 'gods' arriving throughout the novel; her heroine has 'soft bright hair', described as standing out 'round her head halo-wise' (p. 28) and as surrounding her face 'like a halo' (p. 343); and, most importantly, the novel takes suffering, transformation and growth to maturity as its theme. But in Hamilton's novel, the gods arrive for Katherine Fleming only when she gives up her aspirations to be an independent woman and a political activist and returns to her role as man's helpmate. This, of course, is how Wharton's novel opens, with Halo surrendering her own identity in order to support Vance's writing, but it is not how it ends. Halo, as we have seen, learns with considerable pain that she must attain emotional independence before she and Vance can relate to each other as mature adults. Vance is a far more complex and interesting character than the priggish and self-righteous Richard Franklin and his transformation is hard-won. Both Katherine Fleming and Halo Spear, however, suffer social disapprobation and castigation when they try to exercise their intellects and assert their independence. In an implied comparison of the two works, Wharton might well be ironically pointing to the fact that things had not changed a great deal for intelligent women between 1897 and 1932 despite the social, economic and political advances achieved by women in the United States and in Europe during that period.

While the various readings of the novel's conclusion are interesting and often persuasive, they ignore what Wharton considered a fundamental premise for the creation of good art – a premise that is emphasised by Vance Weston's successes and failures as an author – that writers must work within yet develop their own place in the literary tradition. If we re-read the ending of *The Gods Arrive* in this light, it becomes clear that – like many authors before her – Wharton deliberately tempers realism with allegory and the prosaic with the mysterious in her late work. Like Dante, Shakespeare, Goethe and Dostoyevsky, she is more interested, at this stage of her career, in psychological realism than in social verisimilitude. Thus Halo is presented as a redeeming presence in a manner that evokes not just a Madonna figure but also Beatrice in Dante's *Paradiso*, Helen in Goethe's *Faust*, Hermione in Shakespeare's *The Winter's Tale* and Sonia in Dostoyevsky's *Crime and Punishment* (all works that Wharton knew well). Beatrice, Dante's ideal woman, guides him through the nine celestial spheres of heaven in *Paradiso*, the third and final part of his *Divine Comedy*. In this allegorical work, the last line of the last canto celebrates 'The Love which moves sun and the other stars'. In Goethe's *Faust*, Helen is the ideal woman, with the Mothers representing the origin of all life as well as rebirth and transformation: the second part of the drama ends with the appearance of the Virgin Mary and the words 'Eternal Womanhood/ Draws us on high' (p. 239).[49] Shakespeare's Hermione in *The Winter's Tale*, apparently dead from a broken heart after her husband, Leontes, has brutally and unjustly imprisoned her, actually lives hidden from him for 16 years. Not until Leontes has learnt remorse and wisdom through isolation and suffering is she restored to him. Their reunion, effected through the trick of a statue coming to life, is presented as a resurrection: as Paulina says to Hermione, 'Bequeath to death your numbness, for from him/ Dear life redeems you' (Act V, sc. iii). In *Crime and Punishment*, Dostoyevsky provides an Epilogue to the novel in which Sonia, previously tormented and ill-treated by Raskolnikov, becomes his only hope of redemption and moral regeneration. Again, the language of resurrection is used to suggest a new beginning:

> How it happened he did not know, but suddenly something seemed to seize him and throw him at her feet. He embraced her knees and wept. At first she was terribly frightened, and her faced was covered by a deathly pallor...But at one and at the same moment she understood everything ...in those sick and pale faces the dawn of a new future, of a full resurrection to a new life, was already shining. It was love that brought them back to life: the heart of one held inexhaustible sources of life for the heart of the other.[50]

Failure to recognise the last scene of *The Gods Arrive* as continuing this powerful tradition within European writing is to disregard how that tradition informed Wharton's work more emphatically as she matured as an author. Wharton here – as ever – consciously engages with the figure of woman as redeemer, leaving the reader to ponder on how such a tradition might relate to matters of gender and creativity in the twentieth century. In that sense, like most of her late novels, *The Gods Arrive* provides no neat solution; rather, like Shakespeare's late plays, it offers problems for contemplation. But, above all, this last scene positions *The Gods Arrive* within a European framework so that novel itself provides continuity with a European legacy despite the fact that Halo and Vance are American and that they choose to return finally to the United States. The references are not only to earlier texts by other authors, however. As previously noted, one of the most powerful presences in *The Gods Arrive* is that of Wharton's first American novel, *The House of Mirth*. Here Lily Bart's final epiphany concerns the failure of herself as an individual and of the society in which she lives to build 'any real relation to life'.

The conclusion of the Vance Weston diptych responds to Lily's dying, clarifying vision:

> In whatever form a slowly-accumulated past lives in the blood – whether in the concrete image of the old house stored with visual memories, or in the conception of the house not built with hands, but made up of inherited passions and loyalties – it has the same power of broadening and deepening the individual existence, of attaching it by mysterious links of kinship to all the mighty sum of human striving.[51]

As Vance realises at the end and as Halo understands from the beginning, in Frenside's words: 'We most of us need a frame-work, a support' (p. 317). Halo repeats his words to herself when thinking through her relationship with Vance after Frenside leaves her at Oubli: 'They might have a child, and then there would be something about which to build the frame-work' (p. 323). The return to the Willows, the reunion of lovers, the imminent birth of the child, and the 'kinship' of human suffering derived from St Augustine and others is physically enacted in Miss Lorburn's library; Lily Bart's ghost is stilled as Halo and Vance accept each other with 'the strength not to pretend' (p. 438).

The conclusion to *The Gods Arrive* also carries a political and cultural dimension. In *French Ways and their Meaning*, Wharton had argued that 'we should cultivate the sense of continuity, that "sense of the past" which enriches the present and binds us up with the world's great stabilising traditions of art and poetry and knowledge'.[52] This is the agenda of *Hudson River Bracketed* and *The Gods Arrive*. Like the poetry of T.S. Eliot, Wharton's novels are 'shaped by a sense of the alienation caused by modern culture, a desire for an order that would serve as a counterpoint to this culture's chaos, and a belief that the past held the key to artistic integrity'.[53] If we ignore the multiple evocations of literary tradition at the end of *The Gods Arrive* we repeat, in miniature, the very rejection of tradition that is castigated within the novel itself. In the return of Vance and Halo to the Willows the reader is asked to turn back to the past; as T.S. Eliot expressed it in 'Little Gidding', 'the end of all our exploring/ Will be to arrive where we started/ And know the place for the first time'. And it is a past enriched not only by the literary and cultural work of others but also by the fictions of the writers present here, at the end of their long journeys, whether Vance Weston or Edith Wharton.

6
The Buccaneers

'the rich low murmur of the past'[1]

Wharton's last and unfinished novel, *The Buccaneers*, is the only one set in England. Given Wharton's own old New York background, the fact that it took the whole of her writing career before she finally arrived creatively in a parallel social milieu, amongst the English aristocracy, is in many ways surprising. This is not the only distinctive feature, however, of *The Buccaneers*; the novel breaks the pattern of Wharton's fiction in a number of ways. In three of the late novels – *The Mother's Recompense, The Children, The Gods Arrive* – Wharton sets major parts of the action in Europe, but the Europe of these novels is the traveller's Europe, providing the backdrop for an essentially American cast of characters; the texture of the landscape and its inhabitants play very little part in the narrative. Central to *The Buccaneers*, however, is the life-changing immersion in another culture of its main protagonist, Nan St George. In her final novel Wharton's continuing exploration of relationships between men and women also takes a new turn. The focus is on a number of marriages and their outcomes rather than the complications, often triangular, of a single relationship. Although the novel seems to begin with a somewhat conventional courtship and marriage plot, Wharton is actually much more interested in the compromises and failures which follow. Also highly significant here is the importance of relationships between women. The narrative is driven by women, for women. There is cooperation between women, both intergenerational and between peers, which is unique in Wharton's longer fiction.

The thematic strain of the growth to maturity through emotional suffering that dominates the novels of the 1920s and 1930s is continued in *The Buccaneers* but it goes beyond the point of consummation of, separation

135

from, or resignation to, a long-term relationship. Very little of courtship and marriage is visible before we discover that Nan St George has become Annabel Tintagel. In a scene that provides one of the many echoes in the novel of Henry James's proto-modernist *The Portrait of a Lady* (1881), Annabel is seen, at the beginning of Book III, as suddenly more than two years into her marriage, just as Isabel Osmond is encountered, in Chapter 37, after an interval of three or so years since her wedding. The intervening events in the married lives of the two women – the death of a child for Isabel, a miscarriage for Annabel, the breakdown of relations with their husbands – these are narrated retrospectively by Wharton and James, although the past, as ever in James's writing, is not depicted with anything approaching straightforward hindsight. Both women marry into a fixed milieu: where, for Isabel, a way of life that she had nuanced as offering a kind of transcendence above nation and location has instead been reified, or indeed fetishised, into a rigid conventionality by her fatally Europeanised American husband; and where, for Annabel, the inherited obligations of the role of Duchess weigh so heavily that she cannot even begin to provide the necessary ballast.

There is, again, in this novel, an emphasis on the importance of continuity. The Willows of *Hudson River Bracketed* and *The Gods Arrive* – and all that it represents in terms of literary and historical heritage and continuity – is replaced not only by Honourslove[2] and the ruins of Tintagel in *The Buccaneers*, but also by codes of conduct which regulate and direct lives. Annabel, for instance, recognises, despite her instinct to continue wrangling with her husband or her mother-in-law, that the demands of her role – that of Duchess – prevent her from self-indulgence:

> Yes; in spite of her anger, in spite of her desperate sense of being trapped, Annabel felt in a confused way that the business of living was perhaps conducted more wisely at Longlands – even though Longlands was the potato-field she was destined to hoe for life. (p. 296)

In this sense, the novel's settings and the customs it portrays are as important as its story and even when Wharton is revealing the negative aspects of tradition and custom, there is still respect for and investment in continuity. The literal role of the literary is also of paramount importance: allusions and points of comparison with predecessor texts – such as *The Portrait of a Lady* – abound, many of which have a role in moving the narrative forward and expressing individual character. Wharton sets a framework in which Nan's aesthetic education, at the hands of Laura Testvalley, provokes a series of sensuous revelations. The first, most important, literary influence is that facilitated in plot terms by Laura being a part of an extended family of Italian exiles that includes Dante Gabriel Rossetti. Nan, as a consequence, is exposed to Rossetti's poetry and by the age of 19 has read all his work, including *The House of Love*. Also woven throughout the text are quotations from the poetry of Keats – a major influence on Rossetti – which signify moments of illumination. Both poets combined the intensely sensual with mystic vision in their work and, during their lifetimes, provoked a good deal of personal as well as professional controversy. In a review article published in 1871, written under the name of Thomas Maitland, Robert Buchanan grouped Rossetti with Morris and Swinburne as 'The Fleshly School of Poetry'.[3] The salience of this description of their work or, at least, its grip on popular perceptions of the work of Rossetti and others, is clearly demonstrated in the text when, shortly before he leaves for South America, Guy Thwarte describes to his father how Nan quoted from the poetry as they stood in front of the Rossetti painting which hangs at Honourslove. Sir Helmsley responds: 'So the Fleshly School has penetrated to the backwoods! Well, I don't know that it's exactly the best food for the family breakfast' (p. 139). *The House of Love* sequence, part of which was published in 1870 in *Poems by D.G. Rossetti*,[4] shocked many readers by its overt references to sex, although Rossetti himself rebutted any accusation of coarseness, pointing to the inseparability of soul and body in his sonnets. However, Sonnet V of the sequence, entitled 'Nuptial Sleep', clearly describes the languid pleasure of post-coital sex;[5] it is, then, not surprising that Laura Testvalley advises Nan not to 'proclaim in public' (p. 165) that she has read all of Rossetti's work. Late Victorian society would certainly have censured knowledge of *The House of Love* in a young unmarried woman, as Sir Helmsley's comment makes clear.

Structurally then, Rossetti, one of Wharton's favourite poets,[6] is a key link between four important characters. Nan, highly influenced by Laura, discovers early on that Guy Thwarte has read all the Pre-Raphaelite's work and that he thinks some of the sonnets in *The House of Life* superior to 'The Blessed Damozel'. In contrast, Ushant, Duke of Tintagel, Nan's future husband, has 'very little time to read poetry' (p. 182), provoking Nan to judge him as 'one of the stupidest young men I've ever met' (p. 187). Laura Testvalley is familiar with all her cousin's poetry, although Rossetti's stoutness and tendency to cause 'all the family a good deal of trouble' (p. 90) result in her having a more measured attitude towards it than Nan – familiarity here, indeed, breeding contempt. Nan, on the other hand, responds feverishly to the sensuous dimension of poetry by both Keats and Rossetti and allows herself to be influenced by an idealised view of love. Rossetti is also key in bringing together the unlikely combination of Sir Helmsley Thwarte and 'the little brown governess' (p. 235) through the former's patronage of the artist's work and Laura's intimate knowledge of and access to it. Indeed, every phase of Nan's development and many of the twists and turns of plot are predicated through hers or others' responses to literature or painting. Nan's imagination, her interior life, has been shaped by her reading and so, for instance, she responds to Laura's suggestion that they visit Tintagel in Cornwall with a delighted reference to the Knights of the Round Table and Tennyson's *The Idylls of the King*, a melancholy and romantic rendition of Arthurian legend. She even becomes amenable to the suggestion that she could be mistress of Tintagel – after Ushant is given the chance to redeem himself from first impressions – because of her susceptibility to myth and legend. Like the Lady of Shalott, who 'weaves by night and day/A magic web with colours gay' while standing 'at the casement' of the 'many-tower'd Camelot', Nan – made vulnerable by her love of words, images, ideas – is predisposed to, and therefore at serious risk of, infatuation.

As well as endowing Nan with her own deep love of language and literature, Wharton also endows her with her love of English history, including a reverence for old houses and gardens which, alongside the English poetic tradition, had always fired her imagination. Wharton had, after all, modelled the only home she ever commissioned *ab initio* on Belton House in Lincolnshire.[7] Nan is depicted in the lexis of Wharton's private enchantments, the language, imagery and quotations which permeate the autobiographical piece, 'Life and I'. The 'rich, low murmur of the past' (p. 249) which Tintagel breathes upon Nan, the fact that Tennyson's *Idylls of the King* 'had been one of Nan's magic casements' (p. 166) – the phrase 'magic casements' taken itself from Keats' 'Ode to a Nightingale' – all build a portrait of a young woman who, like the youthful Edith Wharton, is trying to make sense of the relationship between her internal and external beings and whose best attempts come through the aesthetic – whether found in the Correggios in the Duchess's sitting room or the poetry of Rossetti.[8] One of the persistent laments in Wharton's writing about her own fragmented education was the constant need she felt to make sense of her world. In 'Life and I', when describing her own reading she rationalises her choice of texts thus:

> I can only suppose it answered to some hidden need to order my thoughts, and get things into some kind of logical relation to each

other...It originated, perhaps, in the sense that weighed on my whole childhood – the sense of bewilderment, of the need of guidance, the longing to understand what it was all about. My little corner of the cosmos seemed like a dark trackless region where 'ignorant armies clash by night'...[9]

As ever, at moments of high emotion, Wharton, like many of her characters, expresses the personally difficult through poetry. Here she draws on Matthew Arnold's 'Dover Beach', just as Guy Thwarte, struggling to readjust to life at Honourslove after his return from Brazil, takes words from another poem by Matthew Arnold, describing himself as 'between two worlds yet – "powerless to be born"' (p. 264).[10]

Wharton spent a creative lifetime addressing the deficits in her own education; her appetite for the written word was without limit and in her final book she continued to weave her hard-won aesthetic principles and powers of allusion into the linguistic and structural fabric of her writing. In *Italian Backgrounds* (1905), Wharton speculates that in Italian art of the early Renaissance, the background was often more important than the foreground:

One must look past and beyond the central figures...to catch a glimpse of the life amid which the painting originated. Relegated to the middle distance, and reduced to insignificant size, is the real picture, the picture which had its birth in the artist's brain and reflects his impression of the life around him.[11]

Part of that middle distance here is, of course, the novel of English manners, a selection of which Wharton had been reading whilst working on *The Buccaneers*, arguably her most nineteenth-century novel in tone and content. In *The Writing of Fiction*, she describes Jane Austen as 'one of the great English observers', a 'delicate genius' and an 'impeccable' novelist.[12] '"Ah, Jane, you sorceress", she exclaimed, after listening to [Robert] Norton read aloud from *Sense and Sensibility* over a series of January evenings in 1934', a year in which she was deeply immersed in writing *The Buccaneers*.[13] In focusing on a group of young women of marriageable age whose mothers' greatest desire is to see their girls suitably matched, the novel evokes the sardonic humour and astute social observations found throughout Austen's work – perhaps Nan's first and fateful reaction to the wildness and ruins of Tintagel is an ironic reference to Elizabeth Bennett's dating of her serious interest in Mr Darcy to the first sight of the very orderly Pemberley in *Pride and Prejudice*.

There are other writers who influence the text; during 1934 Wharton had returned, when deep in *The Buccaneers*, not only to Austen but also to Trollope's *Can You Forgive Her?* and *The Prime Minister* – '& oh, how good they are!'. During 1937, when she was, in her own words, 'struggling toward the Cresta run' of *The Buccaneers*, she persuaded Granville-Barker to pick up Thackeray's *Esmond* and read aloud 'the 3 great – greatest – scenes' in the novel'.[14] Wharton is perhaps closest to Thackeray in her last novel particularly as regards the more explicit revelations about the illicit sexual lives of her protagonists. In Austen's work those who are ruined or adulterous are generally kept off-stage; she certainly would not have portrayed in any detail the equivalent of Lord Richard's night-time liaisons, whether at Allfriars or in the hotel in Saratoga; Lady Idina Churt's well-known position as Lord Seadown's mistress; Conchita Marable's string of lovers, ending with 'old Blasker Tripp'; or the drain on the family fortune of Sir Helmsley Thwarte's adventures with younger women.

As well as ensuring that the resonances and the insights of great poetry and prose are embedded in the texture of the novel Wharton researched the 'middle distance' of *The Buccaneers* with immense care. The year in which the novel opens, 1873, was a moment of economic crisis in America, with the rest of the decade remaining volatile economically.[15] This accounts for both the rise in fortunes of Colonel St George and the increasing financial difficulties faced by Mr Closson over the five-year period covered by the novel. Anxious to portray accurately the social life of Saratoga and New York at this time, Wharton sent a list of questions on the topic to Frantz Gray Griswold, an old New Yorker in both senses of the word. He responded precisely to her queries and provided an extra two pages of information.[16] For her portrayal of the country houses and their inhabitants in the England of the 1870s, Wharton drew on the long stretches of time she spent there between 1906 and 1913. Indeed, as a confirmed lover of all things English – as she observed in a letter to Sara Norton, 'And in England I like it *all* – institutions, traditions, mannerisms, conservatisms, everything but the women's clothes, & the having to go to church every Sunday'[17] – she had seriously explored the possibility of living permanently in England during that period, her interest in acquiring a suitable property given added impetus by the fact that Henry James had been for many years a resident. She also had American friends who had married into the English nobility, which provided material to be stored away until she wrote *The Buccaneers*. R.W.B. Lewis suggests Consuelo Yznaga, who became the Duchess of Manchester, and the Jerome sisters, 'a cluster of comely trans-Atlantic invaders in the 1870s', as possible models for her characters[18] – and, famously, 1873 saw the marriage of Jennie Jerome, daughter of a wealthy Wall Street speculator and his heiress wife, to Lord Randolph Churchill, despite opposition from his father, the Duke of Marlborough.[19] In the closing years of the nineteenth and early years of the twentieth centuries this very particular form of emigration to the UK could easily have been mistaken for an export trade. Marriages between American women and British men grew exponentially in number, especially in the peerage. According to Kathleen Burk, between 1870 and 1915 sixty peers and forty younger sons of peers married wealthy American brides and in total 454 American heiresses married into British families.[20] Adeline R. Tintner has argued persuasively that Wharton drew for material on the marriage of the American heiress Consuelo Vanderbilt to the ninth Duke of Marlborough, which took place in 1895 but which very quickly resulted in mutual unhappiness and public scandal; early separation followed although the couple did not divorce until 1920.[21] The pecuniary basis of the marriage was no secret; as Tintner notes: 'William K. Vanderbilt had written in the marriage contract that he would deliver over to the Duke of Marlborough two million five hundred thousand dollars', handed over, as Hermione Lee observes, in the form of railway stock.[22] Of course, Wharton was not the first novelist to portray such transatlantic liaisons. Frances Hodgson Burnett's *The Shuttle*, for example, published in 1907 and which Wharton might well have read, focuses on two American sisters, one of whom marries Sir Nigel Anstruthers of Stornham Court, a bullying English aristocrat in desperate need of money. Some years later, she is rescued from unhappiness by her younger sister, Bettina Vanderpoel, whose historical imagination and 'genius for living' anticipate Nan St George, although 'Betty' is less vulnerable and impressionable than Wharton's character.[23] Guy Thwarte might also owe something to Hodgson Burnett's hero, Lord Mount Dunstan, in that both men are set to inherit family estates which have been neglected by rather irresponsible male relatives. Both novels also contain typhoid episodes. However, *The Buccaneers* is a much more subtle work than *The Shuttle*: Hodgson Burnett's characters are less developed than Wharton's and her novel often drops into melodrama and sentimentality. The complex relationship between America and England, which Wharton was to delineate through the histories and characters of the two nations, is much simplified in *The Shuttle*. Hodgson Burnett's novel exudes unqualified enthusiasm for American energy and resourcefulness; Wharton's critique of both America and England was to be more nuanced. Nor does Hodgson

Burnett attempt to portray the influence of European writers and artists on the American imagination, a crucial aspect of *The Buccaneers*.

Wharton might well have drawn on such precursor texts when planning her last novel but there is no doubt, as Lee confirms in her recent biography of Edith Wharton, that she also drew heavily on historical facts and actual people when writing *The Buccaneers*. In addition to her aristocratic friends, she knew several American expatriates living in England who might well have provided a template for the character of Jacqueline March, a living reminder that the marriage trade between continents had been active for at least 30 years by the time the novel opens. Wharton also clearly enjoyed observing the rich comedy of English society through mixing with the nobility, at one point turning down the opportunity to meet May Sinclair in favour of the Duchess of Sutherland.[24] At the same time, her sharp eye and practical experience as a woman used to managing large establishments alone enabled her to note the difficulties that many owners of large estates were having in trying to maintain their stately homes and inherited estates in the countryside, not to mention the obligatory houses in London.

There are, as already indicated, several good reasons why Wharton chose to open her novel in 1873 and not the 1880s or 1890s, which might have seemed more obvious decades, given the prominence of the Vanderbilt affair during that period. A boom in railroad construction had followed the American Civil War, resulting in about 35,000 miles of new track being laid across the country between 1866 and 1873. Much of the craze in railroad investment was driven by government land grants and subsidies to the railroads. Many speculators made large amounts of money at this time, although the financial risks were significant. The result was a new class of *nouveau riche* – embracing families such as the St Georges and the Elmsworths – in the big cities, who created a social environment quite different from the polite and traditional world of Old New York.[25] But 'the Panic of 1873' marked the start of a serious nationwide economic depression in America (known as the 'Long Depression') that lasted until 1879. Many people had invested too much of their capital in long-term projects; the combination of this factor with an economic crisis in Europe (which affected the American inter-bank lending rate) and the Coinage Act of 1873 (which reduced the domestic money supply) led to the failure of thousands of businesses between 1873 and 1875 and unemployment reaching 14 per cent by 1876. The decade was marked by strikes and bankruptcies; it was only in 1879 – which probably would have marked the end of Wharton's novel had she lived to finish it – that the depression began to lift.

During the course of the novel the economic boom is clearly shifting from the United States to Brazil; Latin America is the land of golden opportunity for both ambitious Americans and members of the aristocracy in England who are looking desperately for new money with which to shore up their old homes. It is no coincidence that both Lord Richard Marable and Guy Thwarte go to Brazil – newly opened up to trade with America – in order seek their fortunes. Brazil offered plenty of money-making opportunities in agriculture and the railways although, of course, Richard Marable is also sent out there as a punishment for having forged one of his father's cheques, probably to pay off gambling debts. Guy Thwarte, having rejected a diplomatic career, joins a firm of civil engineers who specialise in railway building in 'Far Eastern and South American lands...Guy's experience in Brazil had shown him that in those regions there were fortunes to be made by energetic men with a practical knowledge of the conditions' (p. 109). Indeed, it is only Guy's success in Brazil and the conveniently early death of his wealthy Brazilian wife that rescue him from the obvious recourse described by Laura Testvalley to Nan: 'The only way for Guy Thwarte to keep up his ancestral home will be to bring a great heiress back to it' (p. 164).

Wharton's heroines in *The Buccaneers* have been socially isolated in their own country, without the means to gain access to what Wharton would have called the 'best society'. By setting the novel in the England of the 1870s Wharton is able to play on the fact that the girls are a social novelty; their money is a huge attraction for an increasingly cash-poor English aristocracy and their manners are fresh in the dull drawing rooms of Belgravia. Whilst Wharton went to great trouble to represent an accurate historical picture of aspects of England and America in the 1870s she wanted to explore – as ever – failures of imagination, failures of language and, on an international scale, misalignments of economic and material values, as well as tradition and expectation. All these mis-understandings had been exposed to satirical scrutiny since travel had opened up between continents, notably in the writings of Oscar Wilde, whose poetry and plays were well represented in Wharton's library, including a volume of his poetry inscribed 'Edith Wharton – from W.B.' (Walter Berry).[26] Wilde had written, in 1887, in 'The American Invasion':

On the whole, the American invasion has done English society a great deal of good. American women are bright, clever, and wonderfully cosmopolitan...They insist on being paid compliments and have almost succeeded in making Englishmen eloquent. For our aristocracy

they have an ardent admiration; they adore titles and are a permanent
blow to republican principles...As for their voices, they soon get them
into tune...She can talk brilliantly upon any subject, provided that
she knows nothing about it. Her sense of humour keeps her from
the tragedy of a grande passion, and, as there is neither romance nor
humility in her love, she makes an excellent wife.[27]

Wilde's targets are American women, women he characterises as unsen-
timental and business-like in their pursuit of marriage and their conduct following it. Wharton satirises the aristocracy mercilessly, both in
America and England – the disdainful and painfully status-conscious
Mrs Parmore no less than Lady Brightlingsea – but she largely spares the
girls. Although it opens in 1873, *The Buccaneers* also had contemporary
resonances in the late 1930s given that an English king had abdicated
in 1936 in order to marry an American divorcee.[28] Wharton ventures
a topical joke when Mrs Elmsworth is made to conjecture that 'beauty
such as Lizzy's (because it was rarer, she supposed) had been known to
raise a girl almost to the throne' (p. 156). 'Almost', indeed.

It is in the English 'middle distance' of the novel, its social milieu,
that the satiric thrust of Wharton's vision is located. But her satire is
not merciless or pitiless here. Until she allows Nan St George to depart
with her lover, Guy Thwarte, Wharton had, throughout her writing life,
successively denied her characters the chance of perfect happiness. In
The House of Mirth, Lily Bart is dead before Lawrence Selden can reach
her to tell her that he has transcended the petty restrictions of society's
prejudices; Justine Brent must make do with a compromised vision
of the marriage of true minds she thought was hers in *The Fruit of the
Tree*; Ethan Frome and Mattie Silver lead crippled and tortured lives
instead of finding transcendence in life or death; Ellen Olenska will
wait unrequited for Newland Archer to find the place where they can
live together in *The Age of Innocence*. However, if Nan wins happiness,
this is counter-balanced by the destruction of Laura Testvalley's hopes
for a physically and intellectually stimulating union after a lifetime of
service to her family and her employers. She and Nan together have
the spirit, imagination and determination to rise above their material
and economic destiny but, according to Wharton's plan for the end of
the novel, only one of them will succeed. Nan and Laura Testvalley are
both 'outsiders', Laura because of her lowly status and her revolutionary and artistic family heritage, and Nan because she has the ability to
transcend the mundane, to experience what she herself describes as a
'sense of beyondness' (p. 137) in a landscape which yields its beauty to

her. In a world where most matches are made for status or for money, a certain sad irony attaches to the fact that it is her lively historical imagination that draws Nan into a relationship with the Duke of Tintagel and therefore into a desperately unhappy marriage. The girls have come to England specifically for the purposes of self-advancement and enhanced social status and, remarkably, they all achieve their goals. Laura Testvalley, however, loses everything: her job, her reputation and the man she has come to love because she is, in Wharton's words, 'the great, old adventuress' who gives her all in order to see 'love, deep and abiding love, triumph for the first time in her career' (p. 358). This act of self-sacrifice marks another hugely significant distinction between this novel and its predecessors: the warmth of the relationship between the older woman – Laura is nearly 40 – and the younger – Nan is 16 years old when the novel opens. This intimacy is unique in Wharton's novels; nowhere else is the state of affairs between women anything other than one of either rivalry or neglect. The many strained relationships between mothers and daughters in Wharton's oeuvre, most notably those between Kate and Anne Clephane in *The Mother's Recompense*, Judith and Joyce Wheater in *The Children* and Pauline and Nona Manford in *Twilight Sleep*, are here redeemed by one that has no tie of blood. Laura develops the desire to protect and nurture Nan very early in their relationship: '"She might have been my own daughter", the governess thought, composing her narrow frame to rest, and listening in the darkness to Nan's peaceful breathing' (p. 90). It is not only in this relationship, however, that there is sympathy and cooperation. The girls work together, even when it might be to one or other's individual disadvantage, and this is nowhere more evident than in the confrontation between the Buccaneers and Lady Idina Churt at Runnymede.

Wharton opens the chapter which contains this most dramatic of scenes with a lengthy description of the character, background and ambitions of a young 'Conservative M.P. for one of the last rotten boroughs in England' (p. 188),[29] Hector Robinson. His wealth, deriving from the family cotton industry in Lancashire, in which he is a partner, is 'new' money and thus the English equivalent of Colonel St George's fortune. He faces similar hurdles in London to those the St Georges and the Elmsworths encounter in New York when trying to break into polite society, although it is clear that his 'aspiring and impatient' nature (p. 190), combined with his elected position, make it likely that his determination to turn his father's knighthood – awarded for services to industry – into a baronetcy, will be realised. This would indeed guarantee his entry into 'the elect' (p. 191) social circles of England. He is a very British buccaneer – one of the many English gentlemen 'with short pedigrees and long purses' (p. 189) looking to climb the social ladder. Frequenting Runnymede, full of 'golden youths' (p. 191), proves useful to his strategy of self-advancement. Using Hector Robinson as her focaliser in this scene enables Wharton to present events from the perspective of an intelligent outsider, but one who is also very sensitive to social and class nuances. Robinson's astuteness allows him to see the ultimately destructive self that lies beneath Idina Churt's beauty and sophistication – 'her avidity, her disorder, her social arrogance and her spiritual poverty' (p. 210). One minute taken aside by Mabel Elmsworth in order to enlist his support for Lizzy Elmsworth in a possible battle with Virginia St George for Lord Seadown, the next marvelling at Lizzy's decisive intervention, he recognises the potential for dynamism in the girls in a way inconceivable to the privileged members of the upper classes. Of Lizzy Elmsworth he thinks: 'What a party-leader she'd make' and is quietly glad that, in deliberately sacrificing her own chance of marriage with Lord Seadown, she will not 'be thrown away on this poor nonentity' (p. 208). Although he ably plays the game of tradition and convention in order to advance his career, he is a more modern man than either Ushant or Lord Seadown, and Wharton presents his marriage to Lizzy Elmsworth in an extremely positive light at the end of the novel – these two interlopers finding a frank and full happiness together. The Runnymede episode is full of dramatic tension and great irony but it also illustrates the young American women working together to achieve a collective advantage, much to the surprise of the admiring Robinson.

The unexpected arrival of Lady Churt at the cottage turns a lazy August day into a scene charged with tension in which a game of poker becomes a metaphor for the bold strategies adopted by young women competing for well-born husbands. Borrowing money from Lord Seadown, her companion and lover, Idina, despite being 'too emotional for a game based on dissimulation' (p. 202), tries her hand at poker and loses to Miles Dawnly, but it is clear to all that the 'stakes...were higher than usual' (p. 202). In fact, the real stake is Lord Seadown who, by the end of the morning, has been manoeuvred by Conchita and Lizzy into announcing his engagement to Virginia. Idina's over-emphatic announcement that, having lost the game, she is 'completely ruined', ironically presages her wounding emotional defeat at the hands of two sharp-witted young Americans, despite her cavalier assertion to Conchita that money means more than love to her: 'Heart, my dear? I assure you I've never minded parting with that organ. It's losing the shillings and pence that I can't afford' (p. 204). In fact, she makes very little attempt to contain her fierce anger at having lost her prestigious if dull lover, as Robinson observes: 'Poor woman...She'll have another try for Seadown, of course – but the game's up, and she probably knows it' (p. 210). In setting the scene at Runnymede, the site that witnessed in 1215 King John's signing of Magna Carta, Wharton imbues the action with a larger and predominantly ironic significance. This document required the King to institute certain rights for all Englishmen, to respect certain legal procedures, and to accept that his own will could be bound by the law. Implicitly supporting what became the writ of *habeas corpus*, which allowed appeal against unlawful imprisonment, it formed the foundation of constitutional law in the English-speaking world, including the United States, which based its Constitution on Magna Carta, as Wharton would have known. It is against the backdrop of Runnymede, the birthplace of Western democracy and civil liberties, that the American girls forfeit their freedom in exchange for marriage, their only career option. In order to secure their husbands, however, the girls behave not like their mothers – between whom the relationship is one of rivalry – but like their fathers. They recognise that they need each other and, led by the example of Conchita in whose 'easy nature' 'there was not an ounce of jealousy' – '"We've each got our own line," she said to Lizzy Elmsworth, "and if we only back each other up we'll beat all the other women hands down...If we stick to the rules of the game, and don't play any low-down tricks on each other..."' (p. 158) – they quickly realise that the cooperative principles upon which they should act are the same as those which allowed their fathers to succeed both in Wall Street and at the poker table.

In another shift from the works of the 1920s and early 1930s, albeit in a historical novel, Wharton affirms appropriate generational sexual attraction. Sir Helmsley Thwarte goes so far as to shed both the 'hospital nurse' and the 'Gaiety girl' after 'a career over-populated by the fair sex' for 'a little brown governess...who...had eyes like torches' (p. 271), drawn by Laura's intellect as much as by her revivified sensuality. And although we know that Laura has had her own intergenerational indiscretions, Conchita's husband, Lord Richard, having been a night-time visitor to her bedroom when she was his sisters' governess, she does not experience the jealousy of a Kate Clephane, whose daughter's lover was once her own, or of a Pauline Manford, for the youth and beauty which are no longer hers. There is, in addition, no judgement made on Laura here for having indulged her sexual appetites, rather the reverse:

The Lord Richard chapter was a closed one and she had no wish to re-open it. She had paid its cost in some brief fears and joys, and one night of agonizing tears; but perhaps her Italian blood had saved her from ever, then or after, regarding it as a moral issue. In her busy life there was no room for dead love-affairs; and besides, did the word 'love' apply to such passing follies? Fatalistically, she had registered the episode and pigeon-holed it. If she were to know an abiding grief it must be caused by one that engaged the soul. (p. 75)

Wharton locates the moral compass in this text in such a way that the only sin is failure to engage the soul. Sex fulfils a physical need, as for Laura here, or it is a part of a bargain, as it is for Ushant whose taste in women is clearly for the passive and childlike; he fears, as he tells Nan, 'beautiful women' (p. 338). There is no moral outrage expressed either here or in relation to Conchita and her lovers; this is a society in which Idina Churt is a figure of pathos rather than a ruined woman and Sir Helmsley's indiscretions are a matter of some amusement. For the author who once received angry letters from readers demanding to know if she had ever known a decent woman after allowing her heroine (Lily Bart) to have tea alone with a bachelor,[30] this is a shift that illustrates very neatly the distance travelled over a writing career that spanned 40 years of enormous social change. Wharton, while composing *The Buccaneers*, was forced to think about the difference in manners and morals between her early and current work because she was writing a new Introduction for a 1936 edition of *The House of Mirth*. She notes there that re-entering the world of her first American novel was 'like going back to the Pharoahs' (p. v), so far distant were its moral precepts and tone. Love, however, is as fragile a thing in *The Buccaneers* as it was in *The House of Mirth*. Lady Brightlingsea feels that her son, Richard Marable, has been cheated out of a fortune and excuses his affairs with other women on the grounds that 'as he says, he's been deceived'; 'Miss March knew that this applied to Lady Richard's money and not to her morals, and she sighed again' (p. 100). When we first encounter Lord Richard he is totally besotted with Conchita; however, his love for her swiftly disappears, as does he from the narrative, once they arrive on English soil. The passion that develops between Sir Helmsley and Laura is also doomed to a short life. Whilst it lasts it clearly has a physical effect on Laura; her hair is braided less tightly, her skin, like Conchita's when in love, 'is suffused with a soft inner light' (p. 336). Wharton – as elsewhere in the novel – expresses the erotic fulfilment of their relationship obliquely by Sir Helmsley's acquisition, through Laura's good offices, of the first study of Rossetti's 'Bocca Baciata'.[31] Featuring a beautiful woman, with full lips and long loose hair, done in the style of Venetian painters such as Giorgione, the painting celebrates sensuality and eroticism. The title, meaning 'the mouth that has been kissed', privileges the woman's sexual experience over innocence, perhaps even emphasises the mature woman's entitlement to erotic pleasure. The words are placed in their original context on the back of the painting, where the relevant lines from Boccaccio's *De Cameron* have been written: '*Bocca baciata non perda ventura, anzi rinova come fa la luna*' – 'the mouth that has been kissed does lose not its freshness; still it renews itself even as does the moon'.[32]

The important use of literary quotation and allusion to advance the narrative in this novel has already been suggested. Wharton also uses allusion proleptically to signal what is to come – in this case disillusion and sorrow. When Laura Testvalley sees the assembled beauties in the unpromising location of the Saratoga Springs railway station her first impression of them is as 'a spring torrent of muslins, sash-ends, and bright cheeks under swaying hat-brims' (p. 41). Surrounded by this 'circle of nymphs', two lines from Keats's 'Song of the Indian Maid' spring to her mind: 'Whence come ye, merry damsels, whence come ye,/ So many and so many, and such glee?' (p. 43). Although the grace, optimism and physical ease of these young women seems appropriately captured by these lines, their provenance is a poem about the transience of pleasure. Moreover, the larger context of that poem is *Endymion*, a 'sensuous, imaginative and fanciful' work,[33] in which Keats uses the conflicting desires of his romantic hero in order to explore the relationship between visionary idealism and the sensuous physicality of love. The brief snatch from the 'Song of the Indian Maid' – for those who know the poem – hints at the disenchantment these young American women will eventually experience. Keats's famous pronouncement in a letter to J.H. Reynolds that 'Sorrow is wisdom'[34] resonates strongly with the mood and meaning of *Endymion*: growth to maturity through sorrow and suffering – the predominant theme of *Hudson River Bracketed* and *The Gods Arrive* – which would also have been realised through Nan's and Laura's later experiences had Wharton lived to finish the novel.

The capacity to grow to maturity if not wisdom is predicated differently in each of the young protagonists, and their development – excepting that of Lizzy Elmsworth – is often seen through the prism of Nan's high standards and values. The sight of her own sister, once 'so secure, so aloof' now – as Lady Seadown – 'enslaved to that dull half-asleep Seadown, absorbed in questions of rank and precedence and in awe – actually in awe – of her father-in-law's stupid arrogance, and of Lady Brightlingsea's bewildered condescensions' (p. 261), fills Nan with despair, but Virginia was 'divinely dull' (p. 138) before her marriage and continues to be so.

Conchita Marable mocks Allfriars, the Brightlingsea seat, describing it as the 'family vault' (p. 102), distracts herself from her unsatisfactory marriage by flinging herself into numerous short-lived affairs and, in the final pages of the novel, is invited to the Robinsons' country house party at Belfield in tandem with the rich, elderly and entertainingly named Sir Blasker Tripp. Although this lifestyle comes at a cost, that cost is felt as unreasonable mainly by Nan rather than Conchita: 'what relation', thinks Nan, 'did the Conchita Closson who had once seemed so ethereal and elusive, bear to Lady Dick Marable, beautiful still, though she was growing rather too stout, but who had lost her lovely indolence and detachment, and was now perpetually preoccupied about money, and immersed in domestic difficulties and clandestine consolations' (p. 261). Conchita herself, however, has a different, much more hard-headed view; she knows all too well the alternative to the life she has made for herself in England. As she tells Nan when asking to borrow £500 to discharge some of her debts to pleasure, she would:

> 'Never! Not for a single minute!' consider going back to New York: 'I'd rather starve and freeze here than go back to all the warm houses and the hot baths, and the emptiness of everything – people and places...ask Jacky March, or any of the poor little American old maids, or wives or widows, who've had a nibble at it, and have hung on at any price because London's London, and London life the most exciting and interesting in the world, and once you've got the soot and the fog in your veins you simply can't live without them; and all the poor hangers-on and left-overs know it as well as we do.' (pp. 303–5)

Conchita, in losing that 'indolence and detachment', has grown up. She might live an entirely worthless life but then the story of Nan's failed intervention with the Linfrey family provides us with a partial explanation of why women in the Tintagel or Brightlingsea households have limited capacity to be useful, even, as in Nan's case, when they want to be. Whilst recognising that 'Her values...were not Conchita's values', her friend's outburst does provide Nan with the opportunity to think seriously about both the 'thinness of the mental and moral air' in her past American life and the reasons for her own deep attachment to England:

> At least life in England had a background, layers and layers of rich deep background, of history, poetry, old traditional observances, beautiful houses, beautiful landscapes, beautiful ancient buildings, palaces, churches, cathedrals. (p. 305)

The difference between English and American landscapes is the closest Wharton comes to producing her own version of the infamous list in Henry James's *Hawthorne* of the things missing from the American scene in the 1850s.[35] It is particularly appropriate that she intimates such differences here because in *Hawthorne* James was describing the impoverishing effect upon the imagination of the absences he denotes and it is the particular bent of her imagination that causes Nan so many of the disappointments in her life. She does not, for instance, have the imagination to think of ways to 'manage' (p. 306) her husband, nor the empathy to understand what the situation of her own mother might have been as regards the emptiness of her married life. Her imagination is otherworldly and so when, in Book III, she figures her life in gothic terms, with images of death, imprisonment, constraint and punishment dominant, a mood and tone distinct and different from the previous two books of the novel is established. However, this shift results very clearly from a personal act of troping. When Conchita, in a moment of histrionic metaphor, designed to extort money from Nan, refers to herself as trapped in 'one of these awful English marriages, that strangle you in a noose when you try to pull away from them' (p. 300), Nan replies 'I'm almost as much as a prisoner as you are, I fancy; perhaps more' (p. 301). The Tintagel family home, Longlands, is described as being 'like a sepulchre to her; under its ponderous cornices and cupolas she felt herself reduced to a corpse-like immobility' (p. 317) and yet earlier in the narrative she had been able to see the beauty beyond the gloomy corners and peeling paint of the other stately homes she had visited. The language of imprisonment and constraint is all Nan's, she configures the other American brides as 'borrowers and beggars' but the hyperbolic language of deprivation and degradation here is undermined by Wharton with the swift reminder of the fact that their cajoling for funds is actually to support a lifestyle in the full glare of Society London's spotlight with which Nan has no sympathy; in actuality, their 'needs did not stir her imagination' (p. 310). At this point the novel seems to shadow – in terms of mood and intent – Jane Austen's *Northanger Abbey*, in which Catherine Morland's determination to find high gothic intrigue and evil-doing in the Tilney family is rendered somewhat comic in relation to the specific, rather mundane and materialistic story of domestic tyranny that is the reality. Nonetheless, at the level of the individual married woman or marriageable girl there are definable horrors to be experienced at the hands of husbands and fathers, horrors which largely derive from the paucity of choice over one's future destiny. For Catherine Morland there is a happy ending with the rational Mr Tilney, whose independence comes from his vocation. However, for women, either in Austen's fiction or Wharton's there is often simply no choice. Moreover, where one might be made, as in the case of Ushant's sister, the Lady Almina Folyat, who has a 'secret desire to enter an Anglican sisterhood' (p. 213) – a much more sincere vocation than Nona Manford's in *Twilight Sleep*, for whom a convent is only a possibility if she can find one where no one believes in anything – she is simply too afraid to express it. Hermione Lee, in her discussion of *The Buccaneers* notes that: 'under its frothy surface is a harsh exposure of society marriage as a form of prostitution and gambling, mothers trading their daughters, sex as a threat and a bargain, marital sadism and neglect, and several kinds of prejudice and racism'.[36] Lee also draws attention to the verdict of two of Wharton's previous biographers on the text: R.W.B. Lewis described the novel as having 'an air of fairy-tale enchantment'[37] and Shari Benstock found it 'arguably the most charming novel Edith Wharton ever wrote'.[38] It is not clear that the view at either of these extremes does justice to what Wharton is attempting in her last novel. She is in fact walking a very fine line between parody and sincerity, between the use of predecessor texts to signify disillusion and suffering but also enlightenment, solace and consolation; between the use of the lexis of claustrophobia and imprisonment for a superficial dramatic effect but also to express real, if naive despair; between the contradictions of a public moral code and a private code of amorality. One of Nan's difficulties lies in her incapacity for trivial transgression; she has no appetite for affairs, for gambling, for running up bills at the dressmaker. When she sins, she does so dramatically and irrevocably. However, in Laura's terms and the terms in which Wharton constructs the value system of the novel, the real sin would be Nan's failure to follow her heart.

The difficulty of asking her husband for the considerable sum of five hundred pounds for Conchita is a useful illustration of Nan's other-worldliness; she has never had any need for money because it has always been in a plentiful enough supply to provide her wants; consequently she has no idea of the monetary value of anything. What follows her request, the assumption by Ushant that he can expect a favour – and a sexual favour at that – fails to reach the level of the gothic drama that Nan's linguistic turn might promise. Any hyberbolic language is again undercut by her own, self-confessed, understanding of the reality, which is that Ushant is so little of a villain: 'Nan had noticed before now that anger was too big a garment for him: it always hung on him in uneasy folds' (pp. 315–16). Both Duke and Duchess are inexperienced and naive. When Nan leaves the house to find solitude after this conversation in the temple of Love – rather heavy-handedly described as 'derelict' – within the grounds of Longlands, she configures her situation again in high gothic terms: 'But think out what? Does a life-prisoner behind iron bars take the trouble to think out his future?' However, Wharton is clear here that this is Nan 'sinking into depths of childish despair – one of those old benumbing despairs without past or future which used to blot out the skies when her father scolded her or Miss Testvalley looked disapproving' (p. 318).

This is the moment at which, despite the childishness of her reaction, she recognises beyond doubt that she made a mistake in marrying Ushant, Duke of Tintagel. Marriage has brought only unhappiness and a loss of authenticity: '…vanished out of recognition…Annabel of the Grand Union had vanished' (p. 261). Furthermore, she sees herself as dead and her previous self as a ghost: 'Yes – a ghost. That was it. Annabel St. George was dead, and Annabel Tintagel did not know how to question the dead, and would therefore never be able to find out why and how that mysterious change had come about…' (pp. 241–2). Her own ghost haunts her with intimations of what might have been, tapping 'against the walls which had built themselves up about the new Duchess' (p. 262); visiting Honourslove with Laura Testvalley and Lady Glenloe, she 'seemed to see her own pitiful figure of four years ago flit by like a ghost' (p. 344). To Guy she confesses: 'I'm a strange woman, strange even to myself, who goes by my name' (p. 321). As in *The Mother's Recompense*, Wharton here uses the ghost to signify the loss of a securely located self. Nan, like Kate Clephane, belongs neither to the United States nor to Europe, she belongs neither to the past nor to the future. In what is clearly depicted as a period of depression following the loss of her baby, a loss coterminous with the death of the Linfry child and any pretence she might have had that she could lead a useful and productive life, she is left in a state where 'the only things that seem real are one's dreams' (p. 284).

It is clear, however, from Wharton's portrayal of Ushant that Nan is not the only one suffering from a crisis of personal identity and purpose. Ushant, for whom marriage is a grim necessity, a duty – 'He must marry, have children, play the great part assigned to him' (p. 174) – is no more comfortable with intimacy than Nan. Aware of his own deficiencies, he 'craved the stimulation of a quicker mind' (p. 175) but feared the clever and the beautiful. While wanting his bride to be 'of ancient lineage and Arcadian innocence' (p. 176) – not such an outlandish requirement when it is remembered what was expected of the bride of a British heir to the throne late in the twentieth century, that is, to have a history but no past – he is unwilling to accept that such innocence would one day inevitably be lost. Although Nan is not the product of an ancient family, she is young and innocent for her years and stays young even after marriage; she is always described as a child, even by Guy Thwarte after his return from Brazil, and a child who 'didn't measure what she was saying' (p. 284) at that.

The histrionic language and imagery used by Ushant mirrors that used by Nan. He refuses to meet his mother's choice of bride, Jean Hopeleigh, describing himself as being hunted 'for the sake of his title' and, warming to his theme, 'being tracked like a wild animal' despite, as Wharton cannot resist adding, looking 'excessively tame' (p. 170). Just as Nan's susceptibility to the romance of the Arthurian legend has been instrumental in her acceptance of the Tintagel title, so an equally arbitrary circumstance drives Ushant to take his courtship of Nan to a higher level by visiting the cottage at Runnymede: 'If he had not learned, immediately on his return to Longlands, that Jean Hopeleigh and her parents were among the guests expected there, he might never have gone up to London, or taken the afternoon train to Staines. It took the shock of an imminent duty to accelerate his decisions; and to run away from Jean Hopeleigh had become his most urgent duty' (p. 218). Duty drives him, more perversely than positively, as he reserves the right to determine for himself what that duty consists of and seeks a solution to the obligation upon him to marry which will involve the least commitment of self. Ushant is, by choice, an isolate, metaphorically and literally an island as Wharton slyly demonstrates whilst also providing yet another connection between the American girls and Ushant via her research for the novel. The Duke of Tintagel's first name derives from a small island off the coast of Brittany, surrounded by rocks and strong tides. As it is a very uncommon name,[39] it is likely that Wharton took her inspiration from John Esquemeling's *The Buccaneers of America*, a copy of which she held in her library at Ste-Claire, and which provided the title for her novel. In it, Esquemeling clearly paints the seas round Ushant as perilous:

> After this we came to an anchor in the Bay of Conquet, in Brittany, nigh unto the Isle of Ushant, there to take in water. Having stored ourselves with fresh provisions at this place, we prosecuted our voyage, designing to pass by the Ras of Fonteneau and not expose ourselves to the Sorlingues, fearing the English vessels that were cruising thereabouts to meet us. This river Ras is of a current very strong and

rapid, which, rolling over many rocks, disgorges into the sea on the coast of France, in the latitude of eight-and-forty degrees and ten minutes. For which reason this passage is very dangerous, all the rocks as yet being not thoroughly known. (p. 10)[40]

Ushant is trapped by his family's history; he lives in fear of any kind of demand being made upon him which is why he is attracted to Nan; they share an aversion to Society but, more importantly, they share the characteristic of the 'rocks' in 'as yet being not thoroughly known' – they both have some growing up to do and much of what they will become is as yet indistinct. Ushant's further development as a character was something that Wharton probably had in mind, had she lived to complete the novel. In her dramatisation of *The Buccaneers* for the BBC in 1995, the writer Maggie Wadey completed the narrative so as to endow upon Ushant an explicitly homosexual identity, although one that is, unsurprisingly, covertly prosecuted. Wharton certainly portrays the Duke as asexual and physically diffident to the point of inertia. As Richard A. Kaye notes:

Wharton expressed 'perverse' male desire through depictions of men steeped in indecision on matters of the heart, a hesitancy often expressed as coquettishness, a trait traditionally gendered as feminine and thus, by implication, effeminately denaturalized.[41]

Despite Ushant's determination to marry Nan it is clear that it is a reactive courtship provoked by the fear of a worse alternative. However, he is warned by Laura that Nan, as she is when he meets her, is not the finished article: 'I only want you to understand that Nan is one thing now, but may be another, quite different, thing in a year or two. Sensitive natures alter strangely after their first contact with life'. Laura's plea for him to 'wait, to give her time to grow up' (p. 227) fails to dissuade him, however, because he thinks that he can arrest her development if he marries her. His only interest in women is because 'a Duke must have an heir, that it is the purpose for which Dukes make the troublesome effort of marrying' (p. 259) and this is why he makes such a poor gothic villain, being sent away from the marital bed in short order even when he thinks he has bought five hundred pounds' worth of procreative activity. Wharton describes Ushant, at the point at which he encounters Nan in the ruins of Tintagel, as going 'in fear of the terrible beauty that is born and bred for the strawberry leaves' (p. 179). Unlike the creative and passionate Nan, or Guy, or Laura or Sir Helmsley, Ushant cannot express any truths about his own condition and feelings through direct poetic allusion; poetic language is applied to him here by the narrator in order to express not a sense of 'beyondness', but circumscription. Wharton compresses phrases from different poems by W.B. Yeats, focusing them into a single sentiment which would seem to indicate that he is looking for a female countenance that he can regard as 'safe', a face from which he can be 're-assured' (p. 179) that there will be no dramatic changes in store and that love will neither blaze nor die.[42] In the stultifying world of the English aristocracy, innovation and challenge are seen as inappropriate and even threatening: '"It has always been like that" was the Dowager's invariable answer to any suggestion of change' (p. 246), and Ushant is his mother's son.

Just as Sir Helmsley's and Laura's relationship is expressed through the Rossetti painting in combination with Boccaccio's words, so the incipient sexual relationship between Guy and Nan is configured in their sharing of reactions to the paintings by Correggio in the Duchess's private sitting-room – a sequence entitled 'Earthly Paradise': 'in the half-dusk of an English November they were like rents in the clouds, tunnels of radiance reaching to pure sapphire distances' (p. 246).[43] In the dark days of winter and her unhappy life as the Duchess of Tintagel – 'and there were many' (p. 246) – these paintings sustain Nan and stimulate her senses as well as her imagination.[44] Besides the direct visual appeal of Correggio's figures, with their 'golden limbs...parted lips gleaming with laughter [and] the abandonment of young bodies under shimmering foliage' (p. 246), the language in which they are described is charged with sensuality, providing a powerful contrast to a marriage in which sexual relations have nothing to do with pleasure and where physical intimacy does not exist. As she gazes at Correggio's figures, lines from a Rossetti sonnet comes to Nan's mind:

> Beyond all depth away
> The heat lies silent at the brink of day:
> Now the hand trails upon the viol-string
> That sobs, and the brown faces cease to sing,
> Sad with the whole of pleasure. (p. 246)

This sonnet, 'For a Venetian Pastoral by Giorgione', records Rossetti's reaction to seeing Giorgione's painting 'The Pastoral Concert' in the Louvre.[45] An immensely sensual painting, it depicts four figures within an Arcadian setting. Against an idealised pastoral background, two almost naked women, one of whom plays a pipe and one of whom is filling a jug of water from a fountain, frame two seated men, one of whom wears peasant's clothes and the other, dressed aristocratically, is playing a lyre. In the middle ground a shepherd guides his flock of sheep. The painting captures a moment of tranquillity, aesthetic beauty and physical sensuality; for Rossetti such moments expressed something timeless and eternal, something beyond mere humanity – 'Life touching lips with immortality' as the last line of the sonnet puts it. Awareness of such perfection is inevitably tinged with melancholy as the moment is transient; the poem, like the painting, thus carries a strong sense of the elegiac. This experience of 'a moment of secular and sensual illumination', in George P. Landow's words,[46] constituted an epiphany for Rossetti which Nan is able to share imaginatively while, nevertheless, doubting its veracity. Gazing at the Correggios, which have brought both Rossetti's poetry and therefore Giorgione's painting to mind, she wonders: 'Were there such beings anywhere...save in the dreams of poets and painters, such landscapes, such sunlight?' (p. 246). Yet, through their shared pleasure first in Rossetti, then in the Correggios, she and Guy are able to establish a profound intimacy, culminating in the coming together of their feelings about Goethe and, in particular, Clärchen, the heroine of *Egmont*, whose famous song expresses her emotional volatility ('Blissful And tearful, with thought-teeming brain; Hoping And fearing In passionate pain...'). As they talk about Goethe so Nan is able to recognise, finally, that her mistakes are not terminal, that she can have a second chance. Again, the shared literary moment produces an advance in the action of the novel as Guy moves to reassure her that there will always be fresh opportunities, however many mistakes one makes: 'Goethe was a very young man when he wrote Clärchen's song. The next time I come to Champions I'll bring *Faust* with me, and show you some of the things life taught him' (p. 346). This is Wharton's *imprimatur* on the growing intimacy between Nan and Guy and her assurance to the reader that Nan – now recognising that one must take responsibility for one's own mistakes – has grown out of the dreamy other-worldliness of the Pre-Raphaelites and has matured sufficiently to embark upon a truly adult relationship.

Despite the sacrifice required of Laura Testvalley so that Nan and Guy can be together, Wharton's final novel does not condone self-sacrifice in women. The marital misery experienced by the Dowager Duchess is constantly referenced – that she had longed to lock the door against her husband, that she had longed to ask him for money, that she had longed to escape from her duties, just for a few days – all these revelations accompany Ushant's complaints to her about the state of his marriage and his wife's obduracy. Mrs St George is similarly miserable, at the mercy of the Colonel's superior tactical and fiduciary powers; indeed, she charts the course of her marriage through the pieces of jewellery with which he has bought her compliance. In the 'middle distance' of the novel, however, Wharton suggests how change might be effected so as to improve the position of women – not through revolution or insurrection – but through changes in attitude and in the law. Chapter XXIX, near the end of the novel as we have it, shows us Lizzy Elmsworth in conversation at breakfast with her husband, Hector Robinson. They are engaged in a relaxed, bantering relationship, full of laughter and easy intimacy. Discussing Nan's impending visit, and her flight from Ushant, Lizzy comments: 'I suppose he can't keep his wife actually chained up, can he, with all these new laws, and the police prying in everywhere?' (p. 352) – a reference to the 1870 Married Women's Property Act, which granted British women the right to own and control personal property.[47] Nan, it is intimated, will become a beneficiary of that Act. It is clear that Hector Robinson is a man who fully appreciates his wife's political acumen as well as her 'regal head' (p. 152): 'He now regarded as a valuable asset the breezy independence of his wife's attitude, which at first had alarmed him...The free and easy Americanism of this little band of invaders had taken the world of fashion by storm, and Hector Robinson was too alert not to have noted the renovation of the social atmosphere' (pp. 353 and 355). Lizzy Elmsworth is far from Oscar Wilde's American wife as object of mockery and derision; she is a dynamic and effective operator who will be a force for change, as is Bettina Vanderpoel in Hodgson Burnett's *The Shuttle*.

Maturity results, as Wharton was at pains to make clear in her last novel, not just from intelligence, education and experience but from openness to other cultures, languages and countries. In this respect, the novel carries a strong cosmopolitan agenda. If the Robinson marriage is presented as a positive model in a novel dominated by unhappy marriages, then those characters open to other cultures redeem the ignorance and narrow-mindedness of their compatriots, whether they are English or American. Similarly Lady Glenloe's marriage is one in which she has not only been free to travel but also to effect substantial social improvements in her home community. In order to imagine a happy future for Nan and Guy we have to read beyond the putative ending of the novel. For a sense of how Wharton would like the world to change, we have only to focus on its 'middle distance', which suggests that wisdom comes from the capacity to free oneself from insularity, whether that derives from national identity, gender or class. In each other

Nan and Guy find the strength to leave all that they value in the landscape and history of England; they achieve 'a deep delicious peace' (p. 350) which transcends place, a transcendence which they can only realise, however, because they can hear and feel, wherever they are, 'the rich low murmur of the past' (p. 249), a past that does not inhibit but that liberates them.

Conclusion

Short stories and 'unchronicled lives'[1]

We suggested at the beginning of our first chapter that although Edith Wharton's interest in the older woman is marked throughout her writing career, her focus on women and ageing intensified during the 1920s, by which time she was in her sixties. Nowhere is this more evident than in her short stories, particularly in those late gothic tales in which the difficulty for older women in maintaining a sense of authentic identity – including sexual identity – is rendered iconoclastically through use of the spectral and the uncanny. Indeed, Wharton's distinctive use of gothic devices in the short fiction written during the last twelve years of her life goes hand in hand with a tempering of realism and alongside the move to hybridity, genre experimentation and boundary blurring in her late novels.

As we have noted elsewhere,[2] in 'Mr. Jones', a tale published first in 1928 in the *Ladies' Home Journal* and republished in *Ghosts* (1937), Lady Jane Lynke wants to assert a claim to the right to tell a different kind of story. Her family history has been, as she acknowledges, a set of male narratives in which women's lives are marked only by omission:

> A long tale, to which she was about to add another chapter, subdued and humdrum beside some of those earlier annals, yet probably freer and more varied than the unchronicled lives of the great-aunts and great-grandmothers buried there so completely that they must hardly have known when they passed from their beds to their graves. 'Piled up like dead leaves,' Jane thought, 'layers and layers of them, to preserve something forever budding underneath.' (*CS 2*, p. 503)

In her late novels and stories Wharton gives voice to those mute, inglorious women whose stories are 'forever budding underneath'. In the late ghost stories in particular, she is intent on challenging stereotypical images of the ageing woman in order to reveal energies and desires that have been constrained by a lifetime of conforming to the expectations of others. She also, however, shows older women on the margins of society whose identities have become forced, even warped, through long adherence to those very stereotypes. She does so with compassion as well as fierce humour. Such stories form an interesting comparison with earlier, more realist, tales featuring older, unfulfilled women.

'The Pelican' (1898), for example, covers several decades in the life of Mrs Amyot who, intelligent, beautiful and born into a family of intellectually gifted women, but denied any career outlet for her gifts, uses her son as the excuse for her continued desire to study and lecture – even, to his acute social embarrassment, when that son is in his thirties. In the first half of the story, Wharton's satire is aimed mainly at the complacent and condescending male narrator through whom all events are focalised. Regarding himself as worldly and successful, he later forgets her entirely – 'she had dropped like a dead leaf from the bough of memory'[3] – even though it is clear that, while not admitting it to himself, he had, in the past, found her sexually attractive. The second half of the story sees Mrs Amyot's lecturing career going into decline and the narrator as ill, ageing and less judgemental: his final meeting with her and her son reveals starkly the son's anger at what he sees as his mother's continuing fantasy concerning her need to work. Wharton leaves the reader to decide whether Mrs Amyot's fabrication is an ingenious solution to a cultural misogyny that confines women to their homes and to being pretty and dependent, or whether the ageing Mrs Amyot is simply self-deluding and foolish. Seen in the context of Wharton's other work, the story seems to suggest that the reason why Mrs Amyot determinedly clings on to the myth that allows her a public life is because there are no suitable outlets for the energies of intelligent women. Pauline Manford, of course, is a later and more developed variation on this theme.

Despite their lower social status, Evelina and Ann Eliza Bunner are similarly undone by their constrained lives. The short story, 'Bunner Sisters', published in 1916, charts the emotional vulnerability of two older women who run a dressmaker's shop in New York – 'a shrunken image of their earlier ambitions' (*CS 2*, p. 167) – to the machinations of Mr Herman Ramy, a covert drug addict, who marries Evelina, having been refused by her older sister. The marriage turns out badly: Mr Ramy takes Evelina to St Louis where, having lost his job, he spends the sisters' savings on opium. Not hearing from Evelina for many weeks, Ann Eliza fears that her sister is dead, 'thrust away under the neglected mound of some unknown cemetery, where no headstone marked her name' (*CS 1*, p. 228) – anticipating the reference to the inevitable oblivion facing the lives of girls and women in 'Mr Jones'. The story ends with Mr Ramy having run off with a younger woman and Evelina, in the final stages of consumption, returning to her sister, who nurses her until she dies in their modest home. In her last few days, Evelina reveals the misery of her marriage, which included being beaten by her husband and seeing her one-day old baby die. Wharton's tale implies that had the two sisters not been confined to such dull, impoverished lives they might have been able to resist seeing marriage as a triumph, the crowning achievement of a woman's life. But they have been socialised, as women, not to demand too much: Ann Eliza is 'well-trained in the arts of renunciation', although listening to her sister's sad tale confronts her with 'the awful problem of the inutility of self-sacrifice' (*CS 2*, pp. 179 and 236). Their fear of becoming lonely 'spinsters' in a society which does not value older women in general and the unmarried in particular, also plays a large part in the sisters' tragedy; Ann Eliza especially is acutely aware of age and loneliness closing in on her and the relentless march of time itself is emphasised in the story by the constant ticking of the clock.

Apart from the occasional use of gothic metaphor in these tales – for example in 'The Pelican' the narrator thinks of the older Mrs Amyot 'as one of those pathetic ghosts who are said to strive in vain to make themselves visible to the living' (*CS 1*, p. 86) – the earlier stories about older women do not engage either with the gothic mode or with the forces of supernature although they do look at those who are socially marginalised. From the mid-1920s, however, Wharton turned increasingly to 'the fun of the shudder' (*CS 1*, p. 834). Drawn since childhood by what she called 'my intense Celtic sense of the super-natural',[4] in the last stage of her writing career Wharton appropriated and often parodied the gothic mode in her stories as well as in her novels in order to interrogate the values at the heart of American society. Her experimental strategies in these tales mark their affinity with the late novels; both the mode of narration and the portrait of older women in her late short stories are more subtle and complex than in her earlier short fictions.

For example, in 'Miss Mary Pask', first published in 1925 in *Pictorial Review 26*, the narrator of the tale, a young male friend of Mary Pask's brother-in-law, Horace Bridgeworth – the object of some considerable homo-social esteem – is prepared for an encounter with the uncanny by a journey in thick fog, at night, with a terrified and pusillanimous local guide, in a hostile and ominously named landscape. He is greeted by Miss Mary Pask – shortly after recalling the fact that she had died the previous year – but who 'still practised the same arts, all the childish wiles of a clumsy capering coquetry', despite her blue fingernails and her hands like 'pale freckled toadstools...' (*CS 2*, p. 315). Like the elder Bunner sister, Mary Pask is a spinster; indeed, much narrative time is taken up with highlighting the differences – all of which disadvantage her – between her single life and that of her married sister. Events in that life are also precipitated by the fact of her sister's marriage – Mary's self-imposed exile to France for instance, as well as her loneliness, her irrelevance. Wharton makes no attempt to communicate any sense that Grace leads a particularly fulfilling life; the children, the husband, these are decorative features of a 'dull' existence where emotions are displayed rather than felt, as she smiles 'through a veil of painless tears' (*CS 2*, p. 321). Mary's 'capering', on the other hand, in spite of the derogatory language with which the focalising voice characterises her, is at least inspired by real longing, by an intense craving for physical fulfilment. In the later story, 'All Souls'', the dour, somewhat elderly Agnes, long-serving retainer to the wealthy widow whose life is irrevocably changed by her exposure to the existence of illicit sexual appetite, has been infected with such 'desire', such 'uncontrollable longing', that 'all inhibitions' (*CS 2*, p. 820) are broken by the promise of the kind of ecstasy attendance at a coven can provide. Or, at least, that is how the somewhat prurient narrator, who has taken a cue from the 'history of witchcraft', sees it (*CS 2*, p. 820). Mary, however, has reason to be less inhibited than Agnes, who is guaranteed sexual ecstasy at least once a year, because men do not often come her way, especially after her 'death', and she has to grasp at what she can. Both she and Agnes inhabit a liminal zone between nature and supernature where they find it possible to express or even fulfil sexual longing. It is not insignificant, of course, that Mary Pask lives literally in a liminal space in her cottage on the edge of a wild and remote part of the Brittany coast. Both older women are equally physically unappealing in the eyes of respectable society and live at the edge of civilisation, or in the interstices between reality and fantasy; they are, however, sufficiently liberated to express what, in the case of Mary Pask, 'the living woman had always had to keep dumb and hidden' (*CS 2*, p. 319). Indeed, Mary's ghoulish articulation of her new post-death lifestyle, mimics the ways of the vampire, just as the story itself parodically mimics the gothic tale:

I hate the light...And so I sleep all day. I was just waking up when you came...Do you know where I usually sleep? Down below there – in the garden...There's a shady corner down at the bottom where the sun never bothers one. Sometimes I sleep down there till the stars come out. (*CS 2*, p. 317)

The narrator – still believing Mary Pask to be dead – is terrified, however, by her playful rendition of vampiric qualities and seeks immediate escape, despite her increasingly desperate pleas for him to stay. In fact, her pleas revolve as much around loneliness as sexual frustration:

I used to think I knew what loneliness was...I said to myself then: 'You couldn't be lonelier if you were dead'. But I know better now... There's been no loneliness like this last year's...none! (*CS 2*, p. 318)

As in 'The Pelican', the narrator here represents entrenched cultural attitudes that render the mature woman both invisible and absurd – doomed, therefore, to loneliness. Her clinging to him, her invitation to him to indulge in graveside capers – 'No one need know...no one will ever come and trouble us' (*CS 2*, p. 319) – is on one level comic and the storyline is resolved neatly in a Radcliffean explanation of a cataleptic trance being mistaken for death, combined with Grace's failure to let even her close friends know that Mary is alive. However, on another level the story is deeply subversive: it is clear throughout that Mary is unwilling to relinquish her undead status, presumably because it offers a new freedom of expression. In embracing the role of the undead, Mary Pask asserts her right to an active sexuality, refusing to accept ageing as a narrative of decline and, instead, celebrating it as 'a nice new devil'.[5] Her role-playing is, however, a response to the cruelties and neglect of the real world and as such, not to be dismissed as one of the old 'tales and legends' featuring 'the bride of Corinth, the medieval vampire' that float through the narrator's mind – although even he finds it hard to attach such 'names to the plaintive image of Mary Pask!' (*CS 2*, p. 320). Despite her failure to live up to the figurative expectations of the narrator, Mary still, however, manages to invade his consciousness and disturb his preconceptions and even his understanding of the boundaries between life and death or the acceptable and the forbidden. He talks of an awakening, almost an epiphany, in describing the: 'revelation of the dead Mary Pask who was so much more real to me than the living one had been' (*CS 2*, p. 320). Vampiric behaviours concealing sexual transgression also appear in Wharton's story, 'Bewitched' (1925) where Venny Brand impersonates her dead sister in order to lure Saul Rutledge into an adulterous relationship.

Wharton's story set on All Hallows' Eve, 'All Souls'', the most sophisticated of her gothic parodies, was the last fiction she wrote before she died in 1937. Here she calls up the forces of supernature again to express the inexpressible about the sexual appetites of the older woman, and an older woman, to boot, without any claims to attractiveness, status or independence. Equally, the '"fetch"'[6] who comes to summon Agnes, as well as the maid and the chauffeur, to the coven, is an unlikely procuress, being completely unglamorous and also impervious to social control, for she only laughs when Sara Clayburn refuses her access to the house or its inhabitants. This woman is actually the embodiment of sexual desire for a group of people who are otherwise refused its expression[7] – an embodiment which proves all too much for Sara Clayburn, the mistress of Whitegates, trapped in a set of rigid class attitudes and afraid of any loss of control, social or sexual.

Edith Wharton published 'Bewitched' and 'Miss Mary Pask' when she was 63 years old and 'All Souls' aged 75. As a mature woman she was writing about transgressive sexual behaviour through the lens of the gothic which – like melodrama and opera, but unlike naturalism or realism – allowed her to express 'emotion in the pure histrionic form of dreams'.[8] As many critics have pointed out, the gothic mode, in mingling emotional opposites such as humour and terror, can reflect the psychic world more accurately than realist writing. Indeed, Philip Stevick suggests that while the heightened, distorted and sometimes comic quality of gothic texts – deriving from their likeness to dream narratives – might make the story seem ridiculous, even amusing, 'the coexistence of mythic seriousness, psychic authority and laughter' reflects the disturbing authenticity of insight gained through an unconscious process.[9] It is also pertinent, of course, that 'Miss Mary Pask' and 'All Souls'' deal with the twin spectres of loneliness and death, both of which were beginning to haunt Wharton herself during the 1930s. Following the loss of her little dog, Linky, in April 1937, the year of her death, she confessed to William Tyler that 'I feel for the very first time in my life, quite utterly alone and lonely'.[10]

The issues of desire, power and narrative control, both cultural and literary, are central within these late stories, particularly in relation to women. We have argued throughout this book that the matter of female desire and ageing was close to Wharton's heart in the last 12 years of her writing career. We need to remind ourselves that this was still a taboo topic in the early twentieth century. Indeed, after documenting the energy and continued sexual vitality of older women in her study *La Vieillesse*, published in 1970, Simone de Beauvoir noted that: 'Neither history nor literature has left us any worthwhile evidence on the sexuality of old women. It is an even more strictly forbidden subject than the sexuality of old men'.[11] For Beauvoir, the histories of ageing women remained 'unchronicled lives' even in the late twentieth century. Wharton did not want, of course, to portray in vivid physical detail the sexuality and sexual relations of older women – that would not have interested her; nor did she wish to stray into the territory of philosophy and social theory, like her contemporary, Charlotte Perkins Gilman or, later, Simone de Beauvoir. However, she used her fiction to challenge the taboos surrounding female desire, just as she challenged the rise in America of materialism and a consumer culture; the 'junking' of history and literary tradition; the lack of opportunity for clever women in a supposedly democratic society; society's obsession with youth and youthfulness and its concomitant embrace of ageism; the 'flapper' culture and the sexual promiscuity that went with it; intellectual and cultural isolationism; and, above all, the rigid stereotyping of women, especially of older women. In the hybrid, experimental novels and short stories of her last 12 years she used irony, satire and parody in order to express such challenges with wit and passion. They still have much to teach us about the world in which we live.

Notes

Introduction

1. Edmund Wilson, 'Justice to Edith Wharton' (1938; reprinted in *The Wound and the Bow*, 1947) cited in Pamela Knights, *The Cambridge Introduction to Edith Wharton* (Cambridge: Cambridge University Press, 2009), p. 128; R.W.B. Lewis, *Edith Wharton: A Biography* (London: Constable and Company Ltd, 1975), p. 523. Cynthia Griffin Wolff held that Wharton's late novels 'are not as strong as her earlier work' (*A Feast of Words: The Triumph of Edith Wharton* (New York and Oxford: Oxford University Press, 1977), p. 343) and Elizabeth Ammons concluded in *Edith Wharton's Argument with America* that Wharton's late novels 'do not compare favourably with her earlier ones' (Athens, GA: University of Georgia Press, 1980), p. 167. For a more recent dismissal of Wharton's late work see, for example, Claire Preston's descriptions of the plot of *The Buccaneers* in *Edith Wharton's Social Register* as 'too sentimental and romantic to stand up as satire, its improbabilities merely silly and amusing' and of *Hudson River Bracketed* and *The Gods Arrive* as 'very weak novels indeed' (Basingstoke: Macmillan, 2000), pp. 170 and 209.
2. Dale M. Bauer, *Edith Wharton's Brave New Politics* (Wisconsin: University of Wisconsin Press, 1994). While Bauer's reassessment of Wharton's late work was a ground-breaking study, it differs from our own in its concentration on the American context, early twentieth-century eugenics and the new social sciences.
3. http://www.wsu.edu/~campbelld/wharton/newbib.htm; accessed 8 June 2010.
4. These are: Ellen Pifer, '"Did She Have a Precursor?" Lolita and Edith Wharton's *The Children*', in Jane Grayson, Arnold McMillin and Priscilla Meyer (eds), *Nabokov's World, 1: The Shape of Nabokov's World* (Basingstoke: Palgrave, 2002); Jennifer Haytock, 'Marriage and Modernism in Edith Wharton's *Twilight Sleep*', *Legacy: A Journal of American Woman Writers* 19.2 (2002) 216–29; Suzanne W. Jones, 'The "Beyondness of Things" in *The Buccaneers*: Vernon Lee's Influence on Edith Wharton's Sense of Place', *Symbiosis: A Journal of Anglo-American Literary Relations* 8.1 (2004) 7–30; Judith P. Saunders, 'Evolutionary Biological Issues in Edith Wharton's *The Children*', *College Literature* 32.2 (Spring 2005) 83–102; Jean C. Griffith, '"Lita is Jazz": The Harlem Renaissance, Cabaret Culture, and Racial Amalgamation in Edith Wharton's *Twilight Sleep*', *Studies in the Novel* 38.1 (2006) 74–94; Deborah J. Zak, 'Building the Female Body: Modern Technology and Techniques at Work in *Twilight Sleep*', in Gary Totten (ed.), *Memorial Boxes and Guarded Interiors: Edith Wharton and Material Culture* (Tuscaloosa, AL: University of Alabama Press, 2007); Janet Beer and Avril Horner, '"Wharton the Renovator": *Twilight Sleep* as Gothic Satire', *Yearbook of English Studies* 37.1 (2007) 177–92; Janet Beer and Avril Horner, 'Edith Wharton and Modernism: *The Mother's Recompense*' in Catherine Morley and Alex Goody (eds),

American Modernism: Cultural Transactions (Newcastle upon Tyne: Cambridge Scholars Publishing, 2009), pp. 69–92. This is not to say, of course, that more generally named articles and books do not contain analyses of or comments on Wharton's late work.

5. Percy H. Boynton, *Some Contemporary Americans: The Personal Equation in Literature* (Chicago: University of Chicago Press, 1924), p. 89. Cited by Pamela Knights, *The Cambridge Introduction to Edith Wharton*, p. 127.

6. Box 50, Folder 1501, 'Biographical Sketches', 1937, from an interview with Loren Carroll, published in the Paris edition of the *New York Herald*, November 1937. Edith Wharton Archive, Beinecke Library, Yale University.

7. R.W.B. Lewis and Nancy Lewis (eds), *The Letters of Edith Wharton* (1988) (New York: Collier Books, Macmillan Publishing Company, 1989), p. 481.

8. Knights, *The Cambridge Introduction to Edith Wharton*, pp. 115 and 114.

9. Kristin Olson Lauer, 'Can France Survive this Defender? Contemporary American Reaction to Edith Wharton's Expatriation' in Katherine Joslin and Alan Price (eds), *Wretched Exotic: Essays on Edith Wharton in Europe* (New York: Peter Lang, 1993), p. 87.

10. Richard A. Kaye, *The Flirt's Tragedy: Desire without End in Victorian and Edwardian Fiction* (Charlottesville and London: University Press of Virginia, 2002), p. 211.

11. Hermione Lee, *Edith Wharton* (London: Chatto & Windus, 2007), p. 610.

12. Robert A. Martin and Linda Wagner-Martin, 'The Salons of Wharton's Fiction' in Joslin and Price (eds), *Wretched Exotic*, p. 108.

13. Lee, *Edith Wharton*, p. 586.

14. Kathy A. Fedorko, *Gender and the Gothic in the Fiction of Edith Wharton* (Tuscaloosa, AL: University of Alabama Press, 1995), p. ix.

15. Amy Kaplan, *The Social Construction of American Realism* (Chicago: University of Chicago Press, 1988), p. 66.

16. Edith Wharton, *The Writing of Fiction* (1924; New York: Simon & Schuster, 1997), p. 13.

17. Wharton, *The Writing of Fiction*, p. 109.

18. Maggie Cline, Gary Day and Chris Maguire, 'Decline and Fall? The Course of the Novel' in Gary Day (ed.), *Literature and Culture in Modern Britain Vol. 2: 1930–1955* (London: Longman, 1997), p. 52.

19. *Literature and Culture in Modern Britain Vol. 2: 1930–1955*, p. 50.

20. Stephanie Lewis Thompson, *Influencing America's Taste: Realism in the Works of Wharton, Cather and Hurst* (Florida: University Press of Florida, 2002), p. 90.

21. Sharon Kim, 'Edith Wharton and Epiphany', *Journal of Modern Literature* 29.3 (Spring 2006) 150–75.

22. See Frederick Wegener, 'Form "Selection", and Ideology in Edith Wharton's Antimodernist Aesthetic' in Clare Colquitt, Susan Goodman and Candace Waid (eds), *A Forward Glance: New Essays on Edith Wharton* (London: Associated University Presses, 1999), pp. 116–38, in which Wegener sees Wharton's dismissal of modernist writing as an aspect of her impatience with modernisation generally and of her 'antiliberal, indeed antidemo-cratic' attitude to change. See also Robin Peel, *Apart from Modernism: Edith Wharton, Politics and Fiction before World War I* (Madison: Fairleigh Dickinson University Press, 2005). Peel sees *Ethan Frome*, published in 1911, as standing 'on the verge of modernism' but argues that 'Wharton and modernism have

parted company by 1915' and that she finally became 'opposed to most of what modernism stood for' (pp. 15, 16 and 80).

23. See Candace Waid and Clare Colquitt, 'Toward a Modernist Aesthetic: The Literary Legacy of Edith Wharton' in Paul Lamb and G.R. Thompson (eds), *A Companion to American Fiction 1865–1914* (Oxford: Blackwell, 2005), pp. 547 and 551.

24. See Katherine Joslin's summary of such work in '"Fleeing the Sewer": Edith Wharton, George Sand and Literary Innovation' in Joslin and Price (eds), *Wretched Exotic*, especially pp. 349–53.

25. See Katherine Joslin, '"Embattled Tendencies": Wharton, Woolf and the Nature of Modernism' in Janet Beer and Bridget Bennett (eds), *Special Relationships: Anglo-American Affinities and Antagonisms 1854–1936* (Manchester: Manchester University Press, 2002) and Thompson, *Influencing America's Taste*, particularly ch. 4, 'Edith Wharton's Argument with Modernism'. Joslin draws parallels between Woolf and Wharton, including their dislike of *Ulysses* and their admiration for Proust as well as their interest in 'the psychological complexities of daily living' (p. 210), arguing that both authors 'experiment with a new narrative for females' (p. 212). Thompson rightly claims that Wharton's work foregrounds 'the complex intersections between modernist aesthetics, middlebrow culture, and gender politics that constitute her argument with modernism' (p. 106). This allows her to acknowledge that Wharton's insistence on artistic development as (ideally) rooted in tradition links her with Eliot and Pound (p. 111) while also enabling her to offer a particularly interesting reading of Halo Spear in *Hudson River Bracketed* and *The Gods Arrive* (pp. 114–21) in relation to gender, desire and creativity. See also Jennifer Haytock, *Edith Wharton and the Conversations of Literary Modernism* (Basingstoke: Palgrave Macmillan, 2008), in which Haytock includes Wharton within a modernism 'that recognizes the impact of gender on such issues as a sense of fractured identity, feelings of isolation paradoxically combined with the inherent inextricability of the self from others, and the difficulty of relating experience in words' (p. 17).

26. Martin Halliwell, *Transatlantic Modernism: Moral Dilemmas in Modernist Fiction* (Edinburgh: Edinburgh University Press, 2001; 2006), p. 3.

27. Halliwell, *Transatlantic Modernism*, p. 46.

28. Edith Wharton, *The Ghost Stories of Edith Wharton* (New York: Scribner Paperback Fiction; Simon & Schuster, 1973), p. 8. The Preface to this edition is reproduced from Wharton's posthumously published collection entitled *Ghosts* (1937).

29. Jean-Michel Rabaté, *1913: The Cradle of Modernism* (Oxford: Blackwell Publishing, 2007), pp. 194 and 196.

30. Nancy Bentley, *Frantic Panoramas: American Literature and Mass Culture, 1870–1920* (Philadelphia: University of Pennsylvania Press, 2009), p. 219.

31. Tyrus Miller, *Late Modernism: Politics, Fiction, and the Arts between the World Wars* (Berkeley: University of California Press, 1999), p. 20.

32. Box 65 'Letter', Folder 1794, Edith Wharton archive, Beinecke Library, Yale University.

33. Box 60, Folder 1723: letter to Gaillard Lapsley dated 17 March 1932 and Box 26, Folder 810: letter to John Hugh Smith dated 16 March 1932, Edith Wharton archive, Beinecke Library, Yale University.

34. Lewis and Lewis (eds), *The Letters of Edith Wharton*, p. 547.

35. Box 26, Folder 807: letter to John Hugh Smith dated 7 March 1930; Edith Wharton archive, Beinecke Library, Yale University. Lee notes that one of Wharton's orders to her London bookseller James Bain included a request for Waugh's *Decline and Fall* (p. 611).

36. Waugh quoted in Stephen Wall, 'Aspects of the Novel, 1930–1960' in L.R. Williams (ed.), *The Twentieth Century: A Guide to Literature from 1900 to the Present Day* (London: Bloomsbury, 1992), pp. 230-44, p. 237. See Jennie A. Kassanoff, *Edith Wharton and the Politics of Race* (Cambridge: Cambridge University Press, 2004) for a close and detailed examination of Wharton's early work in the light of what Kassanoff describes as Wharton's 'wide-ranging and intellectually voracious brand of American conservatism' (pp. 35–6).

37. Box 59, Folder 1712: letter to Gaillard Lapsley dated 5 July 1921; Edith Wharton archive, Beinecke Library, Yale University. Two years earlier, T.S. Eliot, in an anonymous review of *Summer*, published in *The Egoist* in 1919, had described Wharton as 'the satirist's satirist'. James W. Tuttleton, Kristin O. Lauer and Margaret P. Murray (eds), *Edith Wharton: The Contemporary Reviews* (Cambridge: Cambridge University Press, 1992), p. 263.

38. Katherine Joslin, *Edith Wharton* (Basingstoke: Macmillan, 1991), p. 115.

39. See note 7 to Chapter 1 for critical readings of Wharton's use of the Demeter/Persephone myth in her work.

40. Margaret Morganroth Gullette, 'Creativity, Aging, Gender: A Study of their Intersections, 1920–1935' in Anne M. Wyatt-Brown and Janice Rossen (eds), *Aging and Gender in Literature* (Charlottesville and London: University Press of Virginia, 1993), p. 27.

41. Knights, *The Cambridge Introduction to Edith Wharton*, p. 115.

1   *The Mother's Recompense*

1. Edith Wharton, *The Mother's Recompense* (London: Virago Press, 1986), p. 276. All quotations from the novel are taken from this edition. Page numbers will appear hereafter in the text. *The Mother's Recompense* was first published by D. Appleton and Company in 1925.

2. Gilbert Thomas, 'New York and London Mixtures', *Nation and the Atheneum*, 28 June 1924, p. 416.

3. R.W.B. Lewis and Nancy Lewis (eds), *The Letters of Edith Wharton* (1988; New York: Collier Books, Macmillan Publishing Company, 1989), p. 443. In a letter to Bernard Berenson, dated 7 June 1921, Wharton writes: 'Apparently every self-respecting American magazine has refused "The Old Maid" on the grounds of immorality!' (*Letters of Edith Wharton*, p. 441).

4. Hermione Lee, *Edith Wharton* (London: Chatto & Windus, 2007), p. 627.

5. See Janet Beer and Avril Horner, '"This isn't exactly a ghost story": Edith Wharton and Parodic Gothic', *Journal of American Studies* 37.2 (2003) 269–85 for a more sustained account of this reading.

6. Edith Wharton, *The Ghost Stories of Edith Wharton* (New York: Charles Scribner's Sons, 1973), p. 141. 'Miss Mary Pask' was first published in *Pictorial Review 26* in April 1925.

7. R.W.B. Lewis refers to Wharton's 'lifelong obsession with Persephone and her sojourn in the Underworld' in *Edith Wharton: A Biography* (London: Constable,

1975), p. 495. See Candace Waid, *Edith Wharton's Letters from the Underworld: Fictions of Women and Writing* (Carolina: University of North Carolina Press, 1991) for a reading of Wharton's use of Persephone as a 'figure for the woman writer' (p. 3). Other critics who have pursued this line of argument include Josephine Donovan, *After the Fall: The Demeter-Persephone Myth in Wharton, Cather, and Glasgow* (University Park: Pennsylvania State University Press, 1989); Carol J. Singley and Susan Elizabeth Sweeney, 'Forbidden Reading and Ghostly Writing: Anxious Power in Wharton's "Pomegranate Seed"', *Women's Studies* 20.2 (1991) 177–203; Judy Hale Young, 'The Repudiation of Sisterhood in Edith Wharton's "Pomegranate Seed"', *Studies in Short Fiction* 33.1 (1996) 1–11; and Jacqueline Wilson-Jordan, 'The Woman Writer and the Struggle for Authority in "Mr Jones"', in Gary Totten (ed.), *Memorial Boxes and Guarded Interiors: Edith Wharton and Material Culture* (Tuscaloosa, AL: University of Alabama Press, 2007), pp. 63–82.

8. Lee, *Edith Wharton*, p. 630.
9. This hidden scenario inevitably evokes Wharton's own sexual awakening at the age of 46 by Morton Fullerton. As Hildegard Hoeller points out: 'Kate's thoughts about her love affair are strikingly similar to Wharton's own words when she described her love affair with Fullerton', citing as an example the way in which Wharton closed 'her love diary by telling Fullerton that "you… have given me the only moments of real life I have ever known"'. *Edith Wharton's Dialogue with Realism and Sentimental Fiction* (Florida: University Press of Florida, 2000), p. 182.
10. Sarah Whitehead, 'Demeter Forgiven: Wharton's Use of the Persephone Myth in her Short Stories', forthcoming, *Edith Wharton Review* 2011. The quotation in this paragraph is from Josephine Donovan's *After the Fall*, p. 47.
11. Henry James, 'The New Novel' (1914; rpt in *Selected Literary Criticism*, ed. Morris Shapira, London: Peregrine Books, 1968), p. 387.
12. Lewis and Lewis (eds), *The Letters of Edith Wharton*, p. 480.
13. Henry Seidel Canby, for example, described Kate Clephane as 'a moral coward' in his review of the novel published in the *Saturday Review of Literature* in 1925 (James W. Tuttleton, Kristin O. Lauer and Margaret P. Murray (eds), *Edith Wharton: The Contemporary Reviews* (Cambridge: Cambridge University Press, 1992), p. 401). In the late twentieth century, Cynthia Griffin Wolff suggested that Kate's determination constantly to renew herself results in a loss of authentic identity – 'she is hollow, then, monstrously empty, and all her delights are built on insubstantial fantasies' (*The Feast of Words: The Triumph of Edith Wharton* (New York and Oxford: Oxford University Press, 1977), p. 362) – and Elaine Showalter judged Kate as lacking 'the moral force, passion, or brilliance necessary to see through and free herself from the conventions of the period' ('Afterword' to the Virago edition of *The Mother's Recompense*, 1986).
14. Lee, *Edith Wharton*, p. 632.
15. Lewis and Lewis (eds), *The Letters of Edith Wharton*, p. 483.
16. Box 11, Folder 305, Wharton Archive, Beinecke Library, Yale University.
17. Box 51, Series 5, Personal Papers, Folder 1523, Wharton Archive, Beinecke Library, Yale University.
18. Thomas Hutchinson (ed.), *Shelley: Poetic Works* (London: Oxford University Press, 1967), p. 225.

19. Although cf. Hildegard Hoeller who, in *Edith Wharton's Dialogue with Realism and Sentimental Fiction*, suggests that Kate should be seen as 'a complex sentimental character' (p. 183) rather than one influenced by the Romantic movement.

20. Edith Wharton, *Twilight Sleep* (New York and London: D. Appleton and Company, 1927), p. 30.

21. See Lee, *Edith Wharton*, pp. 627–8 (Kate admits to having been inspired secretly to visit her daughter by *Anna Karénine* on p. 18 of *The Mother's Recompense*), Adeline Tintner, *Edith Wharton in Context: Essays on Intertextuality* (Tuscaloosa and London: University of Alabama Press, 1999), p. 125 and Hoeller, *Edith Wharton's Dialogue with Realism and Sentimental Fiction*, pp. 173–96.

22. In Henry James's story, a young woman leaves her grandmother's respectable house to live with her mother who, 15 years earlier, had abandoned her three young children in order to follow her lover abroad. On the death of her lover, the mother, Mrs Tramore, had returned to London only to be divorced by her husband and sentenced to a life of social isolation. Mrs Tramore and her daughter, Rose, look remarkably alike physically and the daughter enjoys her mother's company despite the social contempt in which they are now both held. The daughter gradually effects her mother's re-introduction into London society but it is Captain Bertram Jay's marriage to Rose that really re-establishes her mother's social life. The ambiguity of the story's closure is due to the fact that the reader is never really clear whether Captain Bertram Jay has married the younger woman for herself or to be close to the mother, whom he seems to have known previously and whom he thinks pretty and charming. It could be argued that Wharton borrowed James's plot, not only changing the gender of the three protagonists but also spelling out the quasi-incestuous element of his story.

23. Box 15, 'Shorter Works', Folder 439 'Cold Greenhouse' (n.d.), Edith Wharton archive, Beinecke Library, Yale University.

24. Richard A. Kaye notes that in Wharton's *The Reef* (1912), 'Darrow's desires reflect Anna's "illicit", incestuous attraction to her stepson. (The novel undoubtedly represents Wharton's updating of Racine's *Phèdre*).' *The Flirt's Tragedy: Desire without End in Victorian and Edwardian Fiction* (Charlottesville and London: University Press of Virginia, 2002), p. 225.

25. See George Ramsden, *Edith Wharton's Library* (Settrington: Stone Trough Books, 1999), for details of some of the editions in the extant half of Wharton's library.

26. For example, in a letter written to Sara Norton dated 1 March 1906, Wharton comments that she has been reading 'Aspects of Greek Genius with great joy – & am now reading Wilamowitz's translation of the Aeschylus Orestes trilogy, which promises well' (Box 29: 'L' General – Norton, Folder 900). Edith Wharton archive, Beinecke Library, Yale University.

27. Wharton's four sonnets (undated) entitled 'Iphigenia', 'Agamemnon', 'Clytemnestra' and 'Orestes' can be found in Box 21: Shorter Works Continued, Folder 671. Edith Wharton archive, Beinecke Library, Yale University.

28. This comment is from Edith Wharton's outline notes for *Twilight Sleep*, Box 13, Folder 365, Wharton Archive, Beinecke Library, Yale University.

29. Tintner, *Edith Wharton in Context*, p. 128.

30. Henry Seidel Canby, 'Pathos Versus Tragedy', *Saturday Review of Literature*, 1, 23 May 1925, *Edith Wharton: The Contemporary Reviews*, p. 401.

31. Early examples include *The Castle of Otranto* (1764) by Horace Walpole, *The Monk* (1796) by Matthew Lewis, *The Italian* (1797) by Ann Radcliffe, Mary Shelley's 'Matilda' (1819) and 'The Fall of the House of Usher' (1839) by Edgar Allan Poe.

32. Paul Baines, '"This Theatre of Monstrous Guilt": Horace Walpole and the Drama of Incest', *Studies in Eighteenth-Century Culture* 28 (1999) 287.

33. Horace Walpole, *The Mysterious Mother* in Frederick S. Frank (ed.), *The Castle of Otranto: A Gothic Story and The Mysterious Mother: A Tragedy (Horace Walpole)* (Toronto: Broadview Press Ltd, 2003), p. 183.

34. Lewis and Lewis (eds), *The Letters of Edith Wharton*, p. 480.

35. Cf. Adeline R. Tintner: 'Why should a mother living for the past two decades on the edge of the most sophisticated society in Europe regard her daughter's marrying her former lover as horrifying? It can only be because Mrs. Clephane views the lover as a husband, and the coupling of her daughter and the man who represents the husband-figure becomes an incestuous act. The father, as it were, cohabits with his own child. ...Wharton has presented the same pattern of the discovery of incest and consequent horror shown by Oedipus.' *Edith Wharton in Context*, p. 127.

36. Beatrice Cenci (1577–99) was the daughter of Francesco Cenci, an Italian aristocrat, who abused his wife and sons long term and committed incest with Beatrice. Eventually four members of the Cenci family conspired to kill him. The murder discovered, the Pope decreed that the murderers should be punished and Beatrice was beheaded. Often celebrated as a symbol of resistance to aristocratic and familial tyranny, she became the subject of many works of art and literature, including Percy Shelley's *The Cenci: A Tragedy in Five Acts* (1820), a work Wharton refers to in her June 1925 letter to Margaret Terry Chanler when commenting on the novel's epigraph: 'Yes – isn't that Shelley line poignant? And, do you know, it's *not* from the Cenci, as it seems as if it should be, but Prometheus Unbound, that inexhaustible mine of beauty' (Lewis and Lewis, *Letters of Edith Wharton*, p. 483).

37. Cf. Janet Shaffer: 'We shall find that the easily blurred line between familialization and incest links the Gothic and sentimental novel in ways that bring the horror of incest or incestuously-based betrayal close to the heart of sentimental fiction, making it a defining element of sensibility as it is of the Gothic'. 'Familial Love, Incest, and Female Desire in Late Eighteenth- and Early Nineteenth-Century British Women's Novels', *Criticism* 41.1 (1999) 67–99 at p. 69.

38. Horace Walpole, 'Postscript' to *The Mysterious Mother* in Frank (ed.), *The Castle of Otranto*, p. 252.

39. Elizabeth Ammons, *Edith Wharton's Argument with America* (Athens, GA: University of Georgia Press, 1980), pp. 142–3.

40. E.J. Clery, 'Horace Walpole's *The Mysterious Mother* and the Impossibility of Female Desire', in Fred Botting (ed.), *The Gothic* (Cambridge: D.S. Brewer, 2001), p. 36.

41. Cf. Alicia Renfroe: 'Wharton often employs legal discourse, particularly the language of contractual obligations and rights, to depict relationships among characters, to examine the ways in which characters define themselves, and to challenge contemporary accounts of justice'. 'Prior Claims and Sovereign Rights: The Sexual Contract in Edith Wharton's *Summer*',

in Michael J. Meyer (ed.), *Literature and Law* (Amsterdam and New York: Rodopi Press, 2004), p. 193.

42. See the novellas 'Summer', 'The Touchstone' and 'Sanctuary' and the novel *Twilight Sleep* for other works by Wharton which explore the law in this way.

43. Walpole, *The Mysterious Mother*, in Frank (ed.), *The Castle of Otranto*, p. 177.

44. Paul Baines, in his article, '"This Theatre of Monstrous Guilt": Horace Walpole and the Drama of Incest', *Studies in Eighteenth-Century Culture* 28 (1999) 287–309, makes this point forcefully: 'Yet one of the most controversial or culpable elements of the play, as Walpole understood it, was exactly its failure to demonize the Countess in this way' (p. 291).

45. Cf. 'it was a like a Greek face, very pure in outline...if she appeared...his cheek would glow, and his marble-seeming features, though they refused to relax, changed indescribably; and in their very quiescence became expressive of a repressed fervour...'. Charlotte Brontë, *Jane Eyre* (London: The Folio Society, 1965), pp. 311 and 332 (chs 29 and 32).

46. Katherine Joslin, *Edith Wharton* (Basingstoke: Macmillan, 1991), p. 110. Interestingly, Joslin notes in her later essay, 'Embattled Tendencies', that *Mrs. Dalloway* and *The Mother's Recompense* both 'depict the same situation: the effect of ageing of a woman's psyche. What Virginia Woolf presents as pools of half-conscious murmurings, Wharton dramatises as spectral encounters, dressed as ghostly figures that float into the heroine's mind' (p. 215).

47. '...in the 1920s, the right to smoke became a defining feature of feminine modernity', Penny Tinkler, *Smoke Signals: Women, Smoking and Visual Culture* (Berg: Oxford and New York, 2006), p. 99.

48. Lilla's 'unintelligible dialect', indicates a linguistic laxity that Wharton, as Pamela Knights points out, found 'alarming: the sign of wider moral and cultural collapse'. Pamela Knights, *The Cambridge Introduction to Edith Wharton* (Cambridge: Cambridge University Press, 2009), p. 118.

49. Dale M. Bauer, *Edith Wharton's Brave New Politics* (Wisconsin: University of Wisconsin Press, 1994), p. 166.

50. Lee, *Edith Wharton*, p. 178.

51. Dale M. Bauer, *Sex Expression and American Women Writers, 1860–1940* (Chapel Hill: The University of North Carolina Press, 2009), pp. 129–30.

52. Margaret Morganroth Gullette, *Aged by Culture* (Chicago and London: University of Chicago Press, 2004), p. 130.

53. Lewis and Lewis, *Letters of Edith Wharton*, p. 480.

54. As quoted in Tintner, *Edith Wharton in Context*, p. 130.

55. See the chapter entitled 'Defying Economies: Sentimental Fiction Revisited in *The Mother's Recompense*' in Hildegard Hoeller's *Edith Wharton's Dialogue with Realism and Sentimental Fiction*, pp. 173–96 for a very persuasive reading of Wharton's *The Mother's Recompense* and an incisive plot summary of Aguilar's rather tedious novel. Adeline Tintner also offers a summary of the novel's plot in *Edith Wharton in Context*.

56. Edith Wharton, *The Writing of Fiction* (New York: Simon & Schuster, 1997), p. 109.

57. Hoeller, *Edith Wharton's Dialogue with Realism and Sentimental Fiction*, p. 174.

58. Kate Ferguson Ellis, *The Contested Castle: Gothic Novels and the Subversion of Domestic Ideology* (Urbana and Chicago: University of Illinois Press, 1989), p. 7.

59. Dale M. Bauer, *Edith Wharton's Brave New Politics*, pp. 5–6.

60. Edith Wharton, ed. Candace Waid, *The Muse's Tragedy and Other Stories* (New York: New American Library, 1990), p. 415.
61. Hoeller, *Edith Wharton's Dialogue with Realism and Sentimental Fiction*, p. 194.
62. Robert Morss Lovett, 'New Novels by Old Hands', *New Republic*, 43. Tuttleton et al., *Edith Wharton: The Contemporary Reviews*, p. 404.
63. See Lev Raphael, *Edith Wharton's Prisoners of Shame: A New Perspective on her Neglected Fiction* (Basingstoke: Macmillan, 1991), pp. 40–7 for an overview of the various interpretations elicited by the novel's ending up until 1990. Raphael sees Kate's refusal of Fred Landers and her return to France as 'really the acts of a woman fleeing the scene of what must feel like perpetual humiliation' (p. 47). Jennifer Killoran, in *Edith Wharton: Art and Allusion* (Tuscaloosa and London: University of Alabama Press, 1996) refers to Louis Auchincloss's petulant remark in his introduction to the novel that he could not see 'why Fred Landers and Kate Clephane would not have happier and better lives married to each other' and to Michiko Katutani's review of a new edition of the novel in 1986 in which he claims that Wharton sacrifices Kate Clephane 'quite unnecessarily, to some abstract sense of tragedy that has little to do with the compelling novel that went before' (p. 101).
64. Tintner, *Edith Wharton in Context*, p. 126.
65. Janet Montefiore, *Men and Women Writers of the 1930s: The Dangerous Flood of History* (London: Routledge, 1996), p. 152.
66. Dale M. Bauer, *Edith Wharton's Brave New Politics*, p. 6.

2 *Twilight Sleep*

1. Edith Wharton, *Twilight Sleep* (New York and London: D. Appleton and Company, 1927), p. 210. All page references, which will appear hereafter in the text, are to this edition.
2. James W. Tuttleton, Kristen O. Lauer and Margaret P. Murray (eds), *Edith Wharton: The Contemporary Reviews* (Cambridge: Cambridge University Press, 1992), pp. 434–5.
3. Review of *Twilight Sleep*, *The Observer*, 29 May 1927; review of *Twilight Sleep* by L.P. Hartley in the *Saturday Review*, 2 July 1927 (Box 13, Folder 365, Edith Wharton archive, Beinecke Library, Yale University).
4. Gertrude Atherton's best-selling novel, *Black Oxen*, published in 1923, features a woman in her late fifties who undergoes the Steinach ovary treatment in order to make herself look thirty years younger. Like *Twilight Sleep*, it was one of many works in a youth-obsessed decade that focused on turning back the body clock.
5. See Dale M. Bauer, *Edith Wharton's Brave New Politics* (Wisconsin: University of Wisconsin Press, 1994), pp. 92–5 for an explanation of how the drug 'Twilight Sleep' featured in the debate on eugenics post-1914.
6. Hermione Lee, for example, writes of *Twilight Sleep* that its 'screaming laughter over a void is a frightening new note in Wharton; we do not hear it again'. *Edith Wharton* (London: Chatto & Windus, 2007), p. 636.
7. For observations on Wharton's use of palimpsest in other works, see Janet Beer Goodwyn, *Edith Wharton: Traveller in the Land of Letters* (Basingstoke: Macmillan, 1990), pp. 5, 105, 115, 121–2 and 129.

8. R.W.B. Lewis: '*Twilight Sleep*...is the most overplotted of Edith Wharton's novels'. *Edith Wharton: A Biography* (London: Constable, 1975), p. 474.

9. Phillip Barrish, *American Literary Realism: Critical Theory and Intellectual Prestige, 1880–1995* (Cambridge: Cambridge University Press, 2001), ch. 4: 'What Nona Knows', pp. 97–127.

10. Naomi Royde-Smith, 'New Novels', *New Statesman*, 2 July 1927 in Tuttleton et al. (eds), *Edith Wharton: The Contemporary Reviews*, p. 441.

11. Lewis's *Main Street*, published in 1920, was initially chosen as the winner of the 1921 Pulitzer Prize for literature but this decision was rejected by the Board of Trustees who overturned the jury's choice on grounds of the book's 'immorality'. The prize went, instead, to Wharton's *The Age of Innocence*, an event which prompted a warm correspondence between the two authors. See R.W.B. Lewis and Nancy Lewis (eds), *The Letters of Edith Wharton* (1988; New York: Collier Books, Macmillan Publishing Company, 1989), pp. 445, 448–9, 454–6.

12. First reviewer: extract from the programme 'Literary Period and Book Review', conducted by Eugene Konecky (Radio Station WOW), 4 June 1927; second reviewer: anonymous for the *Brooklyn Bugle*, 25 May 1927. (Box 13, Folder 365, Edith Wharton archive, Beinecke Library, Yale University.)

13. Mary Suzanne Schriber, *Gender and the Writer's Imagination: From Cooper to Wharton* (Kentucky: University Press of Kentucky, 1987), p. 176. Cited in Deborah J. Zak, 'Building the Female Body: Modern Technology and Techniques at Work in *Twilight Sleep*', in Gary Totten (ed.), *Memorial Boxes and Guarded Interiors* (Alabama: University of Alabama Press, 2007), pp. 111–32, p. 131.

14. Letter to Gaillard Lapsley, 5 July 1921 in Lewis and Lewis (eds), *The Letters of Edith Wharton*, p. 444.

15. Tyrus Miller, *Late Modernism: Politics, Fiction, and the Arts between the World Wars* (Berkeley: University of California Press, 1999), p. 20.

16. Hermione Lee suggests that real-life models for Pauline Manford included 'Margaret Sanger, organizer of the American Birth Control League and advocate of woman's "self-expression", and Grace Abbott, the head of the Children's Bureau, who worked for the Sheppard-Turner Maternity and Infancy Protection Act'. *Edith Wharton*, p. 634.

17. Helen Killoran suggests that 'Maisie Bruss's name is an allusion to Henry James's *What Maisie Knew*, a daughter sacrificed by parents pursuing sexual pleasure'. *Edith Wharton: Art and Allusion* (Tuscaloosa and London: University of Alabama Press, 1996), p. 107.

18. John Mepham, unpublished paper: 'Strange Intimacies: The Telephone in Fiction, 1920–1950'.

19. In his biography of Wharton, R.W.B. Lewis notes that in *The Writing of Fiction* (published in 1925), she 'returns time and time again to the same cluster of names: Balzac and Stendhal; Jane Austen, Trollope, Thackeray, George Eliot and Meredith; Tolstoy, and though less often, Dostoyevsky'. *Edith Wharton: A Biography*, p. 521.

20. Edith Wharton, *The Writing of Fiction* (1925) (New York: Simon & Schuster, 1997), p. 109.

21. Wharton, *The Writing of Fiction*, p. 153.

22. Cf. Elizabeth Ammons: 'whatever her reasons, during the war [Wharton] turned to Goethe in particular, and his influence lasted through the twenties,

showing up first in *The Age of Innocence*...and last in *The Gods Arrive*, with its closing scene evoking – actually invoking for America – the primal Mothers: figures terrifying but also healing in their insistence on confronting rather than avoiding pain and suffering'. *Edith Wharton's Argument with America* (Athens, GA: University of Georgia Press, 1980), p. 195.

23. Goethe, *Faust Part Two*, ed. and trans. David Luke (Oxford: Oxford University Press, 1994; 2008), pp. 223, 217, 219, 221 and 220. Luke notes that '"anxiety" might in some ways be a better translation than "care"' for the German word 'sorge' (p. lxvi). Nona, of course, represents both care and anxiety in the novel.

24. In the May 1927 issue of *Pictorial Review*, in an article featuring famous women's houses, Mrs Fairbank's guest room in her Chicago home is described as having a colour scheme of 'rose, taupe and black' with curtains 'made of modern French linen in a cubist design...The carpet is black velvet. The bedspreads are of silver tissue...The *fauteuil* is cushioned in black velvet' (p. 63).

25. Phillip Barrish, *American Literary Realism*, pp. 120–1.

26. As in, for example, Horace Walpole's *The Castle of Otranto* (1764), Charles Maturin's *Melmoth the Wanderer* (1820), Nathaniel Hawthorne's *The House of the Seven Gables* (1851) and Sheridan Le Fanu's 'Carmilla' (1872).

27. Horace Walpole, *The Castle of Otranto* ed. E.J. Clery (Oxford: Oxford University Press, 1996), pp. 108–9.

28. *Notebook: 'Notes and Subjects': Jan. 1924–1928'* (Box 22, Folder 702, Edith Wharton archive, Beinecke Library, University of Yale).

29. Walpole, *The Castle of Otranto*, p. 112.

30. Nancy Bentley, *Frantic Panoramas: American Literature and Mass Culture, 1870–1920* (Philadelphia: University of Pennsylvania Press, 2009), p. 246.

31. Kathy A. Fedorko, *Gender and the Gothic in the Fiction of Edith Wharton* (Tuscaloosa: University of Alabama Press, 1995), p. ix.

32. Little theoretical work has been published on the links between gothic and satire, but for work on gothic and the comic see, for example, Sybil Korff Vincent, 'The Mirror and the Cameo: Margaret Atwood's Comic/Gothic Novel, *Lady Oracle*' in Julianne E. Fleenor (ed.), *The Female Gothic* (Montreal and London: The Eden Press, 1983), pp. 153–63; Paul Lewis, *Comic Effects: Interdisciplinary Approaches to Humor in Literature* (Albany: State University of New York Press, 1989), especially ch. 3, 'Humor and Fear in the Gothic', pp. 111–53; Victor Sage, 'Gothic Laughter: Farce and Horror in Five Texts' in Allan Lloyd-Smith and Victor Sage (eds), *Gothick Origins and Innovations* (Amsterdam and Atlanta: Rodopi Press, 1994), pp. 190–203; Avril Horner and Sue Zlosnik, *Gothic and the Comic Turn* (Basingstoke: Palgrave Macmillan, 2005).

33. Allan Lloyd Smith, 'American Gothic' in Marie Mulvey-Roberts (ed.), *The Handbook to the Gothic* (1998; Basingstoke: Macmillan, 2nd edn, 2009), p. 268.

34. See Fred Botting, *Gothic* (London and New York: Routledge, 1996) for a fuller discussion of Gothic writing in this respect.

35. See Kate Ferguson Ellis, *The Contested Castle: Gothic Novels and the Subversion of Domestic Ideology* (Urbana: University of Illinois Press, 1989) for a fuller discussion of Gothic writing in this respect.

36. Killoran, *Edith Wharton: Art and Allusion*, p. 116.

37. Early examples include novels such as Matthew Lewis's *The Monk* (1796) and Ann Radcliffe's *The Italian* (1797).

38. See Jean C. Griffith, '"Lita is-jazz": The Harlem Renaissance, Cabaret Culture, and Racial Amalgamation in Edith Wharton's *Twilight Sleep*', *Studies in the Novel* 38.2 (Spring 2006) 75–94 for a rather different reading of the 'Other' in *Twilight Sleep*. In this article Griffith explores Wharton's portrayal of the 'postwar white elite' as threatened by jazz (representing restlessness, incoherence and hypersexuality) and 'European (especially Italian), Jewish, and, most importantly black' Others (p. 80). See also Barrish, *American Literary Realism*, p. 114 for a reading of the novel as expressing 'white panic about racial and cultural otherness'.
39. See Killoran, *Edith Wharton: Art and Allusion*, p. 119. She notes on p. 202 that 'Amalasuntha (A.D. 498–535) was the daughter of Theodoric, king of the Ostrogoths' and quotes from *The Encyclopedia Britannica* (1962 edn) entry on 'Amalasuntha': 'She devoted herself with special solicitude to the education of [her son]..., but the young heir to the throne threw off the restraints imposed by his mother [and] plunged into debauchery'.
40. Barrish, *American Literary Realism*, p. 113.
41. Lee, *Edith Wharton*, p. 634.
42. George Baker and Walter Driscoll, 'Gurdjieff in America: An Overview', www.bmrc.berkeley.edu/people/rhodges/html/G-baker.html. We are indebted to Dr Michael Tyldesley for helping us to make this connection.
43. R.W.B. Lewis, 'Powers of Darkness', *Times Literary Supplement*, 13 January 1975 (Box 66, Folder 1824, Edith Wharton archive, Beinecke Library, Yale University).
44. Cynthia Griffin Wolff, *A Feast of Words: The Triumph of Edith Wharton* (New York and Oxford: Oxford University Press, 1977), p. 376.
45. Lewis, *Edith Wharton: A Biography*, p. 424.
46. In her notes for *Twilight Sleep*, Wharton envisioned a much more light-hearted ending: 'in a last scene, Nona is lying in bed, her arm in a sling, & all her friends are calling to congratulate her on her escape, & get her to tell the story – which she can now recite by heart, with occasional thrilling variants' (Box 22, Folder 702, *Notebook: 'Notes and Subjects'*: Jan. 1924–1928, Edith Wharton archive, Beinecke Library, University of Yale).
47. The 'Beatrice Palmato' fragment is reprinted in Lewis, *Edith Wharton: A Biography*, as Appendix C, pp. 547–8.
48. For a persuasive and interesting reading of the 'Beatrice Palmato' fragment, which sees it as 'quintessentially Whartonian Gothic', see Kathy A. Fedorko, *Gender and the Gothic in the Fiction of Edith Wharton*, pp. 82–5.
49. See Barrish, *American Literary Realism*, pp. 120–1.
50. Vincent B. Leitch, William E. Cain, Laurie Finke and Barbara Johnson (eds), *The Norton Anthology of Theory and Criticism* (New York and London: W.W. Norton & Co., 2001), p. 916.

3   *The Children*

1. Edith Wharton, *The Children* (1928) (London: Virago, 1985), pp. 154–5. All quotations from the novel are from this edition and appear hereafter in the text.
2. The unpleasant Sybil Lullmer, a highly manipulative woman with a 'vaporous face' (*The Children*, p. 158), who eventually becomes Cliffe Wheater's

third wife, is perhaps based on Sybil Cutting who, according to Jennifer Haytock, 'Wharton believed...to be a vapid, man-hungry type of woman that she herself despised – and envied' but who proved, according to Goodman, Wharton's 'thesis that men naturally prefer a perfectly complected, childish woman to what Paul Bourget, using Wharton as a model, called "the intellectual tomboy"'. See Jennifer Haytock, *Edith Wharton and the Conversations of Literary Modernism* (Basingstoke: Palgrave Macmillan, 2008), p. 78 and Susan Goodman, *Edith Wharton's Inner Circle* (Austin: University of Texas Press, 1994), pp. 30–1 (quoted in Haytock, p. 78). Sybil Cutting had several affairs with men Wharton knew, including Bernard Berenson, and was married first to Geoffrey Scott and then to Percy Lubbock.

3. Arthur Maurice, 'Scanning New Books', *Mentor* 17.2.1929 (54) in James W. Tuttleton, Kristin O. Lauer and Margaret P. Murray (eds), *Edith Wharton: The Contemporary Reviews* (Cambridge: Cambridge University Press, 1992), p. 463. Only one contemporary reviewer had the courage to voice concerns when the novel was published. This was a critic who, in an anonymous review of *The Children* published in the *Times Literary Supplement* on 20 September 1928, praised it as containing episodes and characters 'richly and beautifully done'. The review concluded, however, with a strong reservation, albeit expressed rather obliquely: 'All the same, there is either an element of caricature or a fundamental want of decency in the situation that weakens artistic treatment. Either one must laugh without thinking or one becomes too angry to be amused.' Anon, 'New Novels, *The Children*', *Times Literary Supplement* 20 September 1928, p. 664 in *Edith Wharton: The Contemporary Reviews*, pp. 455–6.

4. R.W.B. Lewis and Nancy Lewis (eds), *The Letters of Edith Wharton* (1988; New York: Collier Books, Macmillan Publishing Co., 1989), p. 518.

5. Scott Fitzgerald, *Tender Is the Night* (Harmondsworth: Penguin Books, 1975), pp. 309–10.

6. Graham Vickers, *Chasing Lolita: How Popular Culture Corrupted Nabokov's Little Girl All Over Again* (Chicago: Chicago Review Press, 2008), pp. 57, 58 and 60. Chaplin's last wife was Oona O'Neill, whom he married in 1953 when he was 54 and she was 18.

7. Vickers, *Chasing Lolita*, p. 60.

8. Vickers, *Chasing Lolita*, p. 64.

9. Lewis and Lewis (eds), *The Letters of Edith Wharton*, p. 490; letter to Gaillard Lapsley dated 11 April 1926. Wharton's comment in this letter that she told a 'Mr. and Mrs. Herbert Fisher' 'that Americans were the only people left who understood the meaning of Leisure' suggests that she might have drawn on the cruise for some of the material in *The Children*.

10. Marilyn French, in her introduction to the Virago edition of the novel, observes that 'Wharton's naming the Princess' college *Lohengrin* suggests she may have been aware of the interest in the eugenics movement in Germany, where Hitler was soon to put it into practice. (Hitler was also a devotee of Wagner, who composed *Lohengrin*, and who was also a racist).' Edith Wharton *The Children* (London: Virago, 1985), p. ix. See also Dale M. Bauer, *Edith Wharton's Brave New Politics* (Wisconsin: University of Wisconsin Press, 1994), pp. 105–10 for a fuller discussion of Wharton's representation of the eugenics movement in *The Children*.

11. Pamela Knights, *The Cambridge Introduction to Edith Wharton* (Cambridge: Cambridge University Press, 2009), p. 118.
12. Hermione Lee, *Edith Wharton* (London: Chatto & Windus, 2007), pp. 655 and 660.
13. Susan Currell, *American Culture in the 1920s* (Edinburgh: Edinburgh University Press, 2009), p. 4.
14. Currell, *American Culture*, pp. 4–5.
15. She was not the only one to voice criticisms of the new age, of course. In a collection of essays entitled *Civilization in the United States*, published in 1922, Harold Stearns noted that 'the most moving and pathetic fact in the social life of America today is emotional and aesthetic starvation' – a result, he claimed, of society being driven by materialism and mass production. See Currell, *American Culture in the 1920s*, p. 5.
16. Interestingly, in Wharton's original summary of the novel's plot, sent to Appleton, her publisher, Boyne was involved in the First World War. She describes him in this document as 'a sensible, shrewd and experienced man, but, having been much away from the big social centres, is only half aware of the great changes which have taken place in behaviour and standards since 1914. (During the war he was on a destroyer, escorting troops to England.)' (Series 1, Box 4, Folder 81 Edith Wharton archive, Beinecke Library, Yale University.)
17. The detached nature of American involvement in the First World War is satirised by Stella Benson in her novel *The Poor Man: A Novel of Character*, published in 1922, which Edith Wharton thought 'brilliant & fatiguing' (Lewis and Lewis, *The Letters of Edith Wharton*, p. 472). During a conversation about shell shock, a Mr Hope thinks back on the fact that 'he too had risked his life for his country in the course of a month in a training camp in Texas' (London: Pan Books Ltd, 1948), p. 11.
18. Nancy Bentley, *Frantic Panoramas: American Literature and Mass Culture, 1870–1920* (Philadelphia: University of Pennsylvania Press, 2009), p. 219.
19. Hermione Lee suggests that Wharton's portrait of Martin Boyne might owe something to one of her French friends, 'Léon Bélugou, a much-travelled civil engineer who had been a teacher (and who married a very young wife)'. *Edith Wharton*, p. 658.
20. Percy A. Hutchison, 'Humor and Satire Enliven Mrs. Wharton's Novel: *The Children* Is a Moving Study of the Effects of Family Discord on Sons and Daughters', *New York Times Book Review*, 2 September 1928, p. 2 in Tuttleton et al. (eds), *Edith Wharton: The Contemporary Reviews*, pp. 450–2, p. 451.
21. Helen Killoran, *Edith Wharton: Art and Allusion* (Tuscaloosa and London: The University of Alabama Press 1996), pp. 127–8.
22. Edith Wharton, *Summer* (1917, London: Constable and Co., 1976), p. 135.
23. Lewis and Lewis, *The Letters of Edith Wharton*, p. 398.
24. Helen Killoran, *Edith Wharton: Art and Allusion*, p. 142.
25. Series 1, Box 4, Folder 81, Edith Wharton archive, Beinecke Library, Yale University.
26. Knights, *The Cambridge Companion to Edith Wharton*, p. 116.
27. Tuttleton et al. (eds), *Edith Wharton: The Contemporary Reviews*, pp. 449 and 453.
28. Tuttleton et al. (eds), *Edith Wharton: The Contemporary Reviews*, p. 451.

29. Cf. '...in the 1920s, the right to smoke became a defining feature of feminine modernity', Penny Tinkler, *Smoke Signals: Women, Smoking and Visual Culture* (Oxford and New York: Berg, 2006), p. 99.

30. Cf. 'Now there is at Jerusalem by the sheep market a pool, which is called in the Hebrew tongue Bethesda, having five porches. In these lay a great multitude of impotent folk, of blind, halt, withered, waiting for the moving of the water. For an angel went down at a certain season into the pool, and troubled the water: whosoever then first after the troubling of the water stepped in was made whole of whatsoever disease he had.' *The Holy Bible*, St John, Book 5, vv. 2–5.

31. The Lemures, or lemurs, were the restless ghosts of the dead according to the ancient Romans. Goethe has Mephistopheles address them as 'my lemur-goblins, patched/ Up semi-skeletons,/ With mouldering sinews still attached/ To move your rattling bones!' Goethe, *Faust Part Two*, Act Five, trans. David Luke (1994; Oxford: Oxford University Press, 2008), p. 221.

32. Series VII, Gaillard Lapsley material (1895–1939) Box 59, Folder 1714, Edith Wharton archive, Beinecke Library, Yale University.

33. Billie Melman, *Women and the Popular Imagination in the Twenties: Flappers and Nymphs* (Basingstoke: Macmillan, 1988), p. 77. See also Faye Hammill, *Women, Celebrity and Culture between the Wars* (Austin: University of Texas Press, 2007) for a fuller description of reactions to the novel and an interesting reading of it as a 'cross-over' text.

34. Margaret Kennedy, *The Constant Nymph* (1924) (London: Virago, 1983; 2007), p. 19. All page references are to this edition and appear hereafter in the text.

35. Beulah Amidon, for example, wrote: 'Ever since *The Constant Nymph*, we have been running into the loosely knit, unconventional family, more or less irregular in constitution and behaviour, half-rooted or not-rooted at all, and always with brilliant, sophisticated, uncared-for children suffering for the social sins of their parents. Well here they are again' (Tuttleton et al. (eds), *Edith Wharton: The Contemporary Reviews*, p. 461). The other text with which contemporary critics often compared *The Children* was Henry James's *What Maisie Knew*.

36. As Billie Melman points out, however, the reviewers – in enjoying the combination of 'juvenile eroticism and actual sexual innocence' – were typical of postwar audiences. As she notes, 'The ambivalence of purity and sensuality is evident in the opposing words comprising the title of the novel'. She also likens Tessa to 'the female child as predestined victim or even saint' (as her name suggests) as well as to 'the Victorian child bride, or the beloved ward' (*Women and the Popular Imagination*, pp. 80, 82 and 87.)

37. Although as Nancy Bentley points out, in Wharton's work 'The gentler ironies attending courtship and marriage in Austen's novels have given way to harsh incongruities and startlingly destructive forms of kinship: compulsive serial divorces (*The Custom of the Country, Glimpses of the Moon*), bizarre intergenerational love triangles (*The Mother's Recompense*), and forms of incest (*Summer, The Children, Twilight Sleep*)'. *Frantic Panoramas*, p. 231.

38. Melman, *Women and the Popular Imagination*, p. 82.

39. Bentley, *Frantic Panoramas*, p. 242.

40. Melman, *Women and the Popular Imagination*, p. 155.

41. Melman, *Women and the Popular Imagination*, p. 88.
42. Melman, *Women and the Popular Imagination*, p. 88.
43. Hammill, *Women, Celebrity and Culture*, p. 125.
44. Knights, *The Cambridge Introduction to Edith Wharton*, p. 119.

4 *Hudson River Bracketed*

1. Goethe, *Faust Part One*, trans. David Luke (Oxford: Oxford University Press, 1987), p. 11.
2. See 'Literature' and 'Life and I' in Laura Rattray (ed.), *The Unpublished Writings of Edith Wharton Vol. 2: Novels and Life Writing* (London: Pickering & Chatto, 2009), pp. 119–81 and 183–204 respectively and Edith Wharton, *A Backward Glance* (1934) (London: Century Hutchinson, 1987).
3. See Penelope Vita-Finzi, *Edith Wharton and the Art of Poetics* (London: Pinter Publishers, 1990) for a thorough exploration of how Wharton's principles concerning order and harmony in literature and life went hand in hand with her ideas on interior décor and architecture in works such as *The Decoration of Houses* (with Ogden Codman Jr; 1897), *Italian Backgrounds* (1905) and *Italian Villas and their Gardens* (1904).
4. Edith Wharton to Desmond MacCarthy, 17 October 1928. Quoted in *Edith Wharton: The Uncollected Critical Writings* ed. Frederick Wegener (Princeton, NJ: Princeton University Press, 1996), p. 174.
5. Sharon Kim, 'Edith Wharton and Epiphany' *Journal of Modern Literature*, 29.3 (Spring 2006) 150–75.
6. Edith Wharton, *Hudson River Bracketed* (London and New York: D. Appleton and Company, 1929), p. 465. All quotations are from this edition of the novel; hereafter page numbers are given parenthetically in the text. As Penelope Vita-Finzi points out in *Edith Wharton and the Art of Poetics* (p. 6), Wharton states in *French Ways and their Meaning* that the four qualities she most admires in the French are taste, reverence, continuity and intellectual honesty.
7. Edith Wharton, 'Tendencies in Modern Fiction', in Wegener (ed.), *Edith Wharton: The Uncollected Critical Writings*, p. 170.
8. Edith Wharton, *The Writing of Fiction* (New York: Charles Scribner's Sons, 1924; New York: Simon Schuster, 1997), p. 109.
9. Wharton, *The Writing of Fiction*, p. 109.
10. See, for example, Chapter 6 in Janet Beer, *Edith Wharton: Traveller in the Land of Letters* (Basingstoke: Macmillan, 1990) and Hermione Lee, *Edith Wharton* (London: Chatto & Windus, 2007), pp. 677–80.
11. Virginia Woolf, *To the Lighthouse* (Harmondsworth: Penguin Books, 1966), p. 237.
12. See, for example, Janet Beer and Elizabeth Nolan, '*The House of Mirth*: Genred Locations' in Janet Beer, Pamela Knights and Elizabeth Nolan (eds), *Edith Wharton's The House of Mirth* (London: Routledge, 2007), pp. 106–15.
13. Edwin Muir, for example, in a review of a recently published biography of George Eliot, remarked in 1928 on her 'unpopularity at present', noting that 'absurdly overrated in her own time; she was compared with Homer and Goethe' yet 'To-day she is hardly allowed any merit at all'. 'George Eliot', *The Nation and Athenaeum*, 28 April 1928, p. 111.

14. See Edith Wharton, 'George Eliot' (1902), originally published in a collection of essays on George Eliot edited by Leslie Stephen; reprinted in Wegener (ed.), *Edith Wharton: The Uncollected Critical Writings*, pp. 71–8.
15. Wharton drew attention to such early critical responses in her introduction to the 1936 World Classics edition of *The House of Mirth*. See Beer et al. (eds), *Edith Wharton's The House of Mirth*, p. 59.
16. Box 8: Folder 220 'Novels', Edith Wharton archive, Beinecke Library, Yale University. This outline of *Hudson River Bracketed* is undated.
17. Box 22: Folder 702 'Notebooks: "Notes and Subjects", No. 2: Jan. 1924–1928'. Edith Wharton archive, Beinecke Library, Yale University.
18. Letter to Elsina Tyler, dated 1 January 1920 in R.W.B. Lewis and Nancy Lewis (eds), *The Letters of Edith Wharton* (1988; New York: Collier Books, Macmillan Publishing Company, 1989), p. 525. In this letter Wharton also expresses her gratitude to John Hugh Smith, who had been 'so patient in reading the early part in type'. The novel is dedicated to him under the initials 'A.J.H.S'.
19. Edith Wharton, *The Writing of Fiction*, p. 58.
20. *The Writing of Fiction*, pp. 59–60.
21. *The Writing of Fiction*, p. 59.
22. For example, Oscar Graeve, editor of *The Delineator* apparently stated that 'with so much that is already unsatisfactory, a special ending to lop it off short would be indeed the last straw': quoted in Wharton's letter to Rutger B. Jewett dated 15 July 1929 (Lewis and Lewis, *The Letters of Edith Wharton*, p. 521).
23. R.W.B. Lewis, *Edith Wharton: A Biography* (London: Constable, 1975), p. 492.
24. Lewis and Lewis (eds), *The Letters of Edith Wharton*, p. 491.
25. Stephanie Lewis Thompson, *Influencing America's Tastes: Realism in the Works of Wharton, Cather and Hurst* (Florida: Florida University Press, 2002), p. 106.
26. Lewis and Lewis (eds), *The Letters of Edith Wharton*, p. 461.
27. Wharton, *The Writing of Fiction*, pp. 11–13.
28. James W. Tuttleton, Kristin O. Lauer and Margaret P. Murray (eds), *Edith Wharton: The Contemporary Reviews* (Cambridge: Cambridge University Press, 1992), pp. 470, 474, 472, 475.
29. Cynthia Griffin Wolff, *A Feast of Words: The Triumph of Edith Wharton* (Oxford and New York: Oxford University Press, 1977), p. 392.
30. Hermione Lee, *Edith Wharton* (London: Chatto & Windus, 2007), p. 677.
31. Janet Beer, *Edith Wharton: Traveller in the Land of Letters* (Basingstoke: Macmillan, 1990), p. 122.
32. Lewis, *Edith Wharton*, p. 490.
33. Cf. Beer: 'The language is weary and simplistic...The easy qualitative superlatives are left to carry the burden of seemingly limitless and ultimately meaningless signification...the idea of continuity contained with the use of "contiguity" is dissipated by the carelessness of the language which surrounds it.' *Edith Wharton: Traveller in the Land of Letters*, pp. 126–7.
34. Lewis, *Edith Wharton*, pp. 493 and 492.
35. Pamela Knights, *The Cambridge Introduction to Edith Wharton* (Cambridge: Cambridge University Press, 2009), p. 119.
36. From a letter Aldous Huxley wrote from Florence to his father, Leonard Huxley, on 26 November 1923. *Letters of Aldous Huxley*, ed. Grover Smith (London: Chatto & Windus, 1969), p. 224.

37. Wegener (ed.), *Edith Wharton: The Uncollected Critical Writings*, p. 274.
38. Letter to Margaret Terry Chanler, 25 March 1932, in Lewis and Lewis (eds), *The Letters of Edith Wharton*, p. 547.
39. Sinclair Lewis, *Babbitt* (New York: Grosset and Dunlap, 1922), p. 13.
40. Lewis, *Babbitt*, p. 401.
41. Hugh Walpole, 'A Note on the Modern American Novel', *The Nation & The Athenaeum*, 17 October 1925.
42. Sinclair Lewis, *Main Street* (New York: Harcourt, Brace & World, Inc., 1920) Preface.
43. Edith Wharton, 'The Great American Novel', originally published in the *Yale Review* in July 1927. Reprinted in Wegener (ed.), *Edith Wharton: The Uncollected Critical Writings*, pp. 153 and 154.
44. Cf. Wharton's statement: 'Novelists of my generation must have noticed, in recent years, as one of the unforeseen results of "crowd-mentality" and standardizing, that the modern critic requires every novelist to treat the same kind of subject, and relegates to insignificance the author who declines to conform.' *A Backward Glance* (1934) (London: Century Hutchinson, 1987), p. 206.
45. Edith Wharton letter to Margaret Terry Chanler, 1 October, 1923, in Lewis and Lewis (eds), *The Letters of Edith Wharton*, p. 470.
46. Aldous Huxley, *Antic Hay* (1923; Harmondsworth: Penguin Books, 1971), p. 8.
47. Wharton, *A Backward Glance* (New York: 1934; rpt London: Constable and Co., 1938), p. 150.
48. Edwin Muir, 'Aldous Huxley', *The Nation and Athenaeum*, 27 February 1926, pp. 743–4.
49. Raymond Mortimer, 'New Novels', *The Nation and Athenaeum*, 22 September 1928, pp. 795–6.
50. Storm Jameson, 'The Decline of Fiction', *The Nation and Athenaeum*, 3 August 1929, pp. 594–5.
51. F. Sidgwick, *The Athenaeum*, 29 October 1920, p. 595.
52. Michael Sadleir, 'The Publisher and the Public', *The Nation and Athenaeum*, 17 May 1924, p. 202.
53. Harold Forrester, 'Booksellers and Bookselling', *The Nation and Athenaeum*, 13 September 1924, pp. 716–17.
54. Laura Rattray (ed.), *The Unpublished Writings of Edith Wharton Vol. 2: Novels and Life Writing* (London: Pickering & Chatto, 2009), p. 196.
55. Jane K. Brown, 'Goethe and American Literature: The Case of Edith Wharton', in Nicholas Boyle and John Guthrie (eds), *Goethe and the English-Speaking World: Essays from the Cambridge Symposium for his 250th Anniversary* (Woodbridge, Suffolk: Camden House [Boydell & Brewer Inc.], 2001), pp. 177–8. She also notes that *The Age of Innocence* begins with a performance of Gounod's *Faust* (p. 183).
56. Lee, *Edith Wharton*, p. 84.
57. Lee, *Edith Wharton*, p. 673.
58. Lee, *Edith Wharton*, p. 673.
59. Lee, *Edith Wharton*, p. 674.
60. As Lee notes, Wharton applies the line 'Two souls, alas, are housed within my breast' to herself '(as in the poem "La Folle au Logis") and to her most autobiographical characters' (p. 673).

61. Wharton's preoccupation with sinking into the depths of the mind as a preliminary to creativity becomes literalised in an idea for a story. In a notebook she used between 1924 and 1928, she outlined a short story, 'formerly called "Plumbing"', about a 'boy from the West' who finds 'Kubla Khan' on the table of a deserted 1840 house in Hudson and comes to realise the power of the past. Box 22, Folder 702 Notebooks; 'Notes and Subjects': Jan. 1924–1928 (No. 2), Edith Wharton archive, Beinecke Library, Yale University.
62. Lee, *Edith Wharton*, p. 673.
63. Henry James, *The Question of our Speech* (Boston and New York: Houghton, Mifflin & Co., 1905), pp. 44–5.
64. Edith Wharton, *The Custom of the Country* (New York: Charles Scribner's Sons, 1913), p. 81.
65. Charlotte Brontë, *Villette*, ed. Tony Tanner (1853; London: Penguin Books, 1979), p. 175.
66. A.J. Downing, *Cottage Residences: or, a Series of Designs for Rural Cottages and Cottage-Villas and their Gardens and Grounds; Adapted to North America* (New York and London: Wiley & Putnam, 1842), pp. 99 and 106. http://www.archive/org/details/cottageresidence00downrich; accessed 25 November 2009.
67. A.J. Downing, 'On the Moral Influence of Good Houses', *Horticulturalist* 2 (February 1848) 345–47. http//:www.fandm.edu/x10620; accessed 25 November 2009.
68. Kim, 'Edith Wharton and Epiphany', p. 175.
69. Wharton, *The Writing of Fiction*, p. 78.
70. Edith Wharton, 'A Reconsideration of Proust', *Saturday Review of Literature*, 27 October 1935; reprinted in Wegener (ed.), *The Uncollected Critical Writings*, p. 183.
71. 'Life and I' in Rattray (ed.), *The Unpublished Writings of Edith Wharton Vol. 2*, p. 188.
72. Letter written from Sainte-Claire, dated 1 January 1930, in Lewis and Lewis (eds), *The Letters of Edith Wharton*, p. 525. The earliest version of this 'theme' is to be found in the chapter outlines and first few chapters of an unfinished novel, *Literature*, held in the Beinecke Edith Wharton archive and recently published by Pickering & Chatto in Rattray (ed.), *The Unpublished Writings of Edith Wharton Vol. 2*, pp. 119–81. Begun about 1913, the novel was interrupted by the war and not taken up again until the 1920s. Like Vance Weston, the hero of *Literature*, Richard Thaxter, early experiences the rhapsody of language and a sense of the numinous through encounters with nature.

5 *The Gods Arrive*

1. Goethe, *Faust Part Two*, trans. David Luke (Oxford: Oxford University Press, 1994; 2008), p. 234.
2. R.W.B. Lewis, *Edith Wharton: A Biography* (London: Constable, 1975), p. 490.
3. Edith Wharton, *The Gods Arrive* (1932) (London: Virago Press, 1987), p. 5. All quotations are from this edition of the novel and page numbers appear hereafter in parentheses within the text.
4. Lewis, *Edith Wharton*, p. 127.

5. The tea party in the grounds of Gardencourt marks the entry of Isabel Archer, the ingénue American, into the narrative. Present at Wharton's tea party is Floss Delaney, whose notion of freedom, unlike Isabel's, centres on the acquisition of those with 'brains or titles or celebrity'. Even her father says of Floss that 'money's her god' and adds, 'I guess there's nothing on God's earth as undemocratic as a good-looking American girl' (p. 234).
6. Edith Wharton, *A Backward Glance* (1934) (London: Constable, 1972), p. 249.
7. See Elizabeth Ammons, *Edith Wharton's Argument with America*, Chapter 7, 'The Mothers', for an interesting reading of how Wharton resolves the figures of the Furies into those of the Mothers in *The Gods Arrive*. In her last completed novel, Ammons suggests, Wharton finally confronted 'her own notion of inherent female superiority and develop[s] it into an intellectually provocative, even if fundamentally conservative, concept' (p. 195).
8. The quotation 'The gods approve/The depth, and not the tumult of the soul', which Wharton uses as the epigraph to *The Gods Arrive*, is from Wordsworth's poem 'Laodamia', in which he uses the Greek figures Protesilaus and Laodamia to explore fidelity and constancy in love.
9. Goethe, *Faust Part One*, trans. David Luke (Oxford: Oxford University Press, 1987), p. xxi.
10. Luke, *Faust Part One*, p. xxx.
11. Letter to Bernard Berenson, date 9 April 1937, in R.W.B. Lewis and Nancy Lewis (eds), *The Letters of Edith Wharton* (1988; New York: Collier Books, Macmillan, 1989), pp. 604–5. Wharton continues: 'Oh, how clearly I remember saying to myself that day by the stream, as I looked up at the snow through the pink oleanders: "Old girl, this is one of the pinnacles – " as I did the last time I was at Compostela'.
12. Percy Hutchison, 'Mrs Wharton Probes a Social Period: Her New Novel Is a Searching Study in the Patrician Caste', *New York Times Book Review*, 18 September 1932 in James W. Tuttleton, Kristin O. Lauer and Margaret P. Murray (eds), *Edith Wharton: The Contemporary Reviews* (Cambridge: Cambridge University Press, 1992), pp. 490–3.
13. Tuttleton et al. (eds), *Edith Wharton*, p. 496.
14. Marilyn French, 'Afterword' to *The Gods Arrive* (London: Virago Press, 1987), p. 453.
15. Diana Wallace, 'Ventriloquizing the Male: Two Portraits of the Artist as a Young Man by May Sinclair and Edith Wharton', *Men and Masculinities* 4.4 (2002) 327.
16. Edith Wharton, *The Writing of Fiction* (1925) (New York: Simon & Schuster, 1997), p. 78.
17. Edith Wharton, *A Backward Glance* (1934) (London: Constable, 1972), p. 151.
18. Shakespeare describes Autolycus in Act IV, sc. iii of *The Winter's Tale* as 'a snapper-up of unconsidered trifles'.
19. Penelope Vita-Finzi, *Edith Wharton and the Art of Poetics* (London: Pinter Publishers, 1990), pp. 52 and 53.
20. Edith Wharton, *Italian Backgrounds* (1905) (New Jersey: Ecco Press, 1998), p. 146.
21. It is perhaps worth noting here that Goethe frequently adapts biblical material when writing *Faust*. For example, as David Luke notes in his introduction to *Faust Part One* (p. xxix), Goethe takes the opening of the Book of Job

and reworks aspects of the biblical devil into Mephistopheles, the cynic, the nihilist and the spoiler. By contrast, Faust, like Vance, represents idealism and vision.

22. Laura Rattray (ed.), *The Unpublished Writings of Edith Wharton Vol. 2: Novels and Life Writing* (London: Pickering & Chatto, 2009), p. 186.
23. Wharton, *A Backward Glance*, p. 121.
24. Edith Wharton, *A Motor-Flight through France* (1908) (London: Picador, 1995), pp. 26 and 24.
25. Edith Wharton, 'Tendencies in Modern Fiction' in F. Wegener (ed.), *Edith Wharton: The Uncollected Critical Writings* (Princeton, NJ: Princeton University Press, 1996), p. 170.
26. Vita-Finzi, *Edith Wharton and the Art of Poetics*, p. 14.
27. Wharton, *A Backward Glance*, p. 198.
28. Alexander Gillies, *Goethe's Faust: An Interpretation* (Oxford: Basil Blackwell, 1957), p. 130.
29. See Luke, *Faust Part One*, p. xxxix.
30. Helen Killoran points out in *Edith Wharton: Art and Allusion* (Tuscaloosa and London: University of Alabama Press, 1996) that Wharton probably had Poussin's 'The Inspiration of the Poet' (c. 1636) in mind when she has Vance think of a work by Poussin entitled 'Poet and Muse' (p. 164). Emily J. Orlando, in *Edith Wharton and the Visual Arts* (Tuscaloosa: University of Alabama Press, 2007) sees this as Wharton exposing Vance's self-identification with the central figures of the painting, the poet and the god Apollo, while the muse, 'like Halo...is relegated to the margins' (p. 125).
31. Some ancient thinkers, including Lucian and Pliny, interpreted Endymion's love of Diana as an astronomer's desire to know the moon; later writers (for example, Ben Jonson in *News from the New World Discovered in the Moon*, a masque performed in 1620) often referred to the phenomenon of travelling to the moon in a dream or while asleep as 'Endymion's way' – or what we might think of as a poetic flight of fancy.
32. James Joyce, *A Portrait of the Artist as a Young Man* (1916) (Harmondsworth: Penguin Classics, 2000), p. 186.
33. Cf. Elsa Nettels: 'Female characters rarely objectify men in similes or metaphors but male characters habitually perceive women in the centuries-old figures'. *Language and Gender in American Fiction: Howells, James, Wharton and Cather* (Charlottesville: University Press of Virginia, 1997), p. 116; cited in Dianne L. Chambers, *Feminist Readings of Edith Wharton: From Silence to Speech* (Basingstoke: Palgrave Macmillan, 2009), p. 172.
34. Chambers, *Feminist Readings of Edith Wharton*, p. 47.
35. Cf., however, Emily J. Orlando, who draws attention to the fact that Halo is described by Wharton as short-sighted, suggesting that she, too, is blind to certain aspects of her life and to her objectification by Vance (*Edith Wharton and the Visual Arts*, pp. 118–19). Wharton was not the only female writer at this time to realise that the positioning of women as either subject matter or muse (no matter how lofty the vocabulary) made it difficult for them to realise themselves as authors. H.D., for example, having been the inspiration for the 'dryad' in several of Pound's poems, later rewrote the tale of Helen of Troy in order to deconstruct masculine attitudes to both women and war during the early twentieth century.

36. Hermione Lee, *Edith Wharton* (London: Chatton & Windus, 2007), p. 620.
    Gale was the first woman to be awarded the Pulitzer Prize for Drama, which
    she won in 1921 for her adaptation of her own *Miss Lulu Bett* (1920), a novel
    describing life in the Midwest. She also played an active part in the creation
    of the Wisconsin Equal Rights Law, which prohibits discrimination against
    women.
37. Gillies, *Goethe's Faust: An Interpretation*, p. 129.
38. See Lewis, *Edith Wharton: A Biography*, pp. 509–12 and Lee, *Edith Wharton*,
    pp. 671–2, 712–14 and 743.
39. Lee, *Edith Wharton*, p. 664.
40. Lee notes that 'Wharton's own writing life was, after 1899, so high-voltage,
    so prolific and efficient, that it is startling to find it crowded, too, with
    unfinished novels, plans for unpublished stories, poems that stayed in
    manuscript form, and abandoned sequels to several of her novels' (p. 174).
    Cf. Wharton's description of Halo's life as 'always crowded with projects,
    engagements, fragments of unfinished work' (p. 88). The difference between
    them is, of course, that Halo has less confidence in her own talents and
    never becomes a writer.
41. Lee, *Edith Wharton*, p. 85. Halo reveals her knowledge of Goethe's work by
    quoting eight lines in German from *Faust* on p. 89 of *Hudson River Bracketed*;
    Lee records that Wharton had been reading Goethe since the age of 15 and
    that her 'cruise diary had an epigram from Faust – his expression of longing
    for a magic cloak that would carry him into unknown lands' (p. 84).
42. Jean-Jacques Rousseau, *Emilius and Sophia: or, a New System of Education*,
    trans. William Kenrick, Vol. 4 (London: printed for T. Becket and P. A. de
    Hondt, at Tully's Head, in the Strand, 1763), pp. 19–20 (accessible through
    Eighteenth-Century Collections Online). This work by Rousseau is now more
    commonly entitled *Emile: or, on Education*. Emily J. Orlando also makes this
    connection, commenting: 'Wharton, then, seems to be directly engaging
    Rousseau insofar as Halo's charm evidently invigorates Vance's art' (*Edith
    Wharton and the Visual Arts*, pp. 124 and 219).
43. Abby H.P. Werlock, 'Edith Wharton's Subtle Revenge?: Morton Fullerton and the
    Female Artist in *Hudson River Bracketed* and *The Gods Arrive*', in Alfred Bendixen
    and Annette Zilversmit (eds), *Edith Wharton: New Critical Essays* (New York and
    London: Garland Publishing, 1992), pp. 181–99, pp. 182 and 192.
44. Julie Olin-Ammentorp, 'Wharton through a Kristevan Lens: The Maternality
    of *The Gods Arrive*', in Katherine Joslin and Alan Price (eds), *Wretched Exotic:
    Essays on Edith Wharton in Europe* (New York: Peter Lang Publishing, 1993),
    pp. 295–312; pp. 295, 296, 304, 306, 310.
45. In the oft-quoted letter to Robert Grant, 18 December 1907, Wharton wrote:
    'I conceive my subjects like a man – that, rather more architectonically &
    dramatically than most women – & then execute them like a woman; or
    rather, I sacrifice, to my desire for construction & breadth, the small inciden-
    tal effects that women have always excelled in, the episodical characterisa-
    tion, I mean.' Lewis and Lewis (eds.), *The Letters of Edith Wharton* (New York:
    Collier Books; Macmillan Publishing Company, 1989), p. 124.
46. Stephanie Lewis Thompson, *Influencing America's Tastes: Realism in the Works of
    Wharton, Cather and Hurst* (Florida: University of Florida Press, 2002), p. 117.
47. Thompson, *Influencing America's Tastes*, p. 121.

48. Annie E. Holdsworth Hamilton, *The Gods Arrive* (1897) (New York: Dodd, Mead and Company, 1897; reprinted by University Press: John Wilson and Son, Cambridge, USA, undated), p. 344.
49. A. Gillies describes the end of Goethe's play in the following manner: 'He sees the Holy Virgin encompassed by a halo of stars. She is moving upwards and is surrounded by a company of penitent women. The whole of celestial life is in motion as Faust's soul is brought aloft. Heavenly birth takes place, as does terrestrial birth, as the result of woman's love, the Eternal Womanly, represented at the very highest level by the Madonna herself. We are drawn irresistibly towards the love that is incarnate in her. It alone can satisfy; it alone can obliterate weakness and sin and bring redemption'. *Goethe's Faust*, p. 216.
50. Fyodor Dostoyevsky, *Crime and Punishment* (1866), trans. David Magarshack (Harmondsworth: Penguin Books, 1967), pp. 557 and 558.
51. Edith Wharton, *The House of Mirth* (1905) (New York: Charles Scribners' Sons, 1914), pp. 516–17.
52. Edith Wharton, *French Ways and their Meaning* (1919) (Woodstock, VT: Countryman Press, 1997), p. 97.
53. Thompson, *Influencing America's Tastes*, p. 111.

6 *The Buccaneers*

1. Edith Wharton, *The Buccaneers* (New York and London: D. Appleton-Century Company, 1938), p. 249. All page references are to this edition and appear hereafter in the text.
2. Hermione Lee suggests that Honourslove is based on Stanway, 'the fine eighteenth-century house, near Winchcombe in Gloucestershire', home of Lady Elcho, wife of the Earl of Wemyss. Wharton visited Stanway throughout her life, returning several times in the 1930s: 'For Wharton, it stood for everything she most loved about English traditions and English country-house architecture'. *Edith Wharton* (London: Chatto & Windus, 2007), pp. 235 and 236. See also Suzanne W. Jones, 'The "*Beyondness* of Things" in The Buccaneers: Vernon's Influence on Edith Wharton's Sense of Places', *Symbiosis: A Journal of Anglo-Literary Relations* 8.1 (April 2004) 7–30 for an interesting essay on the connections between the two writers and for the suggestion that Laura Testvalley is based not only on Anna Bahlmann, Wharton's own German governess, but also on Vernon Lee.
3. Thomas Maitland, 'The Fleshly School of Poetry: Mr. D.G. Rossetti', *The Contemporary Review* 18 (August–November 1871), accessible via http://www.robertbuchanan.co.uk/html/fleshly.html. This article was expanded and published a year later as a pamphlet. The review prompted a reply from Rossetti, published as a letter in the *Atheneum* on 16 December 1871 under the title 'The Stealthy School of Criticism'.
4. The completed *House of Life* sequence was published in 1881.
5. *Poems & Translations by Dante Gabriel Rossetti, including Dante's 'Vita Nuova' & the Early Italian Poets* (London: J.M. Dent & Sons Ltd and New York: E.P. Dutton & Co., undated, but probably 1912), p. 105. According to Hermione Lee, Wharton marked up some sonnets in her own copy of Rossetti's *The House of Life* (*Edith Wharton*, p. 669).

6. Lee notes that 'some of Dante Gabriel Rossetti's sonnets from *The House of Life*' were among poems Wharton described in her introduction to the anthology *Eternal Passion in English Poetry* as 'poems read aloud again and again by the winter fireside, and again and again found enchanting and satisfying'. *Edith Wharton*, p. 669. Adeline R. Tintner notes that Wharton's Library included Rossetti's *'Ballads and Sonnets* (Tauchnitz, 1892) and *The Collected Works* (two volumes, London, 1890), the latter with her bookplate'. *Edith Wharton in Context: Essays on Intertextuality* (Tuscaloosa and London: University of Alabama Press, 1999), p. 166.
7. R.W.B. Lewis, *Edith Wharton: A Biography* (London: Constable, 1975), p. 100.
8. In 'Life and I', Wharton wrote of the impact that reading had on her: 'I have always had a sense of the "au delà", & of casements opening on the perilous foam of the seas of magic'; Laura Rattray (ed.), *The Unpublished Writings of Edith Wharton*, Vol. 2 (London: Pickering & Chatto, 2009), p. 190. Wharton also used the phrase 'magic casements' to describe the effect that reading the work of Darwin, 'Huxley, Herbert Spencer, Romanes, Haeckel, Westermarck, and the various popular exponents of the great evolutionary movement' had upon her as a young woman. She goes on: 'But it is idle to prolong the list, and hopeless to convey to a younger generation the first overwhelming sense of cosmic vastnesses which such "magic casements" let into our little geocentric universe'. Edith Wharton, *A Backward Glance* (London: Century Hutchinson Ltd, 1987), p. 94.
9. Rattray (ed.), *The Unpublished Writings of Edith Wharton, Vol. 2*, p. 195.
10. Visiting a monastery in France, the narrator of Arnold's poem, 'Stanzas from the Grande Chartreuse' (1855), finds himself between two worlds, the monastery – which represents a dying world of religious faith – and that to which he must return, a world that has lost faith and is driven by progress, machinery and the industrial revolution. Guy Thwarte's sense of dislocation results from his return to a traditional English way of life, having spent a long period of time in South America.
11. Edith Wharton, *Italian Backgrounds* (1905) (New Jersey: Ecco Press, 1989; third printing 1998), p. 174.
12. Edith Wharton, *The Writing of Fiction* (1925) (New York: Simon & Schuster, 1997), pp. 28, 48 and 76.
13. Lewis, *Edith Wharton*, p. 522.
14. R.W.B. Lewis and Nancy Lewis (eds), *The Letters of Edith Wharton* (1988; New York: Collier Books, Macmillan, 1989), pp. 575 and 602.
15. 1873 also saw the publication of *The Gilded Age: A Tale of Today*, by Mark Twain and Charles Dudley Warner. Coined by Twain and Warner, the term 'the Gilded Age' came to refer specifically to the rapid economic growth of the United States between 1865 and 1901 and was associated with the conspicuous consumption of wealth by America's upper class during this period. In *1913: The Cradle of Modernism*, Jean-Michel Rabaté notes that 'What was denounced by the populists as "the crime of 1873" facilitated the growth of American capitalism while encouraging early globalization' (p. 185).
16. Series 1: Writings. Box 3: *The Buccaneers*, Folder 79: Miscellaneous, n.d. Edith Wharton archive, Beinecke Library, Yale University. Wharton's questions included the following: 'My opening scene is laid at the United States Hotel, Saratoga. Was there already racing there at the time, and if so was it only

trotting races?'; 'Would men of the smart sporting type be there with their families; or did that come only later?'; To what clubs would the relatively unknown fathers of my fast girls belong?'; What would an elderly Wall Street broker wear at a race meeting?'; 'What sort of clothes would they wear in travelling?'; What would a ball at the United States Hotel at Saratoga be like?'; 'Would there be "night life", poker, suppers with demi-mondaines, etc.?'.

17. Letter to Sara Norton, 5 June 1903, in Lewis and Lewis (eds), *The Letters of Edith Wharton*, p. 84.

18. Lewis, *Edith Wharton*, p. 41. Hermione Lee argues for a close parallel between Consuelo Yznaga's marriage to Lord Mandeville, the future Duke of Manchester, in 1876 and that between Consuelo Closson and Lord Richard Marable (*Edith Wharton*, p. 723).

19. Jennie Jerome became the mother of Sir Winston Churchill and was, apparently, a formidable personality in her own right. In her early notes for the novel, Wharton wrote: 'Conquest of England by American adventurous (& adventuress) families in the seventies. Type: Jeromes, Paran (?), Stevens, Yznaga etc.' Box 22, Folder 702, Notebooks: 'Notes and Subjects' Jan. 1924–1928 (No. 2), Edith Wharton archive, Beinecke Library, Yale University.

20. Kathleen Burk, 'Anglo-American Marital Relations, 1870–1945', Gresham Lecture, http://www.gresham.ac.uk/event.asp?PageId=45&EventId=211, accessed 20 July 2010.

21. Adeline R. Tintner, 'Consuelo Vanderbilt and The Buccaneers', *Edith Wharton Review* 10.2 (1993) 15–19. See also Hermione Lee, *Edith Wharton*, p. 723 for more on Consuelo Vanderbilt's marriage to the 9th Duke of Marlborough and its parallels with Nan St George's marriage to the Duke of Tintagel. Lee notes that 'Between 1870 and 1924, about a hundred Americans married into the British peerage, several of them connected to Wharton' (p. 724).

22. Adeline R. Tintner, 'Consuelo Vanderbilt and The Buccaneers', p. 15. Lee, *Edith Wharton*, p. 723.

23. Frances Hodgson Burnett, *The Shuttle* (1907) (Memphis, TN: General Books, 2010), p. 79.

24. Lee, *Edith Wharton*, p. 241.

25. Cf. Steven C. Topik: 'The Gilded Age conjures up images of robber-barons lighting cigars with hundred dollar bills, farmers plowing the Great American Desert into a wheat basket, miners striking pay dirt, and factories belching black, prosperous smoke across a countryside closely knit together by rail and canal. It was a time of excess and contrast: abundant crops followed by drought, industrial boom leading to glut, silver bonanzas cheapened by dwindling prices, wealthy captains of industry in palatial mansions employing impoverished immigrants and freedmen who dwelt in slums'. *Trade and Gunboats: The United States and Brazil in the Age of Empire* (Stanford, CA: Stanford University Press, 1996), p. 11.

26. George Ramsden, *Edith Wharton's Library* (York: Stone Trough Books, 1999), p. 143.

27. Oscar Wilde, *Court and Society Review*, 23 March 1887. See http://www.readbookonline.net/readOnLine/9884/, accessed 10 August 2010.

28. Wharton wrote to Elsina Tyler early in 1937: 'You will be amused to hear that Mrs. Simpson has made my tale "de l'actualité", & that publishers & editors in England & the US are prodding me to finish it!!' Lee, *Edith Wharton*, p. 721.

29. Such boroughs, comprising a very small number of voters, could easily be acquired as a parliamentary seat through bribing the electorate. This tells the reader more about Robinson's ambition than his political integrity; it also signals Wharton's disapproval of a political system which is supposedly democratic but open to such corruption.

30. Edith Wharton, *The House of Mirth* (Oxford: Oxford University Press, 1936), Introduction by the author, p. x.

31. As Adeline R. Tintner notes, 'At the time of Whartons's novel...the famous Rossetti oil, *Bocca Baciata* (1859), was actually in the collection of G.P. Boyce, who had commissioned it, and it remained in his collection until July 1897...It is...likely...that Wharton saw the picture when it was exhibited at the Royal Academy in 1906'. 'Correggio and Rossetti in *The Buccaneers*: Tradition and Revolution in the Patterns of Love' in Tintner, *Edith Wharton in Context*, pp. 162–3.

32. Virginia Surtees, *Dante Gabriel Rossetti, 1828–1882: The Paintings and Drawings. A Catalogue Raisonné* (Oxford: Clarendon, 1971) as quoted in Tintner, *Edith Wharton in Context*, p. 164.

33. Douglas Bush, 'Keats', in Walter Jackson Bate (ed.), *Keats: A Collection of Critical Essays* (Englewood Cliffs, NJ: Prentice-Hall, 1965), p. 23.

34. From a letter written by Keats to J.H. Reynolds, 3 May 1818. http://englishhistory. net/keats/letters/reynolds3May1818.html, accessed 30 July 2010.

35. 'The negative side of the spectacle on which Hawthorne looked out, in his contemplative saunterings and reveries, might, indeed, with a little inge- nuity, be made almost ludicrous; one might enumerate the items of high civilization, as it exists in other countries, which are absent from the texture of American life, until it should become a wonder to know what was left. No State, in the European sense of the word, and indeed barely a specific national name. No sovereign, no court, no personal loyalty, no aristocracy, no church, no clergy, no army, no diplomatic service, no country gentlemen, no palaces, no castles, nor manors, nor old country-houses, nor parsonages, not thatched cottages nor ivied ruins; no cathedrals, nor abbeys, nor little Norman churches; no great Universities nor public schools – no Oxford, no Eton, nor Harrow; no literature, no novels, no museums, no pictures, no political society, no sporting class – no Epsom nor Ascot! Some such list as that might be drawn up of the absent things in American life – especially in the American life of forty years ago, the effect of which, upon an English or French imagination, would probably as a general thing be appalling.' Henry James, *Hawthorne* (London, 1880; rpt. London: Macmillan and Co., 1967), p. 55.

36. Lee, *Edith Wharton*, p. 721.

37. Lewis, *Edith Wharton*, p. 524.

38. Shari Benstock, *No Gifts from Chance: A Biography of Edith Wharton*, p. 460. Cited in Lee, *Edith Wharton*, p. 721.

39. Frances Hodgson Burnett in *The Shuttle* also gives one of her male charac- ters (the son of Lady Rosalie Anstruthers) an uncommon name, 'Ughtred'. Wharton, in her choice of 'Ushant' for one of her male characters, might well have been signalling her engagement with, and reworking of, this ear- lier novel about 'the American Invasion' (*The Shuttle*, p. 55).

40. John Esquemeling's *The Buccaneers of America: A True Account of the Most Remarkable Assaults Committed of Late Years upon the Coast of the West Indies by the Buccaneers of Jamaica and Tortuga*, written originally in Dutch, translated into English in 1684–5. Wharton's copy was that introduced by Andrew Lange, Third Impression, London: George Routledge & Sons Ltd; New York: E.P. Dutton & Co., undated but probably published in 1925. Page references are to this edition.

41. Richard A. Kaye, *The Flirt's Tragedy: Desire without End in Victorian and Edwardian Fiction* (Charlottesville and London: University Press of Virginia, 2002), p. 158.

42. The famous phrase 'a terrible beauty is born' comes from Yeats's well-known poem, 'Easter 1916', about the Republican uprising in Ireland against British rule on Monday, 24 April 1916. The uprising was unsuccessful, and most of the Irish leaders involved were executed for treason. Yeats describes in his earlier poem 'The Falling of the Leaves', how the 'wet wild-strawberry leaves' turn yellow in autumn before dying, just as love wanes before it dies: 'And weary and worn are our sad souls now; Let us part, ere the season of passion forget us...'.

43. As Adeline R. Tintner points out, 'There is actually no such sequence by Correggio' (*Edith Wharton in Context*, p. 165). She goes on to surmise that Wharton imagined the sequence, having probably seen several individual panels by Correggio in galleries in Paris, Berlin and Rome. She also suggests that Wharton took her title for the imagined series from William Morris's long poem, *The Earthly Paradise*, a copy of which she held in her library: 'The stories are those of the loves of the gods and goddesses, covering the same kind of material that Correggio paints on his isolated canvases, but in Morris's poem [Henry] James wrote in a review in *The Nation* that "Fate reserves for the poor storm-tossed adventurers a sort of fantastic compromise between their actual misery and their ideal bliss"' (Tintner, *Edith Wharton in Context*, pp. 165 and 167). James's words resonate strongly with Nan's painful growth to emotional maturity.

44. For an interesting essay on Wharton's use of art, described as '[f]unctioning as a non-human Greek chorus' (p. 444) in *The House of Mirth, Custom of the Country* and *The Age of Innocence*, see Maureen Honey, 'Women and Art in the Fiction of Edith Wharton', *Prospects* 19 (1994) 419–50.

45. The painting is now thought to have been completed by Titian and is documented as such in the Louvre.

46. George P. Landow, '"Life touching lips with immortality": Rossetti's Temporal Structures', http://www.victorianweb.org/religion/type/ch6b.html, accessed 18 May 2010.

47. Before the Act, a woman's property and income would have automatically passed to her husband on marriage and she would have had no legal right to it. Nan's difficulty in obtaining money to help Conchita, however, shows that many husbands still controlled their wives' finances, despite changes in the law. As a character remarks in Hodgson Burnett's *The Shuttle*, 'A man cannot tie his wife to the bedpost in these days, but he can make her efforts to leave him so decidedly unpleasant that decent women prefer to stay at home and take what is coming' (p. 283).

Conclusion

1. *Edith Wharton: Collected Stories 1891–1910 Vol. 2*, ed. Maureen Howard (New York: The Library of America, 2001), p. 503. Hereafter referred to in the text as *CS 2*.

2. Janet Beer and Avril Horner, '"This isn't exactly a ghost story": Edith Wharton and Parodic Gothic', *Journal of American Studies* 37.2 (2003) 269–85.

3. *Edith Wharton: Collected Stories 1891–1910 Vol. 1*, ed. Maureen Howard (New York: The Library of America, 2001), p. 86. Hereafter referred to in the text as *CS 1*.

4. Edith Wharton, 'Life and I' in Laura Rattray (ed.), *The Unpublished Writings of Edith Wharton Vol. 2: Novels and Life Writing* (London: Pickering & Chatto, 2009), p. 191.

5. See Margaret Morganroth Gullette, *Aged by Culture* (Chicago and London: University of Chicago Press, 2004) which carries Winston Langley's words 'Age is a nice new devil' as its epigraph.

6. According to the *Shorter Oxford English Dictionary*, the word 'fetch' dates from the eighteenth century and is 'the apparition, double, or wraith of a living person'.

7. For a fuller reading of this story see Beer and Horner, '"This isn't exactly a ghost story"', pp. 280–4.

8. Eric Bentley, quoted in Peter Brooks, *The Melodramatic Imagination: Balzac, Henry James, Melodrama and the Mode of Excess* (New Haven and London: Yale University Press, 1976; 2nd edn, 1995), p. 12.

9. Philip Stevick, 'Frankenstein and Comedy', in George Levine and U.C. Knoepflmacher (eds), *The Endurance of Frankenstein: Essays on Mary Shelley's Novel* (Berkeley, Los Angeles and London: University of California Press, 1979), p. 239.

10. R.W.B. Lewis and Nancy Lewis (eds), *The Letters of Edith Wharton* (1988; New York: Collier Books, Macmillan, 1989), p. 606.

11. Simone de Beauvoir, *Old Age* (*La Vieillesse*, 1970) trans. Patrick O'Brian (Harmondsworth: Penguin Books, 1985), p. 390.

Select Bibliography

Ammons, Elizabeth. *Edith Wharton's Argument with America*. Athens, GA: University of Georgia Press, 1980.

Baines, Paul. '"This Theatre of Monstrous Guilt": Horace Walpole and the Drama of Incest'. *Studies in Eighteenth-Century Culture* 28 (1999): 287–309.

Barrish, Phillip. *American Literary Realism: Critical Theory and Intellectual Prestige, 1880–1995*. Cambridge: Cambridge University Press, 2001.

Bate, Walter Jackson, ed. *Keats: A Collection of Critical Essays*. New Jersey: Prentice-Hall, Inc., 1965.

Bauer, Dale M. *Edith Wharton's Brave New Politics*. Madison: University of Wisconsin Press, 1994.

——. *Sex Expression and American Women Writers, 1860–1940*. Chapel Hill: University of North Caroline Press, 2009.

Beer, Janet. *Edith Wharton: Traveller in the Land of Letters*. Basingstoke: Macmillan, 1990.

—— and Bridget Bennett, eds. *Special Relationships: Anglo-American Affinities and Antagonisms 1854–1936*. Manchester: Manchester University Press, 2002.

—— and Avril Horner. '"This isn't exactly a ghost story": Edith Wharton and Parodic Gothic', *Journal of American Studies* 37.2 (2003): 269–85.

—— and Avril Horner, '"Wharton the Renovator": *Twilight Sleep* as Gothic Satire', *Yearbook of English Studies* 37:1 (2007): 177–92.

—— and Avril Horner, 'Edith Wharton and Modernism: *The Mother's Recompense*' in *American Modernism: Cultural Transactions* eds. Catherine Morley and Alex Goody. Newcastle upon Tyne, Cambridge Scholars Publishing, 2009: 69–92.

——, Pamela Knights and Elizabeth Nolan, eds. *Edith Wharton's The House of Mirth*. London: Routledge, 2007.

Bendixen, Alfred and Annette Zilversmit, eds. *Edith Wharton: New Critical Essays*. New York and London: Garland Publishing Inc., 1992.

Benson, Stella. *The Poor Man: A Novel of Character* (1922). London: Pan Books Ltd, 1948.

Bentley, Nancy. *Frantic Panoramas: American Literature and Mass Culture, 1870–1920*. Philadelphia: University of Pennsylvania Press, 2009.

Botting, Fred. *Gothic*. London and New York: Routledge, 1996.

Brontë, Charlotte. *Jane Eyre* (1847). London: The Folio Society, 1965.

——. *Villette* (1853). Ed.Tony Tanner. Harmondsworth: Penguin Books, 1979.

Brown, Jane K. 'Goethe and American Literature: The Case of Edith Wharton' in Nicholas Boyle and John Guthrie, eds. *Goethe and the English-Speaking World: Essays from the Cambridge Symposium for His 250th Anniversary*. Woodbridge, Suffolk: Camden House, Boydell & Brewer Inc., 2001: 173–84.

Burnett, Frances Hodgson. *The Shuttle* (1907). Memphis, Tennessee: General Books, 2010.

Bush, Douglas. 'Keats', in Walter Jackon Bate (ed.) *Keats: A Collection of Critical Essays*. New Jersey: Prentice-Hall, Inc., 1965: 13–40.

Chambers, Dianne L. *Feminist Readings of Edith Wharton: From Silence to Speech* Basingstoke: Palgrave Macmillan, 2009.

Clery, E.J. 'Horace Walpole's *The Mysterious Mother* and the Impossibility of Female Desire', in Fred Botting, ed. *The Gothic*. Cambridge: D.S.Brewer, 2001: 23–46.

Cline, Maggie, Gary Day and Chris Maguire, 'Decline and Fall? The Course of the Novel' in Gary Day (ed.), *Literature and Culture in Modern Britain Vol. 2: 1930–1955*. London: Longman, 1997: 50–69.

Colquitt, Clare, Susan Goodman and Candace Waid, eds. *A Forward Glance: New Essays on Edith Wharton*. London: Associated University Presses, 1999.

Currell, Susan. *American Culture in the 1920s*. Edinburgh: Edinburgh University Press, 2009.

Donovan, Josephine. *After the Fall: The Demeter-Persephone Myth in Wharton, Cather, and Glasgow*. University Park: Pennsylvania State University Press, 1989.

Dostoyevsky, Fyodor. *Crime and Punishment* (1866), trans. David Magarshack. Harmondsworth: Penguin Books, 1967.

Downing, A.J. *Cottage Residences: or, a Series of Designs for Rural Cottages and Cottage-Villas and their Gardens and Grounds; Adapted to North America*. New York and London: Wiley & Putnam, 1842. http://www.archive/org/details/cottageresidence00downrich

—— 'On the Moral Influence of Good Houses', *Horticulturalist* 2 (Feb. 1848): 345–47. http//:www.fandm.edu/x10620

Ellis, Kate Ferguson. *The Contested Castle: Gothic Novels and the Subversion of Domestic Ideology*. Urbana and Chicago: University of Illinois Press, 1989.

Esquemeling, John. *The Buccaneers of America: A True Account of the Most Remarkable Assaults Committed of Late Years upon the Coast of the West Indies by the Buccaneers of Jamaica and Tortuga*, written originally in Dutch, translated into English in 1684-5. Introd. Andrew Lange, Third Impression, London: George Routledge & Sons Ltd; New York: E.P. Dutton & Co., n.d.

Fedorko, Kathy A. *Gender and the Gothic in the Fiction of Edith Wharton* Tuscaloosa: University of Alabama Press, 1995.

Fitzgerald, Scott. *Tender is the Night* (1934). Harmondsworth: Penguin Books, 1975.

Gillies, Alexander. *Goethe's Faust: An Interpretation*. Oxford: Basil Blackwell, 1957.

Goethe, Johann Wolfgang von. *Faust Part One* ed. and trans. David Luke. Oxford: Oxford University Press, 1987.

——. *Faust Part Two* ed. and trans. David Luke. Oxford: Oxford University Press, 1994; 2008.

Goodman, Susan. *Edith Wharton's Inner Circle*. Austin: University of Texas Press, 1994.

Griffith, Jean C. '"Lita is Jazz": The Harlem Renaissance, Cabaret Culture, and Racial Amalgamation in Edith Wharton's *Twilight Sleep*', *Studies in the Novel* 38.1 (2006): 74–94.

Gullette, Margaret Morganroth. 'Creativity, Aging, Gender: A Study of Their Intersections, 1920–1935' in Anne M. Wyatt-Brown and Janice Rossen (eds), *Aging and Gender in Literature*. Charlottesville and London: University Press of Virginia, 1993: 19–48.

——. *Aged by Culture*. Chicago and London: University of Chicago Press, 2004.

Halliwell, Martin. *Transatlantic Modernism: Moral Dilemmas in Modernist Fiction*. Edinburgh: Edinburgh University Press, 2001; 2006.

Hammill, Faye. *Women, Celebrity and Culture between the Wars*. Austin: University of Texas Press, 2007.

Haytock, Jennifer. 'Marriage and Modernism in Edith Wharton's *Twilight Sleep*', *Legacy: A Journal of American Woman Writers* 19.2 (2002) 216–29.

——. *Edith Wharton and the Conversations of Literary Modernism*. Basingstoke: Palgrave Macmillan, 2008.

Hoeller, Hildegard. *Edith Wharton's Dialogue with Realism and Sentimental Fiction*. Florida: University of Florida, 2000.

Holdsworth Hamilton, Annie E. *The Gods Arrive* (1897). New York: Dodd, Mead and Company, 1897; reprinted by University Press: John Wilson and Son, Cambridge, USA.

Honey, Maureen. 'Women and Art in the Fiction of Edith Wharton'. *Prospects* (1994) 19: 419–50.

Horner, Avril and Sue Zlosnik. *Gothic and the Comic Turn*. Basingstoke: Palgrave Macmillan, 2005.

Hutchinson, Thomas, ed. *Shelley: Poetic Works*. London: Oxford University Press, 1967.

Huxley, Aldous. *Antic Hay* (1923). Harmondsworth: Penguin Books, 1971.

James, Henry. *Hawthorne* (1880). Rpt. London: Macmillan and Co., 1967.

——. *The Portrait of a Lady* (1881). Harmondsworth: Penguin Books, 1964.

——. *The Question of Our Speech*. Boston and New York: Houghton, Mifflin & Co., 1905.

——. 'The New Novel' (1914) rpt. in Morris Shapira (ed.) *Selected Literary Criticism*. London: Peregrine Books, 1968.

Jameson, Storm. 'The Decline of Fiction', *The Nation & Athenaeum*, 3rd August 1929: 594–5.

Jones, Suzanne W. 'The *"Beyondness* of Things" in *The Buccaneers*: Vernon's Influence on Edith Wharton's Sense of Places', *Symbiosis: A Journal of Anglo-Literary Relations* 8.1 (April 2004): 7–30.

Joslin, Katherine. *Edith Wharton*. Basingstoke: Macmillan, 1991.

——. and Alan Price, eds. *Wretched Exotic: Essays on Edith Wharton in Europe*. New York: Peter Lang, 1993.

——. '"Fleeing the Sewer": Edith Wharton, George Sand and Literary Innovation' in *Wretched Exotic: Essays on Edith Wharton in Europe* ed. Joslin and Price. New York: Peter Lang, 1993: 335–54.

——. '"Embattled tendencies": Wharton, Woolf and the nature of Modernism' in Beer, Janet and Bridget Bennett, eds. *Special Relationships: Anglo-American Affinities and Antagonisms 1854–1936*. Manchester: Manchester University Press, 2002: 202–23.

Joyce, James. *A Portrait of the Artist as a Young Man* (1916). Harmondsworth: Penguin Classics, 2000.

Kaplan, Amy. *The Social Construction of American Realism*. Chicago: University of Chicago Press, 1988.

Kassanoff, Jennie A. *Edith Wharton and the Politics of Race*. Cambridge: Cambridge University Press, 2004.

Kaye, Richard A. *The Flirt's Tragedy: Desire without End in Victorian and Edwardian Fiction*. Charlottesville and London: University Press of Virginia, 2002.

Margaret Kennedy, *The Constant Nymph* (1924). London: Virago, 1983; 2007.

Killoran, Helen. *Edith Wharton: Art and Allusion*. Tuscaloosa and London: University of Alabama Press, 1996.

Kim, Sharon. 'Edith Wharton and Epiphany', *Journal of Modern Literature* 29.3 (Spring 2006) 150–75.

Knights, Pamela. *The Cambridge Introduction to Edith Wharton*. Cambridge: Cambridge University Press, 2009.

Lamb, Paul and G.R.Thompson, eds. *A Companion to American Fiction 1865–1914*. Oxford: Blackwell, 2005.

Lauer, Kristin Olson. 'Can France Survive this Defender? Contemporary American Reaction to Edith Wharton's Expatriation' in Joslin and Price (eds), *Wretched Exotic: Essays on Edith Wharton in Europe*. New York: Peter Lang, 1993: 77–95.

Lee, Hermione. *Edith Wharton*. London: Chatto & Windus, 2007.

Leitch, Vincent B., William E. Cain, Laurie Finke and Barbara Johnson, eds. *The Norton Anthology of Theory and Criticism*, (New York and London: W.W. Norton & Co., 2001.

Lewis, R.W.B. *Edith Wharton: A Biography*. London: Constable and Company Ltd, 1975.

——. 'Powers of Darkness', *Times Literary Supplement*, 13 January 1975.

——. and Nancy Lewis, eds. *The Letters of Edith Wharton* (1988). New York: Collier Books, Macmillan Publishing Company, 1989.

Lewis, Sinclair. *Main Street*. New York: Harcourt, Brace & World, Inc., 1920.

——. *Babbitt*. New York: Grosset and Dunlap, 1922.

Martin, Robert A. and Linda Wagner-Martin, 'The Salons of Wharton's Fiction' in Joslin and Price (eds), *Wretched Exotic: Essays on Edith Wharton in Europe*. New York: Peter Lang, 1992: 97–110.

Melman, Billie. *Women and the Popular Imagination in the Twenties: Flappers and Nymphs*. Basingstoke: Macmillan, 1988.

Mepham, John. Unpublished paper: 'Strange Intimacies: The Telephone in Fiction, 1920–1950'.

Meyer, Michael J. ed. *Literature and Law*. Amsterdam and New York: Rodopi, 2004.

Miller, Tyrus. *Late Modernism: Politics, Fiction, and the Arts between the World Wars*. Berkeley: University of California Press, 1999.

Montefiore, Janet. *Men and Women Writers of the 1930s: The Dangerous Flood of History*. London: Routledge, 1996.

Mortimer, Raymond. 'New Novels', *The Nation & Athenaeum*, 22 September 1928: 795–6.

Muir, Edwin. 'Aldous Huxley', *The Nation & Athenaeum*, 27 February 1926: 743–4.

——. 'George Eliot', *The Nation & Athenaeum*, 28 April 1928: 111.

Mulvey-Roberts, Marie, ed. *The Handbook to the Gothic* (1998). Basingstoke: Macmillan, 2nd edn, 2009.

Olin-Ammentorp, Julie. 'Wharton through a Kristevan Lens: The Maternality of *The Gods Arrive*' in Katherine Joslin and Alan Price (eds.) *Wretched Exotic: Essays on Edith Wharton in Europe*. New York: Peter Lang Publishing, 1993: 295–312.

Orlando, Emily J. *Edith Wharton and the Visual Arts*. Tuscaloosa: University of Alabama Press, 2007.

Peel, Robin. *Apart from Modernism: Edith Wharton, Politics and Fiction before World War I*. Madison: Fairleigh Dickinson University Press, 2005.

Pifer, Ellen. '"Did She Have a Precursor?" Lolita and Edith Wharton's *The Children*', in *Nabokov's World, 1: The Shape of Nabokov's World* eds Jane Grayson, Arnold McMillin and Priscilla Meyer. Basingstoke: Palgrave, 2002: 171–85.

Preston, Claire. *Edith Wharton's Social Register*. London: Macmillan, 2000.

Rabaté, Jean-Michel. *1913: The Cradle of Modernism*. Oxford: Blackwell Publishing, 2007.

Ramsden, George. *Edith Wharton's Library*. Settrington: Stone Trough Books, 1999.

Raphael, Lev. *Edith Wharton's Prisoners of Shame: A New Perspective on Her Neglected Fiction*. Basingstoke: Macmillan, 1991.

Rattray, Laura (ed.) *The Unpublished Writings of Edith Wharton Vol. 2: Novels and Life Writing*. London: Pickering & Chatto, 2009.

Renfroe, Alicia. 'Prior Claims and Sovereign Rights: The Sexual Contract in Edith Wharton's *Summer*' in Michael J. Meyer (ed.), *Literature and Law*. Amsterdam and New York: Rodopi Press, 2004: 193–206.

Rossetti, Dante Gabriel. *Poems & Translations by Dante Gabriel Rossetti, including Dante's 'Vita Nuova' & the Early Italian Poets*. London: J.M. Dent & Sons Ltd and New York: E.P. Dutton & Co., n.d.

Sadleir, Michael. 'The Publisher and the Public', *The Nation & The Athenaeum*, 17 May 1924: 202–3.

Saunders, Judith P. 'Evolutionary Biological Issues in Edith Wharton's *The Children*', *College Literature* 32.2 (Spring 2005): 83–102.

Shaffer, Julie. 'Familial Love, Incest, and Female Desire in Late Eighteenth- and Early Nineteenth-Century British Women's Novels', *Criticism* 41.1 (1999): 67–99.

Shapira, Morris, ed. *Selected Literary Criticism*. London: Peregrine Books, 1968.

Showalter, Elaine. 'Afterword' to *The Mother's Recompense*. London: Virago, 1986.

Singley, Carol J. and Susan Elizabeth Sweeney, 'Forbidden Reading and Ghostly Writing: Anxious Power in Wharton's "Pomegranate Seed"'. *Women's Studies* 20 (2) 1991: 177–203.

Smith, Grover, ed. *Letters of Aldous Huxley*. London: Chatto & Windus, 1969.

Thomas, Gilbert. 'New York and London Mixtures', *Nation and the Athenaeum*, 28 June 1924: 416.

Thompson, Stephanie Lewis. *Influencing America's Taste: Realism in the Works of Wharton, Cather and Hurst*. Florida: University Press of Florida, 2002.

Tinkler, Penny. *Smoke Signals: Women, Smoking and Visual Culture*. Berg: Oxford and New York, 2006.

Tintner, Adeline R. 'Consuelo Vanderbilt and *The Buccaneers*', *Edith Wharton Review* 10.2 (1993): 15–19.

——. *Edith Wharton in Context: Essays on Intertextuality*. Tuscaloosa and London: University of Alabama Press, 1999.

Topik, Steven C. *Trade and Gunboats: The United States and Brazil in the Age of Empire*. Stanford, CA: Stanford University Press, 1996.

Totten, Gary ed. *Memorial Boxes and Guarded Interiors: Edith Wharton and Material Culture*. Tuscaloosa and London: University of Alabama Press, 2007.

Tuttleton, James W., Kristin O. Lauer and Margaret P. Murray eds. *Edith Wharton: The Contemporary Reviews*. Cambridge: Cambridge University Press, 1992.

Vickers, Graham. *Chasing Lolita: How Popular Culture Corrupted Nabokov's Little Girl All Over Again*. Chicago: Chicago Review Press, 2008.

Vita-Finzi, Penelope. *Edith Wharton and the Art of Poetics*. London: Pinter Publishers, 1990.

Waid, Candace. *Edith Wharton's Letters from the Underworld: Fictions of Women and Writing*. Carolina: University of North Carolina Press, 1991.

—— and Clare Colquitt, 'Toward a Modernist Aesthetic: The Literary Legacy of Edith Wharton' in Paul Lamb and G.R. Thompson (eds) *A Companion to American Fiction 1865–1914*. Oxford: Blackwell, 2005: 536–56.

Wall, Stephen. 'Aspects of the Novel, 1930–1960' in Linda R. Williams (ed.) *The Twentieth Century: A Guide to Literature from 1900 to the Present Day*. London: Bloomsbury, 1992: 222–76.

Wallace, Diana. 'Ventriloquizing the Male: Two Portraits of the Artist as a Young Man by May Sinclair and Edith Wharton', *Men and Masculinities* 4.4 (2002): 322–33.

Walpole, Horace. *The Castle of Otranto* (1764) ed. E.J. Clery. Oxford: Oxford University Press, 1996.

Walpole, Horace. *The Mysterious Mother* in Frederick S. Frank (ed.) *'The Castle of Otranto' and 'The Mysterious Mother (Horace Walpole)*. Toronto: Broadview Press Ltd., 2003.

Walpole, Hugh. 'A Note on the Modern American Novel', *The Nation & The Athenaeum*, 17 October 1925: 113–14.

Wegener, Frederick. *Edith Wharton: The Uncollected Critical Writings*. Princeton, NJ: Princeton University Press, 1996.

——. 'Form "Selection", and Ideology in Edith Wharton's Antimodernist Aesthetic' in Clare Colquitt, Susan Goodman and Candace Waid (eds.) *A Forward Glance: New Essays on Edith Wharton*. London: Associated University Presses, 1999: 116–38.

Werlock, Abby H.P. 'Edith Wharton's Subtle Revenge?: Morton Fullerton and the Female Artist in *Hudson River Bracketed* and *The Gods Arrive*' in Alfred Bendixen and Annette Zilversmit (eds), *Edith Wharton: New Critical Essays*. New York and London: Garland Publishing, Inc., 1992: 181–99.

Wharton, Edith. *The Age of Innocence* (1920). Ed. Candace Waid. New York: W.W. Norton, 2002.

——. *A Backward Glance* (1934). London: Century Hutchinson, 1987.

——. *The Buccaneers* (1938). New York and London: D. Appleton-Century Company, 1938.

——. *The Children* (1928). London: Virago, 1985.

——. *The Custom of the Country* (1913). New York: Charles Scribner's Sons, 1913.

——. *French Ways and their Meaning* (1919). The Countryman Press, Woodstock, Vermont: 1997.

——. 'George Eliot', *Bookman*, May 1902. Rpt. in Wegener, Frederick ed. *Edith Wharton: The Uncollected Critical Writings*. Princeton, NJ: Princeton University Press, 1996: 71–8.

——. *The Ghost Stories of Edith Wharton*. New York: Scribner Paperback Fiction; Simon & Schuster, 1973.

——. *The Gods Arrive* (1932). London: Virago Press Ltd, 1987.

——. 'The Great American Novel', *Yale Review*, July 1927. Rpt. in Frederick Wegener (ed.) *Edith Wharton: The Uncollected Critical Writings*. Princeton, NJ: Princeton University Press, 1996: 151–8.

——. *The House of Mirth* (1905). New York Charles Scribners' Sons, 1914.

——. *Hudson River Bracketed* (1929). London and New York: D. Appleton and Company, 1929.

——. *Italian Backgrounds* (1905). New Jersey: Ecco Press, 1998.

——. 'Life and I' in Laura Rattray (ed.) *The Unpublished Writings of Edith Wharton Vol. 2: Novels and Life Writing.* London: Pickering & Chatto, 2009.

——. 'Literature' in Laura Rattray (ed.) *The Unpublished Writings of Edith Wharton Vol. 2: Novels and Life Writing.* London: Pickering & Chatto, 2009.

——.'A Little Girl's New York', *Harper's Magazine* 176 (March 1938): 356–64. Rpt. in Wegener, Frederick ed. *Edith Wharton: The Uncollected Critical Writings.* Princeton, NJ: Princeton University Press, 1996: 274–88.

——. *The Mother's Recompense* (1925). London: Virago Press, 1986.

——. *A Motor-Flight through France* (1908). London: Picador, 1995.

——. *The Muse's Tragedy and Other Stories* ed. Candace Waid. New York: New American Library, 1990.

——. 'A Reconsideration of Proust', *Saturday Review of Literature*, 27 October 1934. Rpt. in Frederick Wegener (ed.) *Edith Wharton: The Uncollected Critical Writings.* Princeton, NJ: Princeton University Press, 1996: 179–83.

——. 'Tendencies in Modern Fiction', *Saturday Review of Literature*, 27 January 1934. Rpt. in Frederick Wegener (ed.) *Edith Wharton: The Uncollected Critical Writings.* Princeton, NJ: Princeton University Press, 1996: 170–4.

——. *Twilight Sleep* (1927) New York and London: D. Appleton and Company, 1927.

——. *The Writing of Fiction* (1924). New York: Simon & Schuster, 1997.

Whitehead, Sarah. 'Demeter Forgiven: Wharton's Use of the Persephone Myth in her Short Stories', *Edith Wharton Review* 2011.

Williams. Linda R. (ed.) *The Twentieth Century: A Guide to Literature from 1900 to the Present Day.* London: Bloomsbury, 1992.

Wilson-Jordan, Jacqueline. 'The Woman Writer and the Struggle for Authority in "Mr Jones"' in Gary Totten (ed.), *Memorial Boxes and Guarded Interiors: Edith Wharton and Material Culture.* Tuscaloosa: University of Alabama Press, 2007: 63–82.

Wolff, Cynthia Griffin. *A Feast of Words: The Triumph of Edith Wharton.* New York and Oxford: Oxford University Press, 1977.

Woolf, Virginia. *To the Lighthouse* (1927). Harmondsworth: Penguin Books, 1966.

Wyatt-Brown, Anne M. and Janice Rossen (eds), *Aging and Gender in Literature.* Charlottesville and London: University Press of Virginia, 1993.

Young, Judy Hale. 'The Repudiation of Sisterhood in Edith Wharton's "Pomegranate Seed".' *Studies in Short Fiction* 33 (1) 1996: 1–11.

Zak, Deborah J. 'Building the Female Body: Modern Technology and Techniques at Work in *Twilight Sleep*', *Memorial Boxes and Guarded Interiors: Edith Wharton and Material Culture*, ed Gary Totten. Tuscaloosa, AL: The University of Alabama Press, 2007: 111–32.

Index

CPSIA information can be obtained at www.ICGtesting.com
Printed in the USA
LVOW070228201212

312529LV00015B/318/P